DATE DUE

Learning for Earning

Your Route to Success

John A. Wanat
Consultant and Author on Occupational Education
Jackson, New Jersey

E. Weston Pfeiffer
Consultant on Technical and Vocational Training
Lambertville, New Jersey

Richard Van Gulik
Superintendent
Hunterdon County Polytech
Flemington, New Jersey

Publisher
The Goodheart-Willcox Company, Inc.
Tinley Park, Illinois

Library of Congress Cataloging-in-Publication Data
Wanat, John A.
Learning for earning : your route to success / John A. Wanat, E. Weston Pfeiffer, Richard Van Gulik.
p.cm.
Includes index.
ISBN 1-56637-939-3
1. Vocational guidance. 2. Finance, Personal. 3. Students—Life skills guides. I. Pfeiffer, E. Weston. II. Van Gulik, Richard. III. Title.
HF5381 .W2135 2004
646.7--dc21
2002021472

ABOUT THE AUTHORS

John A. Wanat is executive director of an education innovation for the over-55 population and author of numerous textbooks, articles, and audiovisual materials. Previously he managed several New Jersey State Department of Education bureaus and implemented a statewide program that found jobs for 10,000 high school graduates not bound for college. Wanat's career has included coordinating degree and nondegree programs for the Center of Occupational Education at Jersey City State College. He also has served as vice president of a security training institute and publisher/editor of two national education magazines.

E. Weston Pfeiffer provides consulting services to major corporations, the World Bank, and numerous education agencies. Pfeiffer began his career as a teacher, then joined the New Jersey Department of Education's Division of Vocational Education. There he was state supervisor of cooperative industrial education, lead program specialist for trade and industrial education, and state director for apprentice training. Recently Pfeiffer has served as advisor for the U.S. Department of Labor on technical and vocational training programs in Europe and the Middle East. He is a founding member of the Cooperative Work Experience Education Association.

Richard Van Gulik is superintendent of Hunterdon County Polytech, the newest school district in New Jersey to provide vocational technical programs. Previously, while serving as Salem County Vocational School principal, his school was recognized by the U.S. Department of Education as one of the top 10 vocational programs in the nation. Van Gulik also served as program specialist in trade and industrial education for New Jersey's Department of Education. He is a leader in initiating programs that address the employment needs of his county and in creating school-to-work and mentoring opportunities for students in vocational programs.

INTRODUCTION

Learning for Earning is designed to introduce you to the skills you will need to succeed in school, on the job, and on your own. It will serve as a guide as you prepare for a career and become a productive member of the workforce.

Success in a career begins with an understanding of the world of work. This text will explain the important changes taking place in the workplace and how they apply to you. It will cover the variety of careers available to you. Skills that are important in work and in your life will be identified as well as ways to acquire them.

Being a member of the workplace involves a whole new set of responsibilities as you strive to become an independent adult. You need to know how to manage your income to meet your needs. *Learning for Earning* provides practical information about following a budget and using banking services. This text also discusses how to use your income to satisfy your housing and transportation needs.

Once you know what type of work you want, you are ready to begin exploring job options. You will learn how to find work suitable to your skills, personality, and personal priorities. You will also gain the knowledge needed to become successful at work and advance in your career.

CONTENTS IN BRIEF

CONTENTS

Part One
Exploring the World of Work

Part Four
Acquiring Workplace Skills

Part Five
Developing Personal
Skills for Job Success_____

Chapter 18
Time Management and
Study Skills _____ 268

Chapter 19
Communication Skills _____ 280

Chapter 20
Your Appearance _____ 298

Part Six
Managing
Your Money _____

Part Seven
Growing Toward
Independence _____

PART ONE
Exploring the World of Work

1

The Importance of Work

Objectives

After studying this chapter, you will be able to

- distinguish the difference between a job and a career.

- identify three reasons why people work.

- explain how work influences identity and lifestyle.

- describe ways in which work provides satisfaction.

- discuss how work keeps the economy strong.

- identify the workplace competencies.

Words to Know

work
job
career
career ladder
income
needs
wants
identity
lifestyle
self-esteem
economy
workplace competencies
competent
transferable skills

What Is Work?

What is work? ***Work*** can be defined as an activity done to produce or accomplish something. People do an activity, or work, in order to gain something in return. Everyone works.

As you go to school, you work. You do homework, read books, give reports, and study for tests. That is the work you do to accomplish passing grades.

At this point in your life, schoolwork is very important. You are preparing yourself for your future work—your career.

A Job or a Career?

A ***job*** is something you may do to earn money. You might have a job in a store or delivering newspapers. In your working life you may have many jobs. Many of your jobs may be temporary or part-time. You may take a job just to earn a few dollars for holiday presents. Nevertheless, a job is not a career.

A ***career*** is a series of jobs, usually in the same or related fields. A good way to display the steps of a career is with a career ladder. A ***career ladder*** shows a sequence of work in a career field, from entry to advanced levels. Each rung of the career ladder is another step in the progression to a better job. Each step in your career may require that you learn new and more complex jobs. Reaching your final career objective may take many years and require considerable training.

Careers may be in *professional, public,* or *business* areas. Doctors and lawyers are examples of a professional career. Your community's mayor and teachers have public careers. The service station manager has a business career and so does the mechanic that repairs all types of car problems. A mechanic that only fixes brakes, however, has a job, not a career. Careers require that many jobs be learned to progress in a chosen area.

No matter what path you choose, advancing in a career will require that you learn increasingly more complex tasks. See 1-1. Chapter 5, "Types of Careers," has more information about career opportunities.

work
An activity done to produce or accomplish something.

job
The work a person does to earn money.

career
A series of jobs, usually in the same or related fields.

career ladder
An illustration that shows a sequence of work in a career field, from entry to advanced levels.

Career Ladder for Interior Design

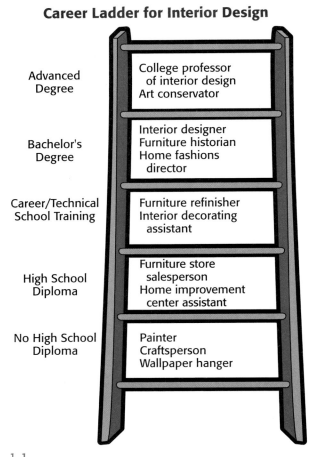

Advanced Degree	College professor of interior design Art conservator
Bachelor's Degree	Interior designer Furniture historian Home fashions director
Career/Technical School Training	Furniture refinisher Interior decorating assistant
High School Diploma	Furniture store salesperson Home improvement center assistant
No High School Diploma	Painter Craftsperson Wallpaper hanger

1-1

This career ladder shows how a person can advance from one job to another in the field of interior design.

There is a direct link between how well you do in school now and your future in the work world. Prospective employers will consider your school records when they make hiring decisions. See 1-2. That's why it is important to make every effort now to do well in school.

Work Provides Income

The purpose of work is to produce or accomplish something. That *something* could be job satisfaction or personal gain. Other reasons for working include a sense of obligation, commitment to a goal, or a sense of pride. The list could go on, but for most people, income is the key reason for working.

Income is the amount of money a person receives for doing a job. With the money people earn from working, they buy things they need or want.

While you are still in school, you may have a part-time job. If so, it probably would allow you to earn spending money and save some money for the future. After you graduate from high school, you will probably find that you must have a full-time job to meet your needs. *Needs* are the basics you must have in order to live. You may need a car, a place to live, money for food, and tuition for further education. Eventually you may need enough income to support a family. Satisfying these needs usually requires income from a job.

1-2
Success in school paves the way for future success in a career.

In addition to your needs, you also have wants. Wants go beyond actual needs. *Wants* include items you would like to have but do not require. For instance, while you may need a car, you may want a new sports car. You may also want a big apartment, stylish clothes, and fun vacations. Affording your needs and wants requires earning a living by working.

Work Influences Identity

Look around the community where you live. You will find many successful people in all types of occupations. Some people work for others. Some people work for themselves. Some of the businesses are big, while others are medium-size or small.

The work you choose to do is likely to influence your identity. Your *identity* is the sum of traits that distinguish you as an individual. Your identity is two-fold. It is the way you see yourself. It is also the way others see you. When you describe yourself, you are talking about your identity. For instance, you may say that you are a daughter, sister, student, and member of the swim team.

income
The amount of money a person receives for doing a job.

needs
The basics a person must have in order to live.

wants
The items a person would like to have, but are not required.

identity
The sum of traits that distinguishes a person as an individual.

As an adult, your job will be an important part of your identity. Your work will influence the way you think of yourself and the way others see you. It is important to choose work that will allow you to respect yourself and develop a positive identity.

Work Influences Lifestyle

How do you spend your time? What activities do you enjoy? Where do you live? What is important to you? Your answers to these questions will help you describe your *lifestyle,* or typical way of life.

The work you choose to do will affect your lifestyle in many ways. It will affect where you live. For instance, if you want to be a flight attendant, you will need to live near an airport.

Your work will also affect the

1-3

The amount of time you have to enjoy leisure activities will depend on your work schedule.

people you meet and the time you have to spend with your family and friends, 1-3. Some jobs may require working nights and weekends. Others may involve overtime hours or out-of-town travel. Some work schedules are fixed—they are firmly set. Working hours and days do not change. Other work schedules are flexible, with work hours and days changing frequently.

Income is another factor that influences lifestyle. The more money you make, the more elaborate your lifestyle may be. You may be able to afford a nice house, expensive clothes, and new cars. If you work too much, however, you may not have time to enjoy your purchases. How you balance your work and nonwork hours depends on your lifestyle decisions.

Work Provides Satisfaction

One of the most important reasons for working is to gain satisfaction. Doing a job well helps you build *self-esteem,* which is confidence in yourself. When you have self-esteem, you feel good about yourself. You are proud of who you are and what you do.

Work also provides a feeling of accomplishment. When you complete a job and do it well, you feel good about it. Others recognize excellent work and commend you for it. That's why you should always put your best possible effort into any work you do.

Another kind of satisfaction from work comes from being with other people. Most types of work allow occasional opportunities to socialize with others.

Work also provides the satisfaction of feeling useful. You can feel useful by earning money to support yourself. You can also feel useful by doing work that you believe is important. Work that provides a public service gives workers a strong sense of usefulness. Some examples include helping people in need, enforcing the law, fighting fires, and cleaning the environment. See 1-4.

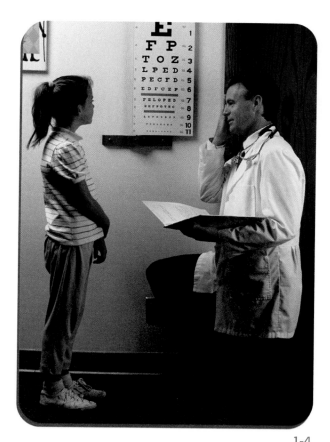

1-4

People in health careers gain satisfaction from helping others.

lifestyle
A person's typical way of life.
self-esteem
The confidence a person has in himself or herself.

1-5
This is one example of people in your community who work to help society.

Many people judge their success in terms of satisfaction rather than income. They do not feel they have to become wealthy to be successful. Many successful people have limited financial resources. They receive their rewards in seeing others helped. They take pride in their jobs and in their accomplishments.

Many of the most famous people in history dedicated their lives to helping society without expecting financial rewards. These people are regarded as society's heroes. See 1-5.

Work Keeps the Economy Strong

The workers of a country are the people who keep that country's economy going. A country's *economy* is its way of producing, distributing, and consuming goods and services.

When people go to work, they make products and perform services that others buy. They also earn money that allows them to buy whatever they need, such as cars, homes, clothes, and food. By making these purchases, people recycle their earnings back into the economy. This process is one big cycle, 1-6. The income you earn from working goes back into the economy when you buy something.

Individuals and businesses in the United States depend on each other. Both must do their parts to keep the economy healthy. Businesses put goods into the marketplace and pay workers for their labor.

Enthusiastic workers help keep the economy strong in two ways. They help businesses succeed by providing labor. They also buy goods and services in the marketplace when they shift from the role of *worker* to *consumer*.

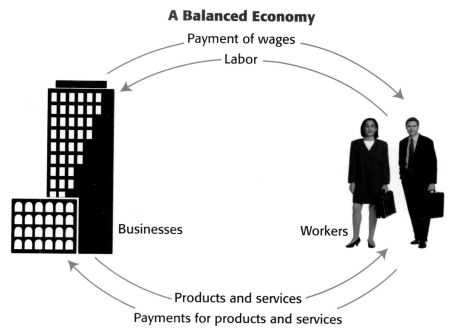

A Balanced Economy

Payment of wages

Labor

Businesses

Workers

Products and services

Payments for products and services

1-6

A strong economy depends on the balance between the production and consumption of goods and services.

You can do your part to keep the economy strong by taking your work role seriously. This will include performing your job correctly, being willing to learn, and having a good attitude.

Work Requires Know-How

Before you are hired, the employer will ask, "What can you do?" This short question requires much thought. The answer must convey all that you can bring to the workplace.

Answering this question is easier when you know what employers seek in their employees. The U.S. Department of Labor identified the job skills and abilities expected in today's workers. These are called *workplace know-how*. See 1-7 on the next page. The list was developed with the help of educators as well as business and labor leaders.

economy
The way goods and services are produced, distributed, and consumed in a society.

Workplace Know-How

Workplace know-how includes five competencies and a three-part foundation of skills and personal qualities needed for solid job performance.

Workplace Competencies

Effective workers are able to use the following:

- Resources—allocating time, money, material, space, and human resources

- Interpersonal skills—working on teams, teaching others, serving customers, leading, negotiating, and working well with people from culturally diverse backgrounds

- Information—working on teams, teaching others, serving customers, leading, negotiating, and working well with people from culturally diverse backgrounds

- Systems—understanding social, organizational, and technological systems, monitoring and correcting performance, and designing or improving systems

- Technology—selecting equipment and tools, applying technology to specific tasks, and maintaining and troubleshooting technologies

The Foundation

Developing competence requires the following:

- Basic skills—reading, writing, arithmetic and mathematics, speaking, and listening

- Thinking skills—thinking creatively, making decisions, solving problems, visualizing, knowing how to learn, and reasoning

- Personal qualities—individual responsibility, self-esteem, sociability, self-management, and integrity

1-7   *U.S. Department of Labor*

Employers want their employees to have these skills and abilities.

Notice that workplace know-how contains two parts. The top part lists ***workplace competencies***. These are the skills needed for workplace effectiveness and success. The bottom part lists foundation elements. These are skills and qualities workers need before they can develop the competencies.

Workers Need a Foundation

Developing skillfulness in the workplace requires all the basic skills plus key thinking skills. Several personal qualities are also needed. See the bottom of 1-7. These skills and qualities form a foundation on which workplace competencies can be developed.

- *Basic skills* allow you to express your thoughts and communicate with coworkers. The key skills are reading, writing, arithmetic, mathematics, speaking, and listening.

- *Thinking skills* allow you to develop ideas and solve problems. The key skills are thinking creatively, making decisions, solving problems, visualizing ideas, knowing how to learn, and reasoning.

- *Personal qualities* shape the way you work and the kind of worker you are. The key qualities are individual responsibility, self-esteem, sociability, self-management, and integrity.

Much of your work as a student is aimed at developing a foundation so you are ready for the world of work.

Workers Need Workplace Competencies

Today's workplace needs workers with strong on-the-job skills. Workers ready for today's challenging workplace are competent with the following:

- resources
- interpersonal skills
- information
- systems
- technology

workplace competencies
Skills needed for workplace effectiveness and success.

The five areas listed encompass all workplace competencies. The term derives from the word **competent**. It means having the ability to respond appropriately. See the top section of 1-7 for more details on what these skills involve.

Workplace competencies are sometimes called *employability skills*. However, many believe that term is too limited because it implies a focus on just getting a job. Sometimes the term *career-success skills* is used. That term is a good substitute since having workplace skills yields lifelong success at work.

The workplace competencies, with the foundation skills and qualities on which they depend, are a means to a satisfying career. Employers will expect workers to have these skills, no matter what their career fields are.

As a student preparing for the world of work, look for ways to develop these skills in yourself. The activities recommended at the end of each chapter will help you. Because the five workplace competencies interrelate, it is almost impossible to focus on just one. You will find that as you develop one, you will also perfect others.

Your school is not the only place where these important skills are learned. Workplace competencies are also developed through extracurricular activities and community involvement. The competencies can even be developed through routine activities at home. By acquiring the skills employers expect, you will have no difficulty answering, "What can you do?"

Workplace Competencies Are Transferable Skills

Skills used in one career that can be used in another are called **transferable skills**. This term highlights the usefulness of a workplace competency to many different types of work.

Workplace Competencies are examples of transferable skills because these broad skills apply to all careers. Workers may also have specialized skills that are transferable. Being able to speak a second language is an example of a specialized skill.

Identifying transferable skills is important to your future career success. That's because few jobs last forever. You are likely to switch jobs, and possibly career paths, several times during your life. Sometimes people tire of a career and desire something different. Often a person's interests expand, prompting a search for new opportunities.

Whatever the reason for a job change, you will need to examine which of your skills carry over to the new position you desire. Consider a chef's artistic skills. Knowing how to apply the principles of design to make food attractive is a must. Similar artistic skills are needed by advertising managers, interior decorators, and fashion designers. However, their focus is something other than food. See 1-8.

1-8

A florist is another example of a career that requires artistic skills.

Another example of a transferable skill is the ability to persuade people. This is important to lawyers as they argue a case in court. Being persuasive is also important for salespeople. The same skill is used by doctors and nurses who deal with difficult patients.

Most people underestimate their skills. Be sure to take the time to identify all your skills in your search for a rewarding career. This text will discuss other transferable skills in Part 4, "Acquiring Workplace Skills," and Part 5, "Developing Personal Skills for Job Success."

competent
Having the ability to respond appropriately.
transferable skills
Skills used in one career that can be used in another.

Summary

In your working life you will surely have many different jobs. A job may or may not be related to your career. A career requires that you learn increasingly more difficult jobs related to a chosen field. Careers exist in professional, public, and business areas of life. A career can be compared to a ladder. Each step is a progression toward a career objective.

Work is important for several reasons. It allows you to earn an income so you can buy things you need and want. It influences how you see yourself and others see you. Work also affects where you live, when you work, what you do, and whom you meet.

One of the most important reasons for working is to gain satisfaction. Satisfaction from work comes in many different forms. The work satisfaction you seek may be different from the satisfaction others seek.

Work is needed to keep the country's economy strong. Every person who earns money and spends it plays a role in keeping the economy healthy. Workers who do their best on the job help make their employers successful. This makes the economy stronger.

Successful workers have workplace know-how. They are the skills required in today's world of work. Students who want success in their future jobs can develop workplace skills and personal qualities through their schoolwork, extracurricular activities, community involvement, and at-home activities.

Reviewing the Chapter

1. In your own words, define *job* and *career*.
2. Why is your schoolwork important at this point in your life?
3. For most people, what is the key reason for working?
4. Show the difference between needs and wants by listing three needs and three wants.
5. Describe three ways in which work influences lifestyle.
6. How do you feel when you have self-esteem?
7. Why should you always put your best possible effort into any work you do?
8. Satisfaction from work can come from _____.

   A. being with other people

   B. earning money

   C. doing work that helps others

   D. All of the above.

9. Explain how work keeps the economy strong.
10. List the five workplace competencies and give one example of each.

Building Your Foundation Skills

1. Write a one-page paper about the satisfaction that work provides.
2. Read a current magazine story about the role workers play in keeping our economy strong. Summarize the story in a brief oral report.
3. Ask three people in different careers how their work affects their lifestyles. Write a paper explaining what you learned. Also, identify the kind of lifestyle you prefer and the type of career that would allow you to achieve it.
4. Work with your classmates to make a list of reasons for working.
5. Identify five careers and describe workers in those careers. Join a class discussion about ways that career choices can influence people's identities.

Building Your Workplace Competencies

Work with two classmates to research career information and present it to the class. Together, select one career from each category: professional, public, and private. Decide as a team how to divide the work. Prepare a written plan outlining who does what. Find the following facts for each career: the predicted job growth or decline, the anticipated earnings, and the skills and academic preparation required. Present the findings to the class using charts, graphs, or pictures. *(This activity develops competence with resources, interpersonal skills, information, systems, and technology.)*

The Changing Workplace

Objectives

After studying this chapter, you will be able to

- compare and contrast employment opportunities in the free enterprise system with other world economic systems.

- identify five new directions that are shaping the world of work.

- describe six factors that affect the labor market.

- explain the importance of technology to the workplace.

- describe what is expected of workers in today's workplace.

Words to Know

free enterprise system
profit
global economy
services
family-friendly programs
flextime
self-sufficient
diversity
outsourcing
technology
computer revolution
CAD/CAM
PC
telecommuting
Internet
e-mail
lifelong learning

Free Enterprise System

You live in a country that operates as a *free enterprise system*. That term describes an economy in which individuals and businesses play a major role in making decisions. In a free enterprise system, people can operate any type of business they choose, provided it is lawful.

Economic Freedom

What does a free enterprise system mean to the people who live and work in it? The following are five reasons that the U.S. economy is based on the free enterprise system:

- People are free to be creative and choose where they work. They can choose to be their own boss or to work for someone else.
- People are free to own private property and buy whatever they want. Just think of all the choices available for any product you desire.
- The government allows people to buy or sell whatever they wish, so long as it doesn't harm others.
- Consumer *wants* and *needs* determine what products are desired in the marketplace.
- Businesses can compete against each other to make money. Those who sell successful products and services make a profit. A *profit* is the money left after all expenses are paid. Competition is good for consumers, too, because it promotes better products at lower prices.

The freedom to own property and freely buy and sell goods began with the founding fathers. The free enterprise system is an outgrowth of their spirit of independence. This economic system is also called a *market economic system*.

The desire to make a profit and earn a good living is called the *profit motive*. See 2-1. In countries where the government (or a central authority) controls the production of goods, it also controls their price and distribution. Under such a system, people must follow the government's dictates reagarding how to work and live.

> **free enterprise system**
> An economy in which individuals and businesses play a major role in making decisions.
>
> **profit**
> The money left in a business after all expenses are paid.

2-1
A child's lemonade stand is a simple example of the profit motive in action under the free enterprise system.

New Directions for the Workplace

The U.S. workplace is continually changing. New types of jobs are created each year. New tools are used to work faster and more efficiently. Companies have new ideas about how to find customers and how work should be done.

The question no longer is: Will change occur? Instead, it is: How will change occur? The one thing you can count on in today's exciting workplace is *change,* and you will be a part of it.

A Global Perspective

Companies once reached no further than their neighborhoods to find customers. Then, companies searched for more customers beyond their towns and states. Today that search takes them beyond the nation's borders to every part of the world. Instant communications through phones, faxes, and computers makes this possible.

Customers are just one focus of the new global perspective. The other is labor. Companies constantly look to other nations for labor services. It generally costs less to make goods in another country because pay scales are much lower. Only a few countries in the world have wage rates that nearly match the rates here.

Cheaper labor in other countries has forced U.S. businesses to change their practices and manufacture many goods elsewhere. Once the United States was the manufacturing center of the world. Factories and production lines were a part of practically every U.S. worker's experience.

Nowadays, most manufacturing is done in various production centers in other countries. These centers fill orders placed by businesses located around the world.

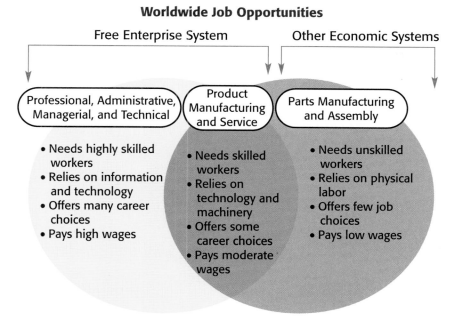

2-2
U.S. jobs generally call for skilled labor because work requiring low skills is handled in other parts of the world.

The centers make small items and parts for complex products. The parts are then sent to wherever the final product is assembled. This manufacturing process makes goods more affordable. See 2-2.

U.S. cars and other large items are often assembled in U.S. factories from parts made in other countries. Most small items are made entirely outside the country and shipped to a store near you. This is evidence of a global economy. A ***global economy*** is a financial interconnection among the countries of the world. It means that parts or entire products are created in one country for sale to customers in other countries.

The global economy has caused a major shift in the U.S. workforce. It has reduced the need for unskilled labor since a vast supply exists in other parts of the world. Instead, skilled, well-educated U.S. workers are needed to plan, develop, and deliver the products and services of tomorrow. Skilled workers are also needed for assembling large, complex products such as cars.

global economy
Goods and services created by companies in one country are sold to customers in other countries.

The Service and Information Economy

The decline of the manufacturing sector paved the way for a new economy based on services and information. *Services* are nonmaterial assistance for which people are willing to pay. This sector of the economy has grown very rapidly in recent years. It will remain the area of greatest job growth for the near future.

Nearly 20.2 million of the 22 million new jobs that will exist by 2010 will be service oriented. See Figure 2-3 for a list of the 10 occupations that will employ the most people in 2010. All are focused on producing some type of service. The only U.S. occupations that produce goods are construction, agriculture, forestry, fishing, manufacturing, and mining.

Occupations Offering the Greatest Number of Jobs, 2000-2010

Occupation	Number of Jobs (in Thousands)	Percent Increase
Combined food preparation and service workers, including fast-food	673	30
Customer service representatives	631	32
Registered nurses	561	26
Retail salespersons	510	12
Computer support specialists	490	97
Cashiers, except gaming	474	14
Office clerks, general	430	16
Security guards	391	35
Computer software engineers, applications	380	100
Waiters and waitresses	364	18

2-3

U.S. Department of Labor

These 10 occupations will see the greatest growth in terms of job openings.

Another focus of today's economy is information. The computer and the Internet are American inventions. These are the tools of the information economy. What we learn with these tools helps us to create new services, improve business methods, and lower costs.

The Commitment to Quality

At every turn, you will hear the word *quality* spoken in the workplace. The pursuit of quality is an all-out effort by employers to be the very best in their field. The company's goal, of course, is to grow and become more successful.

Quality means different things to different companies. In the workplace, *quality work* means doing the job quickly and accurately the first time so there's no need for redoing it. Many of the changes that you will experience on the job will be due to efforts to improve quality.

Building quality into a product or service requires constant attention to the way work is done. You will be expected to watch for ways to do your job better. You will also be asked to suggest ideas for improving quality.

A Teamwork Approach

The old way of managing work developed during the manufacturing era. Supervisors made all the decisions and workers simply followed orders.

Today's workplace uses a team approach as workers jointly seek solutions to problems, 2-4. Employers place high importance on hiring people who work well with others. When interviewing individuals for a job opening, employers look for proof that you have teamwork skills.

The importance of teamwork in your future is so great that one chapter is devoted entirely to the subject. (See Chapter 14, "Being a Team Player.")

Family First

Programs in the workplace that help workers handle the demands of work and family responsibilities are called *family-friendly programs*. Men as well as women seek the flexibility these programs provide. Caring for young children is the main reason for the creation of such programs. Other reasons include caring for elderly parents or sick or disabled family members.

services
Nonmaterial assistance for which people are willing to pay.

family-friendly programs
Work programs that help employees to balance the demand of work and family.

2-4
The teamwork approach is used in many workplace settings

A flexible work arrangement is one type of family-friendly program. *Flextime* is a work schedule that permits flexibility in work hours. See 2-5. Companies that offer flextime generally have a daily core period when all employees must be at the work site. This usually consists of four or five hours in the middle of the day. Employees then can schedule their other work hours before or after the core period, depending on their preference.

Other family-friendly programs that companies may sponsor include the following:

- on-site child care
- vouchers or financial assistance for adult day care or vacation programs for children
- adoption assistance
- on-site shoe repair services, dry cleaners, or employer-sponsored food stores with ready-to-serve food to take home.

Employers are also changing their current policies to make existing programs more family-friendly. For example, many companies no longer require workers to take full weeks of vacation time instead of single days. These companies know that many workers with young families prefer taking Mondays or Fridays off. This gives them long weekends for spending time with the family.

Besides voluntary programs in the workplace, a law requires time off for some employees under certain circumstances. The details of the Family and Medical Leave Act will be covered in the next chapter.

Factors Affecting the Labor Market

Forces beyond any individual's control are constantly at work influencing workers. These forces shape the composition of the workforce and the types of jobs available.

Social Change

Society once frowned on mothers joining the workforce instead of caring for children at home. In fact, women were generally discouraged from full-time work. That social barrier is long gone. Young women today are encouraged to prepare themselves to be self-sufficient. *Self-sufficient* individuals are those who can take care of themselves. This means earning a salary that will support your needs and wants as well as those of your future family.

2-5

A flexible work arrangement lets employees start work early so they can be at home when children return from school.

Except for wartime, the majority of U.S. workers have always been men. However, most new workers have recently been women. This trend will continue, thereby increasing the number of women to nearly 48 percent of the total workforce by 2010. Figure 2-6 on the next page shows this trend.

Population Shifts

Changes in the population as a whole affect the workplace. A significant change underway is the increase in minorities in the U.S. population. Employees of Hispanic, Asian, African-American, or Native American heritage will account for a larger share of the workforce in the future. Other minority groups will likewise increase in size within the workforce.

flextime
A work schedule that permits flexibility in work hours.

self-sufficient
Individuals who can take care of themselves; who can earn a salary that will support their needs and wants as well as those of their future families.

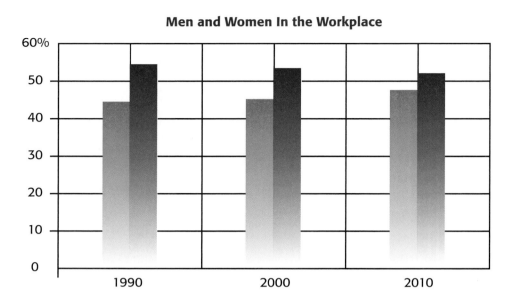

2-6

This chart shows the increasing percentage of women in the workforce, from 45 percent in 1990 to nearly 48 percent in 2010.

Virtually every nation of the world is represented in the U.S. population, making it the most diverse on earth. Diversity is a term commonly used to describe the benefits of working with people different from you. ***Diversity*** is the positive result of people of different racial, ethnic, and cultural backgrounds working together. Business leaders view our diverse workforce as a major resource in dealing with the global market.

The Economy

When the economy is strong, demand is high for goods and services. To meet this demand, employers keep their businesses fully staffed, sometimes working their employees overtime. Workers spend their earnings freely when the fear of unemployment is low. They do not worry about losing their jobs.

A weak economy, on the other hand, can cause unemployment for many employees. During periods of economic uncertainty, the fear of losing one's job causes consumers to cut back purchases. Less money is spent on items that aren't really needed, such as movie tickets, CDs, and eating out. Consumers even postpone buying necessary items.

A widespread slowdown in purchasing will cause employee cutbacks in an industry. For example, if clothing sales decrease, there is less need to put new fashions on display. Consequently, there is less need for salesclerks in the stores, truckers moving inventory, and other workers who help get clothes to market. When economic downturns are prolonged, the poor business in one industry usually affects others.

2-7

Installing water systems, power lines, and new roads are services in which U.S. companies excel.

World Events

An earthquake that destroys roads in Taiwan can mean increased business for road-building experts in this country. See 2-7. At the same time, earthquakes can disrupt the production of computer chips. That disruption can reduce the number of new computers in the U.S. market and may even cause prices to rise.

Whether world events are natural or manmade, they hold opportunities and consequences for U.S. businesses and consumers.

diversity
The positive result of people of different racial, ethnic, and cultural backgrounds working together.

Government Actions

If you own a busy gas station in town and a new expressway interchange is planned five miles away, your station will probably lose business. Government action can, and often does, affect companies. Actions that affect some companies in a positive way may negatively affect others.

It is important to know that rules, regulations, and other government decisions are generally not made suddenly. Issues are considered for many months or years before a plan is announced. Time is always allowed for affected members of the public to comment before a final decision on the plan is made. The smart citizen stays alert to government announcements that may affect his or her livelihood.

The Forces of Competition on Staff Size

Success in the global market means developing and delivering products and services quickly. Often this requires hiring more employees. Deciding how many full-time workers to have is a challenge, especially for smaller companies eager to grow. Employers cannot afford to have employees on the payroll with nothing to do.

Companies often turn to independent consultants before making big changes. Such experts can help companies decide how to best handle a new challenge. If more workers are needed, temporary or part-time help may be considered first. Only when an increased workload is sure to be long-lasting will companies hire more full-time employees.

The reverse is also true. When a company foresees less demand for its products on a long-term basis, it will reduce its workforce.

Sometimes companies turn to other companies for help instead of creating new departments and hiring workers. A company that contracts with another company to handle some work is *outsourcing*. By outsourcing work, companies can get products quickly and often less expensively. Usually one of the terms of the contract is delivery of the products exactly when and where needed.

Companies also contract with service providers for outside help. Outside experts are often used to do payroll tasks, garbage pick-up, and general cleaning. See 2-8. If a company grows unsatisfied with the service provider, it can make changes when the contract expires. Service contracts usually last for one year.

The Technology Revolution

Change is ongoing in the workplace, and technology is the cause of most of that change. *Technology* is the application of scientific principles.

2-8
Using an independent service for a specific task, such as cleanup, can result in a high-quality job at a lower cost to the company.

New Replaces Old

Look around your school and the businesses in your area. You see computers, fax machines, cellular phones, and other signs of modern technology. This society has moved far beyond the steam engine, electricity, and other discoveries that shaped earlier eras. Today's technology affects how you live and work in more dramatic ways than ever.

Technology has a snowballing effect, leading to ever more discoveries. More changes in technology have occurred in the last 25 years than in all the preceding years combined. However, what is new today will be old tomorrow. Technology quickens the pace of change.

At one time, workplace technology consisted of a telephone and a typewriter to supplement the traditional paper and pencil. Today an office with only these tools is a sign of a low-tech workplace.

Some argue that technology causes job losses. Consider the typewriter again and the fact that jobs involving this outdated product are no longer needed. The proper way to judge technology's effect on employment is to compare the number of jobs lost to those created by new technology. In this case, you would compare the total typewriter-related jobs lost to the total computer-related jobs gained. By making a fair comparison, you can see that more jobs result from advances in technology.

outsourcing
The practice of one company contracting with another to handle some work.

technology
The application of scientific principles.

Applications to the Workplace

Much of the technology in today's workplace began with space exploration. The space program created a simple electronic calculator that led to the computer revolution. The *computer revolution* is the total change in the way people live and work caused by computers.

Defense and manufacturing industries expanded the use of that electronic calculator to help with designing new products. This led to computer systems called CAD/CAM (computer-aided design and computer-aided manufacturing). *CAD/CAM* systems use computer technology to run manufacturing systems. They link the production, manufacturing, and control functions of a company. The result is shortened cycles for new product introductions and the ability to bring more goods to market quicker than ever.

The introduction of the *PC*, or personal computer, brought enormous computing power to the top of a desk. This resulted in automating the office and combining systems that formerly were kept separate. Now the work of storing, processing, and communicating information has merged into a single system, allowing several computer users to communicate with each other.

Laptop computers can tap into this system while freeing people from their desks. Laptops are small, notebook-size computers that contain the work of one or more individuals. Workers can take them to the factory, a meeting room, or a project area, and back to their desks. Work can also be done at home, 2-9. All that is needed to send information back and forth is an electronic linkup with the central office. This is known as *telecommuting*.

2-9

Laptop computers are especially useful for salespeople and others who work outside the office environment.

Information can also be sent and received via the ***Internet***, the computer linkup of individuals, groups, and organizations. The Internet has revolutionized the business world. Workers keep each other up-to-date on assignments through ***e-mail***, the feature that allows you to send and receive messages. With the right equipment and connections, workers in different locations can share voice or voice/picture communications anytime and anywhere.

The New World of Work

The workplace has changed as a result of using the tools of technology. Consequently, employers have different expectations of themselves and their employees.

Instant communications, for example, has quickened the overall pace of the business world. Speed is all-important, but so is accuracy. There is no place for slow or wrong responses in today's high-tech environment.

Knowing how to keystroke and operate a computer are skills expected of new employees. You should know how computers are used in the career field you select. You should also know how to access information important in that field.

Only a small percentage of workers will actually work on high-technology assignments. Everyone else will feel the effects of technology in the new tools and processes they use to do their jobs well. Keeping up with advances in technology will require lifelong learning. ***Lifelong learning*** is continually updating your knowledge and skills. It is a term that means your need for learning will never end.

The discussion of technology brings us back to the subject of teamwork. Many firms find that installing the biggest and best equipment does not always guarantee top results. In fact, companies with less advanced equipment but total employee involvement do a better job. This demonstrates that how equipment is used counts most. This also underscores the importance of your future role as part of a work team.

computer revolution
The total change in the way people live and work caused by computers.

CAD/CAM
Systems that use computer technology to run manufacturing systems.

PC
Personal computer.

telecommuting
Working at home through an electronic linkup with the central office.

Internet
The global computer linkup of individuals, groups, and organizations in government, business, and education.

e-mail
A feature of the Internet which allows people to send and receive messages via computer.

lifelong learning
Continually updating your knowledge and skills.

Summary

Several important trends indicate new directions for the workplace. Businesses today operate in a global economy. They search the world for customers as well as affordable labor. Product and service quality is continually examined to make sure it meets customer expectations. Teamwork is the primary way that work is accomplished. Family-friendly programs are helping to lessen the challenge of balancing work and family responsibilities.

Many factors work together to shape the complex labor market. Social changes and population shifts are responsible for more women and minorities joining the work force. Economic conditions directly affect consumer spending habits and employment levels. Government action and world events can positively or negatively affect jobs. Even the forces of competition influence the hiring decisions companies make.

Many high-tech tools are reshaping work, including CAD/CAM, the PC, and the Internet. To be successful in the workplace, employees must know how to use the computer quickly and accurately. They must update their knowledge and skills continually as new tools and processes are used in the workplace. The use of technology on the job is more effective when employees work in teams.

Reviewing the Chapter

1. What sector of the economy will add 20 million new jobs between 2000 and 2010?

2. Name three factors that are causing major changes in the workplace.

3. In 2010, what percentage of the workforce will be women?

4. Companies are *not* likely to outsource _____.

   A. custodial services

   B. landscaping

   C. management functions

   D. payroll services

5. Name four factors beyond an individual's control that affect the labor market.

6. In your own words, define *technology* and *computer revolution*.

7. Technology will *not* _____.

   A. change the way work is done

   B. process information faster

   C. slow the pace of work

   D. link companies and customers around the world

8. True or false. Changes in technology will cause unemployment to increase.

9. True or false. Technology will require workers to constantly keep learning throughout life.

10. Which of the following will *not* be an employment requirement in 2010?

    A. computer ability

    B willingness to learn

    C. teamwork skills

    D. an ability to command

Building Your Foundation Skills

1. Research information about the future of service jobs in our economy and make a brief presentation to the class.

2. Identify one new technology or piece of equipment. Explain in a written report how you think it will influence the workplace.

3. Write a letter inviting a representative from an area business or organization to speak to your class about the general skills desired in new employees today compared to 10 years ago.

Building Your Workplace Competencies

Join a team of three or four classmates to analyze technology changes in the telephone (or similar item) and their effect on the workplace. As a team, determine the five changes you believe were most significant and explain why in a 10-minute presentation to the class. Conclude your presentation with one prediction about future phone capabilities and cite the source of the prediction. Explain how the predicted capability may change the workplace further. *(This activity develops competence with resources, interpersonal skills, information, and systems.)*

The Law in the Workplace

Objectives

After studying this chapter, you will be able to

- define discrimination and list several workplace examples.

- identify the laws that make workplace discrimination illegal in the areas of employment opportunity, pay, physical disability, and age.

- describe two general forms of sexual harassment.

- propose the steps to take to stop any sexual harassment or discrimination at work directed at you.

- list the four conditions addressed by the Family and Medical Leave Act.

Words to Know

discrimination

Equal Employment
  Opportunity Act

EOE

Equal Pay Act

piecework

Americans with
  Disabilities Act

Age Discrimination Act

sexual harassment

Family and Medical
  Leave Act

3-1
The law forbids illegal discrimination in all workplace policies and procedures, beginning with a firm's hiring practices.

What Is Discrimination?

This chapter discusses the laws regarding behavior in the workplace. (Laws concerning health and safety are discussed in Chapter 8, "Keeping Safety First.)

Several laws exist to assure everyone a fair and equal opportunity for employment. These laws protect job seekers and workers from discrimination. **Discrimination** means treating a person or group of people differently from the others. This unequal treatment in the workplace is illegal. See 3-1.

Equal Opportunity

The ***Equal Employment Opportunity Act*** makes discrimination in the workplace illegal when it is based on race, color, religion, sex, or national origin. More recent laws make it illegal to discriminate against people for other reasons. These reasons include physical disability, age, and marital status.

Employers are prohibited from treating workers unfairly in all work practices. These include hiring, training, promoting, and firing employees. For example, an employer cannot reserve certain jobs for men and prevent women from applying or being considered. That is discrimination.

discrimination
Unfairly treating a person or group of people differently.

Equal Employment Opportunity Act
A law that makes it illegal for an employer to discriminate because of race, color, religion, sex, or national origin. More recent laws make it illegal to discriminate against people for other reasons, such as disabilities, age, and marital status.

Some employers include the initials *EOE* in their ads and recruitment materials. *EOE* means *equal opportunity employer.* Of course, all employers must abide by the law and treat all job candidates equally. By including *EOE* in ads, an employer is emphasizing a commitment to equal opportunity.

Employers look for workers with just the right skills and qualifications to do the job well. Employers are not guilty of illegal discrimination when they pass over unqualified jobseekers. For example, an employer can require job applicants for a data processing position to type 60 words per minute. An auto repair shop can require that technicians be certified to do repair work. Employers can legally turn away applicants who do not meet minimum job requirements.

Equal Work, Equal Pay

As a worker, you can count on being paid the same as others for doing the same job. The ***Equal Pay Act*** was a significant step in achieving equal pay protection.

The law was designed to help women get equal pay for equal work, 3-2. It applies to all workers regardless of sex or other differences. Basically, the law does the following:

- It prohibits unequal pay for men and woman doing basically the same work for the same employer.

- The law prevents employers from lowering the wages of either sex to comply with the law. (For example, suppose men are paid more than women for the same work. An employer cannot reduce the men's pay to match the women's level. Instead, the women's pay must be raised to match the men's.)

3-2

The Equal Pay Act requires employers to make pay levels uniform regardless of the race, color, religion, sex, or national origin of the jobholder.

- The law also prevents labor organizations from forcing an employer to violate the law. In other words, unions cannot force companies to pay union members a higher wage than nonmembers receive.

Because of the Equal Pay Act, everyone can be assured of getting the same wage from an employer for doing the same job.

Pay Differences

In some cases, certain factors can be considered that result in different pay levels. The following legal factors can result in higher pay for some people doing the same job:

- length of time with the company
- experience in the job
- advanced training
- productivity, or greater work output

Productivity is most easily measured when a job involves *piecework.* This term refers to a job in which something is produced by an individual that can easily be counted. People who do piecework usually have control over how much they can accomplish. An example of piecework is sewing buttons and buttonholes onto men's shirts. One completed shirt equals one piece.

By considering these four legal factors, employers can reward workers who are faster, better trained, and more experienced. An employer cannot use any practice, however, that unfairly sets pay differences.

A Barrier-Free Workplace

One of a country's greatest resources is its people. Many people with physical disabilities can contribute greatly to society. Enabling a disabled person to work, however, may require certain changes to the workplace. Employers must attempt to accommodate an applicant with a disability.

EOE
Equal Opportunity Employer.

Equal Pay Act
Law that prohibits unequal pay for men and women who are doing essentially the same work for the same employer.

piecework
A job in which something is produced by an individual that can easily be counted.

3-3

Muscular Dystrophy Association

Offices must not restrict workers who need a special chair to move around.

The ***Americans with Disabilities Act*** prohibits employers from discriminating against people with a physical disability. A wheelchair ramp that allows more people to enter and exit the building is one of the most common changes made. Perhaps a piece of machinery may need to be lowered. Employers must make reasonable changes to provide employment free of physical barriers, 3-3.

Medical and physical requirements of workers must be related to business needs. For example, a homebuilder can require a bricklayer to climb scaffolds and read blueprints. The builder cannot, however, require the worker to have perfect hearing since that is not needed for the job. Any physical exam required by an employer must reflect the duties of the job. Consequently, the builder cannot require the physical exam to cover hearing ability.

An employer cannot ask an applicant about a disability. An employer can, however, ask any number of questions about the person's ability to do the job. Employers need not lower their standards or work quality to satisfy the law's requirement. They can make performance a *condition of employment*. This means keeping the job depends on doing what the job requires.

Age Discrimination

This form of discrimination applies most often to people over 40 years old. The ***Age Discrimination Act*** prohibits employers from not hiring older people simply because of their age. It also forbids employers from denying any person a promotion, benefit, or favorable job assignment because of age. The law applies to all employers with 20 or more employees. See 3-4.

Several decades ago, people in their 40s were often considered too old for sales positions. No legitimate reason existed for closing these jobs to people over 40. Instead, it was an industry practice based on discrimination.

Age discrimination continues to draw attention today. The issue usually involves experienced older workers who are left jobless after a company reorganizes. Age discrimination also affects women returning to the workforce after raising their children.

Setting age preferences or limitations as a job requirement is generally unlawful. In certain cases, however, it is legal. For example, if state or federal laws set age requirements, these must be followed. When legal age restrictions are set, they must be applied to everyone in the same manner.

Consider the job of a delivery person. If state law declares 16 as the legal driving age, a 15-year-old cannot be hired no matter how well he or she can do the job. Other restrictions could also be set. For example, it is legal for the job to also require several years of driving experience with a clean driving record.

3-4

Older workers have the same right to employment as everyone else.

Americans with Disabilities Act
Law that prohibits employers from discriminating against people with physical disabilities.

Age Discrimination Act
Law that prohibits employers from not hiring people simply because they are older.

What Is Sexual Harassment?

All forms of sexual harassment in the workplace are against the law. *Sexual harassment* is unwelcome sexual advances. It can be a request for sexual favors. It can also be verbal or physical conduct of a sexual nature. It is illegal in the workplace under the Civil Rights Act and many state human rights laws. The harasser and the victim can be either sex.

Advances from Authority Figures

There are two basic kinds of sexual harassment. The first type is described as *something given for something else*. The legal name is *quid pro quo harassment*. A supervisor or someone in authority usually initiates this kind of sexual harassment. It almost always involves a threat or the promise of a reward.

A group leader may threaten to fire or block a promotion if the victim rejects his or her advances. A supervisor might promise to promote or give a pay raise to the victim. Often sexual harassment involves the use of power to control a new employee or one with less importance or rank in the organization.

A Hostile Environment

The second kind of sexual harassment deals more with the workplace. In this case, a person makes an environment unpleasant enough to interfere with the other worker's performance. Aspects of the workplace that are considered hostile include sexual pictures, signs, objects, and music. A hostile environment also includes offensive language, jokes, gestures, and comments.

Recognizing Sexual Harassment

Threats and rewards for sexual actions are clear and easy to identify. This behavior is always wrong and illegal! Identifying a hostile environment, however, is not as easy. It can even be confusing. The signs of sexual harassment can be physical, verbal, or nonverbal.

- *Physical harassment* is touching, holding, grabbing, and all other unwanted physical contact.
- *Verbal harassment* is telling offensive jokes, using offensive language, and making suggestions of a sexual nature.
- *Nonverbal harassment* involves offensive gestures and actions, such as staring at a person's body or circulating letters, cartoons, or other material of a sexually oriented nature.

Discouraging Sexual Harassment

As an employee, you can discourage cases of sexual harassment by following these guidelines.

- Dress appropriately for the job. See 3-5.
- Become familiar with your right to a workplace free from sex discrimination.
- Know your company's policy and procedures for reporting harassment.
- Conduct yourself in a businesslike manner at all times.

You should receive a copy of the company's sexual harassment policy during your first week as a new employee. If not, ask what the procedure is so you are informed.

3-5

If your job does not require a uniform, you will be expected to wear clothing that is appropriate for that workplace.

Facing Discrimination or Sexual Harassment

Reputable employers want to provide a workplace free of harassment for their employees. It is in their best interest to provide a productive environment. A workplace with constant tension is not productive. Large and midsize companies have at least one person who handles equal rights matters. The personnel office is usually where they work.

> **sexual harassment**
> Unwelcome sexual advances, requests for sexual favors, and other verbal or physical conduct of a sexual nature when it is made a condition of employment or of a person's work performance or environment.

Your greatest weapon against discrimination and harassment at work is to know your rights. When you do, you can confidently proceed.

Action to Take

If you are faced with discrimination or sexual harassment at work, you should follow these steps:

- **Remain professional.** Avoid being too emotional. See 3-6.
- **Speak to the offender.** Let that person know what he or she is doing is illegal and you want it stopped. If the offense continues, send the offender a letter telling him or her what you want stopped and why. Keep a copy of the letter for yourself and file it in a safe place.
- **Record the facts.** Write down all the important details of any continuing event as soon after it occurs as possible. Explain the *who, what, when, where,* and *how* of the incident. Be prepared to provide names of witnesses or others who can support your claims.
- **Report the offense if it does not stop.** Report it to your supervisor, unless he or she is the source of the offense. Then go to someone higher in the company. Contact the person designated by your company to handle such complaints. If you are a union member, you can also go to your union representative. Outside the company, you can contact the Equal Employment Opportunity Commission (EEOC) or your state's Department of Human Rights. Going outside the company is a step to take only after contacting the appropriate source within the company.

As a last resort, the Civil Rights Act gives you the right to take your case to court. If you win the case, you can receive money that you lost because of the discrimination. Loss of money may be due to dismissal, demotion, lost benefits,

3-6

It is important to always act businesslike with coworkers in all settings.

or other reasons. Employers cannot retaliate against employees who file a complaint or testify as witnesses.

The Family and the Workplace

Workplace demands sometimes clash with family demands. How to care for young or sick children while at work is one of the biggest issues facing employees. Child care issues especially affect single-parent households and those with both parents working outside the home. Caring for sick family members and aging parents are additional concerns. See 3-7.

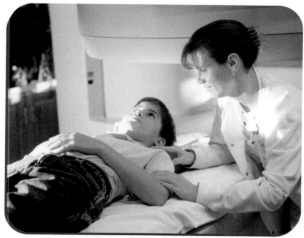

3-7

Too many employees use up all their sick days caring for other sick family members.

Juggling family and workplace demands can cause workers to arrive late or go home early. Employees with special family demands often find it difficult to keep their minds on their work. Often workers use up their sick days caring for other family members.

The *Family and Medical Leave Act* allows some flexibility in the normal work routine to handle special family matters. The law addresses the following four conditions:

- having or caring for a new baby
- adopting a child or adding a foster child to the family
- being unable to work because of serious illness
- caring for a sick child, spouse, or parent

The law applies to employers of 50 or more employees. It generally covers those working at the same company for at least 12 months. Under this law, employees can take a total of 12 weeks off without pay. Also, they can keep their health insurance during the time off and return to their jobs with no loss of benefits or pay.

Family and Medical Leave Act
A law that allows 12 weeks off without pay per year in certain cases to handle special family matters.

Summary

Employers cannot discriminate against anyone in their hiring, training, promoting, or firing practices. Laws prohibit using race, color, religion, sex, national origin, age, a disability, or marital status as a requirement for employment. Discrimination occurs when there is different treatment of one person or group of people.

Discrimination sometimes affects a person's pay. All workers must receive equal pay for equal work with the same employer. Sometimes pay can be higher for some when certain legal factors are considered.

Sexual harassment in the workplace is illegal. It involves unwelcome advances of a physical, verbal, or nonverbal nature. Sexual harassment can affect the way people do their jobs and feel about themselves. When faced with discrimination or harassment, it is important for employees to know their rights under the law and exercise them.

The law also allows greater flexibility in work schedules for some workers with special family demands.

Reviewing the Chapter

1. True or false. It is *not* discrimination if a bank hires only applicants who have a driver's license.
2. True or false. It is *not* discrimination if an employer requires all employees to complete special training programs to be promoted.
3. An employer can pay different wages to people doing the same job if _____.
   A. employees are the same sex and one is a friend of the family
   B. employees are different sexes
   C. one employee has worked at the job longer
   D. the employer wants to impress one of the employees
4. Which of the following is legal under the Americans with Disabilities Act?
   A. Asking job candidates when their disability began.
   B. Asking job candidates how their disability might hinder them on the job.
   C. Requiring a physical exam that tests for more abilities than the job needs.
   D. Requiring job candidates to take a test measuring their ability to do the job.
5. True or false. Sexual harassment only occurs between a man and a woman.
6. List three steps an employee can take to discourage sexual harassment in the workplace.
7. What is the greatest weapon against discrimination and sexual harassment at work?
8. What are the four steps to take if you are the target of discrimination or harassment at work?
9. What government agency is responsible for enforcing the fair treatment of people in the workplace?

10. Suppose a family member becomes seriously ill and requires constant care at home. Based on the Family and Medical Leave Act, which of the following must the employer provide if the company has at least 50 employees?

    A. 12-week leave with pay.

    B. 12-week leave without pay.

    C. Flexible hours.

    D. Less work.

Building Your Foundation Skills

1. Research the psychological effects of discrimination on people. What are the three most important facts you learned? Share them with the class.

2. Write a paper explaining how to distinguish between innocent flirting and sexual harassment involving people your age.

3. Invite an attorney to class to discuss how he or she prepares for a sexual harassment case. What kind of information is needed to substantiate a sexual harassment claim?

Building Your Workplace Competencies

Contact a large employer in your community. Find out who in the organization is responsible for making sure equal employment laws are followed. Schedule a telephone or in-person interview to get answers to the following questions: How does the company make sure the rules regarding sexual harassment and discrimination in the workplace are followed? What training programs are offered to company employees, and who is required to attend? What handouts are given to employees on the subject? Prepare a presentation for your class describing your findings. Use any materials gathered in your contacts. *(This activity develops competence with resources, interpersonal skills, information, and systems.)*

PART TWO

Exploring Career Options

Learning About Careers

Objectives

After studying this chapter, you will be able to

- list factors to consider when choosing a career.
- describe sources for obtaining career information.

Words to Know

traits
education
training
skills
entry-level
advanced training
promotion
fringe benefits
cost of living
online
job shadowing

Basic Job Factors

What do you want to do when you grow up? This is a question you probably began hearing very early in life. It may have inspired you to picture yourself at work in various jobs. Maybe you have already made a mental list of jobs that sound interesting and others that do not.

Choosing the right career is important to your future happiness and success. Making the right choice involves considering several factors. See 4-1.

Job Duties and Responsibilities

The first factor to consider about a job is its duties and responsibilities. These will determine how you will spend your workday. Job duties are often described by the tasks that must be done. Does the job require you to file reports, take photos, or drive a truck? Maybe you would be required to mix chemicals, use power tools, or conduct research.

The duties of common jobs, such as truck drivers and cashiers, are easily described by their tasks. Getting these jobs may depend on previous experience with similar tasks.

Job duties and responsibilities are sometimes described by worker traits. *Traits* are noteworthy characteristics. They are often seen in want ads. The following traits are examples of some common job responsibilities:

- ability to plan and organize
- memory for details
- desire to help people
- ability to persuade

Basic Job Factors

- Job duties and responsibilities
- Job prospects
- Education, training, and skills
- Salary and fringe benefits
- Advancement opportunities
- Work location and environment

4-1

For any career you explore, review these basic job factors.

traits
Noteworthy characteristics.

New or service-oriented jobs are usually described in terms of the traits required. For example, the job responsibilities of a director of customer satisfaction might be described by all four of the traits just listed. Jobs that stress jobholder traits generally do not require previous experience in a similar job. However, you would need to demonstrate that you possess the required traits.

Job Prospects

After you identify a career choice, determine your chances of finding a job in that field. By examining job prospects, you learn about long-term opportunities predicted for the field. What is the outlook for jobs in the next 10 to 20 years for the career you have selected? Will there be openings for job seekers in that field by the time you are ready to enter it? Will this career area grow so you can advance? Only so many teachers, salesclerks, and mechanics are needed at any given time.

You would not want to prepare for a career field in which jobs are quickly disappearing. The Department of Labor continually examines the outlook for all types of U.S. jobs. It reports that manufacturing jobs are declining, which you learned in Chapter 1. Consequently, you would not want to plan on a life-long future in factory work.

Education, Training, and Skills

You will need to prepare yourself to be ready to handle whatever job you choose. This requires knowing what education, training, and skills are required for the career you seek.

Education is gaining knowledge to live and work in today's society. *Training* is applying that knowledge through practice. *Skills* are the abilities that result from education and training. Education and training requirements for jobs are generally divided into the following three levels.

Entry-Level Jobs

Entry-level jobs require no previous training. These are jobs that are easily learned, 4-2. Training for these jobs may be provided on the job. A high school diploma is usually required. These jobs usually pay low wages.

Jobs Requiring Advanced Training

Jobs requiring **advanced training** mean that some job skills are needed. These skills may be obtained in high school through a career or technical program. Skills may also be obtained after high school through a community college. An apprenticeship program offered through a trade, such as carpentry or plumbing, is another way to acquire skills.

Jobs Requiring a College Degree

Jobs requiring a *college degree* mean that a student completes a college or university program of study. College degrees are available for two-year programs, four-year programs, and more advanced studies. Usually when a college degree is a requirement for a job, a four-year degree is assumed. The types of degrees available are discussed in further detail in Chapter 9, "Options for Education and Training."

Other Educational Requirements

Some jobs require you to have a license or the appropriate certification. The local, state, or federal government issues licenses. Certification is obtained through the association that represents the profession. To obtain a license or certification, you generally must

4-2
Painting a house is an example of an entry-level job.

education
Gaining knowledge to live and work in today's society.

training
Applying knowledge through practice.

skills
Abilities that result from education and training.

entry level
A job that requires no previous training.

advanced training
Special skills and training required for a specific job.

meet specific educational requirements. Sometimes you must also meet specific experience requirements, too.

Getting the right education, training, and skills is a big part of career preparation. Because it requires time and effort, it is usually accomplished in steps. For example, a dental hygienist must get a state license in order to work. To get the license, he or she must pass a test that measures knowledge and skills. That person must also be a graduate of a recognized dental hygiene school. However, being accepted by a dental hygiene school requires one or two years of college first. See 4-3.

Some careers require more education and training steps than others. You will need to know what your career choice requires in order to prepare yourself for the job.

Education and Training Requirements for Dental Hygienists

You must have a license from the state in which you will practice, which requires:

- a passing grade on a national written and clinical examination, which requires:

- proof of graduation from an accredited dental hygiene college program, which requires:

- one or two years of study at the college level before being accepted by a school of dentistry

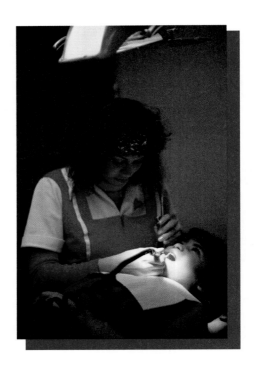

4-3

To understand the education and training required for a specific job, outline the steps needed to fill the requirements. These steps are needed to become a dentist's assistant.

Salary and Fringe Benefits

The starting salary for a job depends on the job specifications and the experience of the applicant. Entry-level jobs usually pay minimum wage, which is set by law. This is the lowest hourly wage that employers are permitted to pay. Your state employment office will be able to tell you what the minimum wage is at the present time. Most unskilled jobs pay minimum wage.

Union wages are set by contract between the employer and the union. If you take a job covered by a union contract, you will receive the pay scale established for that job. The same union jobs in the company will have the same hourly wage scale. Raises are uniform for everyone in the same job category. The size and timing of raises are covered by the union contract.

In most jobs, you will receive an annual review. Your annual review should allow for a raise for satisfactory performance. Check to see how the organization has handled worker reviews in the past. Read the company handbook and talk to employees to learn more.

The best way to make more than the minimum wage is to get a promotion. A *promotion* is a move up to a higher position within a company. Promotions generally result in higher pay. The more promotions you receive, the better your paycheck will look at the end of the week.

A regular hourly wage is normally paid for the first 40 hours of work. Overtime pay usually applies to time worked beyond 40 hours. There also may be a pay difference for evening hours and shift work. Working overtime is usually paid at a time-and-a-half rate, which is 50 percent more. Therefore, a job that pays $6.50 per hour would pay $9.75 per overtime hour. ($6.50 + $3.25 = $9.75)

As you conduct your research, check the organization's policy regarding overtime. Depending on the job, you may be exempt from overtime pay. Check to see if you can receive future time off for working extra hours in a week.

Salaried workers are paid an annual salary. They normally work a 40-hour week. However, they may work evenings and weekends with no overtime pay. The extra hours are figured into their annual salary. Salaried workers may receive bonuses and raises based on their performance and the company's earnings. See 4-4.

promotion
A move up to a higher position within a company.

4-4

Project managers are examples of salaried workers. If they need to arrive early or stay late, they do so without receiving overtime pay.

Fringe benefits are financial extras received in addition to salary or wages. Fringe benefits include paid vacation and sick time, health and life insurance, and pension contributions, to name a few. When you begin working, company-paid pensions and health benefits may not seem important to you. You will probably be more concerned with your paycheck. As you get older, fringe benefits become as important as your paychecks, if not more so.

Advancement Opportunities

Advancement opportunities play a major role in selecting a job. Very few people start at the top pay scale. Your goal should be to move upward at a steady and reasonable pace. The best way to do that is to get promotions for doing an outstanding job. When you research your job choices, ask yourself the following questions:

- Is there opportunity for advancement inside the company, or is it limited?
- Does the company fill openings by promoting its employees, or by hiring outsiders?
- Is there opportunity for advancement outside the firm due to rapid growth in the field?

Look at the opportunities for advancement inside and outside the company. As you master each job function, you become a more valuable worker because of your additional skills and experience.

Work Location and Environment

Another major factor to consider when exploring a career is location and environment. How far must you travel to get to your work location? How much time will it take and what will it cost? Will your salary enable you to live comfortably after paying for travel to the job?

When considering jobs in different areas, compare the differences in the cost of living. The *cost of living* includes rent, food, travel, and other everyday expenses. Living costs may be much higher in a large metropolitan area than in a small town or rural area. Another very important consideration is the quality of recreational facilities and educational opportunities that are available.

Even if you like a job itself, you may still choose not to pursue it if you dislike the day-to-day work environment. The sights, smells, sounds, physical demands, and working conditions of the workplace make up the *work environment.*

Sights may range from a windowless office to sunlight and outdoor views. Smells could involve food cooking, wet paint, or hospital disinfectant. Sounds may include the roar of jet engines or the quiet of a computer keyboard. Physical demands could involve carrying a few lightweight files to lifting heavy bags or boxes. Working conditions may involve a comfortable office or the extremes of outdoor weather.

You can't always know in advance if you will like the location and the work environment. You can, however, ask yourself some questions that can lead to a better decision. See 4-5.

Obtaining Career Information

Your next step in exploring careers is to look for facts about the jobs that interest you. Begin your search by checking the most complete, up-to-date information from the Department of Labor. Then talk with your school counselor. Also, search for more information on the Internet.

fringe benefits
Extra rewards given to workers in addition to salary or wages, such as insurance coverage and paid vacation time.

cost of living
Amount of money needed for rent, food, travel, and other everyday expenses.

Concerns About Work Location and Environment

- Where will I be employed? Is is close to where I live?

- How will I get to work? Can I afford the transportation costs and travel time?

- What is the daily routine of people working in this career?

- Do I like the working conditions? If not, do I like the job enough to tolerate the conditions?

- Does the work require much travel? Are many evenings and weekends spent away from home?

- Is the work stressful or do stressful conditions exist only with certain employers?

- Is there frequent turnover with personnel?

4-5
Finding answers to these questions will help you determine if the career you are considering is right for you.

Department of Labor References

Perhaps the best material on careers is provided by the Department of Labor. Some of the following references exist as publications. Helpful references are available *online,* too. This means they are available through the Internet.

- The *Occupational Outlook Handbook*, updated every two years, is designed to help with decisions about your future work. The *Handbook* describes what workers do on the job, the working conditions, and the training and education required. It also includes earnings information and expected job prospects. The publication's Web site is bls.gov/oco.

- The *Guide for Occupational Exploration* is designed to help people understand what traits are required for certain occupations. The *Guide* categorizes occupations into 12 interest areas that are further divided into work groups. Each work group describes jobs that require the same worker traits. The *Guide* makes it possible to determine how suited you are for a job, based on how well your abilities and interests match job requirements.

■ The Occupational Information Network, called the O*NET, is an excellent online resource from the Department of Labor. O*NET can be used to explore careers, related job skills, and trends. It also provides tools for assessing a person's abilities and interests. O*Net's job-classification system links to other labor market information. Consequently, it is the most complete occupational resource available. Access O*NET at http://online.onetcenter.org/. (O*Net replaces the *Dictionary of Occupational Titles.*)

The Department of Labor offers career information for youth and adults through its Education and Training Administration. The site also links with other helpful sources of career information. Access the Web site at doleta.gov.

School Counselors

Guidance and career counselors are professionally trained to assist you in researching careers. They can save you a great deal of research time by directing your efforts to areas that provide useful facts. Your counselor can help you explore the following areas:

■ careers and their educational requirements

■ colleges and trade or technical schools offering specific programs

■ government service and recruiting information

■ local opportunities to observe jobs in your career field, 4-6

4-6
Watching a work crew in your neighborhood is a good way to see what different jobs involve.

online
Connected to the Internet.

In addition, your school counselor can provide career counseling on a one-to-one basis. Try to schedule a conference early in the school term to speak to the counselor about your career interests.

The Internet and Your Career

The Internet is one of your most valuable sources of career information. Many computers connected to the Internet have all-in-one career sites built into their Web browser. By clicking on the *careers* block, dozens of online career sites are available. Some of the most popular career Web sites follow:

- Job Bank USA (jobbankusa.com)
- America's Job Bank (*ajb.dni.us*)
- *Career* Magazine (careermag.com)
- Career Resource Center (careers.org)

You can also search the Internet for job information provided by many sources. These include unions, professional associations, employment agencies, and companies. Other sources include colleges, universities, government agencies, and hundreds of newspapers and periodicals.

A popular method for getting career and job information from the Internet is through newsgroups and electronic message boards. Newsgroups are special interest groups composed of people with similar interests. Using newsgroups to search for career information helps you limit your Internet search.

Online Internet chat groups and electronic message boards are also useful in gathering career information. Through them, you can talk with others who share your interests.

Additional Ways to Investigate Careers

There are many other ways to learn more about careers. These include researching other sources, talking with people, working in career-related jobs, and attending career events.

Research

Researching careers means gathering information about your career choices before you commit to a specific career. It means weighing the pros and cons of the career. You can use many combinations of the following sources to gather your information:

Libraries

Your school and local libraries carry a wide selection of books, CDs, and videotapes on careers. Classified ads in newspapers, trade magazines, and professional journals provide additional information. Most libraries offer Internet access, too.

Trade Unions and Professional Associations

These organizations offer a great deal of information on jobs in their specific career fields. If you seek a highly specialized career, this is one of the best information sources.

Public Employment Services

These employment service centers exist to help people find employment. You can locate your nearest site by looking in the state government listing of your telephone directory under *Job Service*.

Interviewing Workers

After narrowing your list of career considerations to two or three, contact people who work in these fields. Ask them questions about their careers. A good starting point is your family, teachers, and friends. Do any of them work in a career field that interests you? Ask them to introduce you to anyone they know who works in an area you are investigating.

Generally, people are very eager to talk about their jobs and give advice to interested listeners. Be prepared to ask career-related questions whenever you have an opportunity to discuss a person's job. This opportunity may arise when talking with individuals or when taking part in a career study tour. See 4-7.

Job Shadowing

One of the best ways to investigate a career choice is to accompany workers on the job. This is called *job shadowing*. Job shadowing usually lasts for a short time, only a few days to a week or two. This period is long enough to experience the work environment firsthand and get your career questions answered. You also witness the type of duties commonly performed.

> **job shadowing**
> Accompanying a person to his or her job to learn about that person's job.

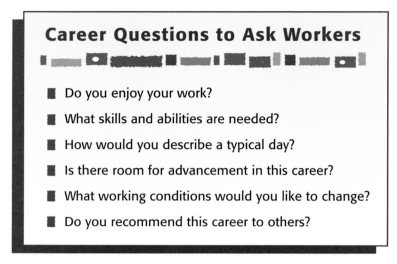

4-7
Some of the most helpful career information you can get is from workers themselves.

Your school counselor might be able to schedule a job-shadowing experience for you. You would stay with a worker at his or her job site during normal work hours. The experience would help you know if a career in the field is worth exploring.

Community/Service Learning

If your dream career involves working with community or service organizations, gaining firsthand experience will be easy. These groups always have work for willing volunteers.

Your school can arrange learning experiences with cooperating agencies in the community. These often include hospitals, senior centers, YMCA/YWCA centers, food pantries, and nursing homes. Through community/service learning, you have an opportunity to use classroom knowledge while performing a service for others. The following activities are just some of the many available to explore:

- Community service agencies need help with their office work.
- Hospitals and health care agencies need helpers to run errands and deliver food to patients.
- Peer tutoring uses students to help other students with their studies. See 4-8.
- Assistants are needed in parks and recreational facilities to serve as referees, camp counselors, and craft instructors.

■ The Habitat for Humanity organization builds homes for those who cannot afford shelter. Youth volunteers are needed to help carry supplies, food, and water to the workers, and litter to trash bins.

Part-Time Jobs

It is not always possible to obtain an entry-level job in the career area you desire. If jobs exist, age or educational restrictions may exclude you. For some career fields, however, entry-level jobs do not exist for teenagers.

You can gain valuable work experience of a general nature by holding a part-time job. You can obtain part-time employment after school, on weekends, or during the summer. You will learn to follow company policies and interact with fellow workers. You will understand more about job performance and expectations. All of these valuable learning experiences will help you find a full-time job when you are ready.

4-8
Helping other students with their studies develops interpersonal and information skills that you can later use in your career.

Career Events

Take advantage of career days, workshops, and tours offered by your school or community. These are excellent ways to investigate specific jobs and employers while learning about different career fields.

Most speakers at career events answer audience questions. They will give you helpful hints on how to learn more about your particular interests. Many presenters bring materials to help you better understand what they do.

Tours to career sites are especially helpful. They let you see firsthand what workers actually do on their jobs. You can also experience the sounds and sights of the work environment.

Summary

Knowing as much as possible about a given occupation will help you make intelligent career choices. Research as much as you can about job duties and job prospects for the careers you are considering. Identify the education, training, and skills necessary. Salary and fringe benefits are very important. Also, consider advancement opportunities, work location, and the work environment.

Begin your career exploration by checking Department of Labor information. Then talk to your school counselor to focus your search.

Check many sources to find out as much as possible. Talk with workers in the career you are considering. Enroll in a job-shadowing program to get a firsthand look at the work environment. To obtain valuable work skills, volunteer for community activities and hold a part-time job. Attend career events to ask questions of the presenters.

Reviewing the Chapter

1. List five factors to explore when investigating basic information about a career.
2. In what two ways are job duties and responsibilities described?
3. Name the three basic levels of education and training.
4. List four fringe benefits.
5. Name the five main qualities of the work environment.
6. List three career references from the Department of Labor.
7. Which Department of Labor publication provides career information in terms of worker traits?
8. Why talk with your school counselor about your career considerations?
9. True or false. Most workers do *not* like to talk about their jobs.
10. Identify six sources of community/service projects to explore.

Building Your Foundation Skills

1. Using the O*NET, research four job titles that interest you. For each, record the Standard Occupational Classification (SOC) code and write a short job description.

2. Give a two-minute presentation to the class on your top career choice. Describe it in terms of the basic job factors.

3. Listen carefully to your classmates' career presentations (described in the previous item). List the pros and cons about their career choices as they apply to you.

4. Organize a community/learning project involving your school and community.

5. Visit an online source for employment information. Record how many openings were listed for your top five job titles.

Building Your Workplace Competencies

Using online and print resources, research your top career choice. Find out what group or organization represents the profession, and phone or write for the name of three people to contact. Indicate that you would like to interview people with practical experience in the career field. Phone the recommended contact people to schedule a phone interview with each. Prepare a list of questions in advance that will provide information you can't get any other way. Summarize your experience in a report to the class. Are you more or less interested in the career as a result of the interviews? Keep your interview findings for future career reference. *(This activity develops competence with resources, interpersonal skills, information, systems, and technology.)*

Types of Careers

Objectives

After studying this chapter, you will be able to

- identify 16 career clusters.

- describe a wide range of occupations within each career cluster.

- determine the requirements for and opportunities in one or more careers that interest you.

Words to Know

career cluster

civil service job

residency requirement

unskilled labor

semiskilled labor

skilled labor

wholesalers

global positioning system (GPS)

Exploring Careers

Studying career clusters is a good way to start learning about the many types of careers. A **career cluster** is a group of careers that are related in some way. In this chapter, you will read about 16 clusters identified by the U.S. Department of Education. The careers in each cluster are based on common interests and skills. If one career interests you, it is likely that other careers in the same cluster will also interest you.

A variety of jobs requiring different levels of education and training exist within each cluster. You may notice that some jobs belong in more than one cluster. For example, *food scientist* belongs in the Agricultural and Natural Resources cluster and the Scientific Research/Engineering cluster.

When you find a career that appeals to you, you will want to find out more about it. You may want to research several career paths. Keep your interests in mind. This will help you choose a career that you will enjoy.

You learned in Chapter 1 that transferable skills can be used successfully in many different careers. For example, foodservice workers, office assistants, and salespeople are just a few of the workers who must know how to schedule activities. Customer service representatives, waiters, and nurses must have good listening skills. If you begin a career and your interests change, many skills used in one career can be used in another.

Using the techniques you learned in Chapter 4, begin exploring the career clusters. The *Occupational Outlook Handbook* and the O*Net contain extensive information to help guide you in choosing a career.

Job Growth

In general, employment between 2000 and 2010 is expected to increase by 22 million jobs. This growth will be seen in some occupational groups much more than others. The chart in 5-1 shows how many new jobs are likely to come from each of the occupational groups. The occupational groups are ranked according to the number of new jobs expected.

career cluster
A group of careers that are related to each other in some way.

Occupations that are classified as *Professional and related* will add the greatest number of jobs to the economy, nearly 7 million by 2020. *Service* occupations represent the second largest group, adding over 5 million new jobs to the economy. The category with the least growth will be *Farming, fishing, and forestry*, with only 51,000 new jobs.

Service occupations in 2000 included more than 26 million jobs. With the additional 5 million jobs expected by 2010, over 31 million people will be holding jobs in this large and growing occupational group. See 5-2 for a breakdown of the many types of service positions available.

Increases in U.S. Employment, 2000-2010

Occupational Group	Number of New Jobs* (Thousands)	Percent Increase*
Professional and related	6,952	26.0
Service	5,088	19.5
Office and administrative support	2,171	9.1
Management, business, and financial	2,115	13.6
Sales and related	1,852	11.9
Transportation and material moving	1,530	15.2
Construction and extraction	989	13.3
Production	750	5.7
Installation, maintenance, and repair	662	11.4
Farming, fishing and forestry	51	3.6
Total of all occupations	22,160	15.2

U.S. Department of Labor

*Note: May not equal the total or 100% due to rounding.

5-1

By 2010, Professional and related occupations and Service occupations will contribute nearly 12 million new jobs.

As you examine the career clusters in this chapter, consider their potential for job growth. When an occupational area is expanding, many new workers are needed. These areas often present the greatest employment opportunities for individuals.

Employment in 2010 Service Occupations

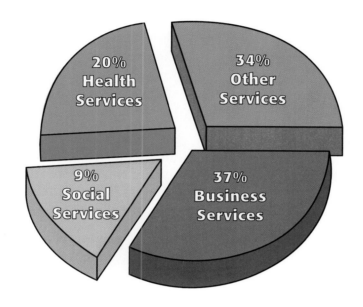

☐ Health care services, hospitals, and offices of health practitioners

☐ Daycare services and residential care services for the elderly

☐ Food preparation and serving, building and grounds cleaning and maintenance, personal care, and protective services

☐ Employment agencies, temporary staffing services, data and systems design and management, and computer consulting

U.S. Department of Labor

5-2
Service jobs in business, health, and social services will account for the majority of service positions in 2010.

Agricultural and Natural Resources

Careers in this cluster involve working with plants and animals. They also focus on the soil, air, water, minerals, and chemicals.

Farmers grow crops and ranchers tend livestock. Foresters plan and supervise the growing and using of trees. Conservationists and environmentalists work on problems regarding the responsible use of air, land, and water. They also preserve marine life and wildlife.

Entry-level jobs are available in this career cluster. Many technical jobs require two or more years of advanced training. Engineers, scientists, and top managers need to complete at least four years of college.

The federal government is one of the biggest employers in this career area. Many specialists work for the Environmental Protection Agency, the National Park Service, and the Fish and Wildlife Service. Other possible employers include landscape nurseries, golf courses, mining and logging operations, and oil exploration companies. More examples of jobs in this career cluster follow:

- ➤ agriculture teacher
- ➤ animal scientist
- ➤ biochemist
- ➤ environmental engineer
- ➤ food scientist
- ➤ veterinarian assistant

Architecture and Construction

People in this career cluster design and build roads, bridges, and all kinds of buildings. They construct homes, offices, shopping centers, hospitals, and factories. Engineers make sure all structures are sound. Careers involving planning, designing, and engineering require college degrees.

Many other workers with special training actually build the structures. These workers include roofers, bricklayers, cement masons, ironworkers, welders, glaziers, and painters. They work on-site wherever structures are built.

Much of their work occurs outdoors and in potentially dangerous conditions.

Most construction workers learn their skills in technical schools or apprenticeship programs. Other examples of jobs in this career cluster follow:

- ➤ architect
- ➤ carpenter
- ➤ contractor
- ➤ electrician
- ➤ heavy equipment operator
- ➤ plumber

Arts, Audiovisual Technology, and Communications

People with careers in the arts include photographers, painters, sculptors, singers, and dancers. Others are cartoonists, stage managers, and lighting directors.

You see the results of work done in the communications field every day. You see newspapers, magazines, books, photographs, and movies. You hear music, radio, and movie sound effects. People in these careers work for publishers, radio and television stations, movie studios, and telephone companies.

Many careers in this cluster are rewarding, creative, and challenging. They are constantly changing, too, because of technological advances. Satellites and computers have led the way for these advances.

The training and education needed are as varied as the careers themselves. Some people have special talents and become instant successes. However, most people spend years training to gain the skills and knowledge needed. Other examples of jobs in this career cluster follow:

- ➤ actor
- ➤ audio engineer
- ➤ journalist
- ➤ printing/graphics technologist
- ➤ telecommunications technologist
- ➤ video producer

Business and Administration

Careers in this cluster involve clerical, computer, accounting, management, and administrative work. An office setting is the most common job site for people working in these careers.

Most entry-level jobs require basic data entry, bookkeeping, and filing skills. Technological advances are forcing workers to upgrade their computer skills. Knowledge of commonly used software programs is especially important.

Administrative assistants, clerks, word processors, and receptionists are needed in all kinds of offices. Some workers input data, organize documents, prepare work schedules, and assemble reports. Managers and administrators solve problems, analyze data, and make decisions.

Jobs in this career cluster occur everywhere there is office work. Business and administration functions exist throughout government, education, and business. Other examples of jobs in this career cluster follow:

- ➤ accountant
- ➤ administrative specialist
- ➤ entrepreneur
- ➤ financial analyst
- ➤ human resource administrator
- ➤ international trade manager

Education and Training

People who enjoy working with and helping people will find this career cluster very rewarding. Do you remember the satisfaction you felt when you helped someone who needed assistance? Teachers and trainers experience that feeling every day.

People with careers in education and training include teacher's aides, parent educators, and librarians. They work with individuals on a one-to-one basis and groups of students. Often the job site is a classroom. However, other sites include offices, gyms, health clubs, private homes, and the workplace itself. Related occupations include occupational trainers and personnel specialists.

Practically all occupations in this career cluster, even for entry-level positions, require training beyond high school. Most occupations require an advanced college degree. Other examples of jobs in this career cluster follow:

- ➤ coach
- ➤ college professor
- ➤ corporate trainer
- ➤ principal
- ➤ school counselor

Finance

People holding jobs in this career cluster generally handle tasks that involve money. Some professionals work for individual clients while others work for various firms and organizations.

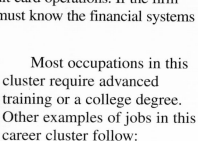

Professionals who work with clients may sell banking services or other financial products. They may give investing advice or arrange a mortgage. They may give credit counseling or process an insurance claim. Whatever their job, they explain the pros and cons of various financial decisions so people can choose what's best for their particular situation.

Every organization, whether profit making or nonprofit, has one or more financial specialists to prepare the required financial reports. They may also manage the accounting and purchasing departments and credit card operations. If the firm buys or sells beyond U.S. borders, these specialists must know the financial systems of other countries.

Most occupations in this cluster require advanced training or a college degree. Other examples of jobs in this career cluster follow:

➤ banker

➤ financial planner

➤ insurance agent

➤ loan officer

➤ stockbroker

➤ tax examiner

Government and Public Administration

Careers in this cluster provide government, legislative, administrative, and regulatory services. All of these services are needed at federal, state, and local government levels.

Many occupations in public service are also called *civil service jobs*. These are government jobs obtained by taking a competitive exam.

Many public service positions have residency requirements. A *residency requirement* demands that an applicant live in a certain area. Usually this is the area served by the branch of government offering the job. For many federal occupations, U.S. citizenship is required.

The qualifications for public service careers vary. Many jobs require education beyond high school. Administrative assistants and secretaries can obtain entry-level jobs, but office training or experience is often expected. Administrators generally need college degrees. Other examples of jobs in this career cluster follow:

- ➤ agency director
- ➤ city manager
- ➤ legislator
- ➤ policy/budget analyst
- ➤ recreation/parks director
- ➤ urban/regional planner

Health Science

The health career cluster offers great opportunities for employment. Jobs are available in hospitals, clinics, and nursing homes. Other workplaces are laboratories, dentists' offices, and drugstores.

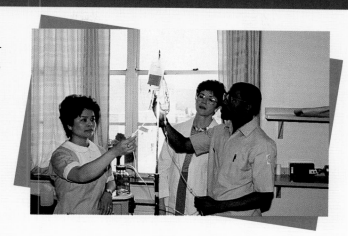

Workers in this cluster help people recover from illness or injury and stay healthy. Dietitians help people meet their nutritional needs. Dentists and orthodontists work on teeth. Podiatrists specialize in the care of feet. Optometrists and ophthalmologists are concerned with people's eyes.

Because the health field is so broad, there are jobs at all levels. Entry-level jobs include those of orderlies and stockroom attendants. Paraprofessionals have one to three years of advanced training. Many of their jobs require licensing. Examples of workers at this level are dental hygienists, practical nurses, paramedics, laboratory assistants, and X ray technicians.

Advanced degrees are usually needed for professions in specialty areas. Other examples of jobs in this career cluster follow:

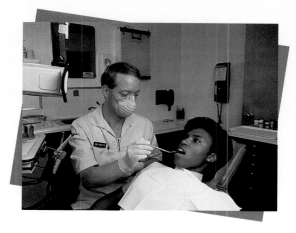

➤ hospital administrator
➤ medical assistant
➤ occupational therapist
➤ pediatrician
➤ physical therapist
➤ radiologic technologist

Hospitality and Tourism

More Americans find ways to enjoy leisure time away from home than ever before. Also, business-related travel is common. Both trends are likely to keep the number of jobs in the hospitality and tourism industry growing.

People in this career cluster work in hotels, restaurants, travel agencies, amusement parks, country clubs, tourist attractions, and on cruise ships. In general, their work focuses on making visitors happy.

Hotel employees from greeters to managers try to make visitors comfortable. Food and beverage service workers satisfy customer appetites. Travel agents, tour guides, and ticket takers make sightseeing trips and vacations enjoyable. People learn to play golf, tennis, and other recreational activities with the help of teaching pros on staff.

Many careers in hospitality and recreation offer on-the-job training. Experience and/or career/technical training may help workers advance. College degrees are usually needed for top jobs. Other examples of jobs in this career cluster follow:

➤ chef

➤ food service manager

➤ leisure and entertainment manager

➤ lodging manager

➤ restaurant manager

➤ travel and tourism manager

Human Services

The many job opportunities available in this career cluster all relate to improving a person's quality of life. Some jobs assist individuals or families. Others involve entire communities.

People in this career cluster work in homes, schools, child care centers, clinics, and community centers. They work with all age groups. Sometimes they work with people who are poor, underprivileged, or have physical or mental disabilities. At times, they serve as consultants to doctors, nurses, and other professionals.

Some occupations in this career cluster require only on-the-job training. Many require career/technical training. Professionals in this field have college degrees, many of which are advanced. Some examples of jobs in this career cluster follow:

➤ social worker

➤ psychologist

➤ child care worker

➤ substance abuse specialist

➤ employment specialist

➤ psychotherapist

Information Technology

Occupations in this career cluster design, develop, and support hardware and software information systems. This career cluster is perhaps the fastest growing and most rapidly changing of all career areas.

Many information technology careers are available for people with strong computer skills. Workers in this field attend computer workshops, seminars, and classes after earning a college degree. They must constantly upgrade their skills because of ever-changing technology. They continue earning various certifications to verify their advanced knowledge and skill level.

Careers tend to cluster in four areas of concentration. Some workers design and run network systems. Some focus on providing technical support and services. Others focus on programming and software development. Yet others concentrate on interactive media. Some examples of jobs in this career cluster follow:

➤ database manager
➤ multimedia producer
➤ network administrator
➤ software engineer
➤ technical writer
➤ Web designer/developer

Law and Public Safety

This career cluster involves planning, managing, and providing judicial, legal, and protective services. Employed by state and local levels, emergency service personnel fight fires and prevent crime. Dispatchers, bailiffs, security guards, and inspectors are some related jobs.

At the federal level, public safety work is more specialized. FBI agents work on cases involving terrorism, organized crime, and violations of federal law. Treasury Department agents investigate the suspicious use of credit cards and illegal gun sales.

Criminal matters plus many other issues are handled by the U.S. court system. Other issues include labor disputes, wills, divorces, business contracts, real estate, and bankruptcy. Lawyers advise clients of their legal rights and represent them in court. Law clerks help research the facts of a case.

Many public service positions require, at minimum, technical training and successful completion of preemployment tests. Some examples of jobs in this career cluster follow:

- ➤ attorney
- ➤ firefighter
- ➤ judge
- ➤ paralegal
- ➤ paramedic
- ➤ police officer

Manufacturing

People in manufacturing careers produce airplanes, cars, and boats. They make appliances, furniture, and toys. They refine ore and produce steel. They knit and weave textiles. They process chemicals and foods. Most people in this career cluster work in factories or plants.

There are three basic types of workers in manufacturing. *Unskilled labor* fills the entry-level jobs. The next level, *semiskilled labor*, requires experience and/or technical training. To qualify for most of the *skilled labor* positions, workers must complete a formal training program beyond high school, such as an apprenticeship or community college program. Companies and trade unions also offer training programs.

Skilled labor positions are called *skilled trades*. Examples of workers in skilled trades are machinists, tool and die makers, drafters, and welders. As was discussed in Chapter 2, technological advances are eliminating entry-level positions in this country while expanding opportunities for skilled labor.

The manufacturing field also employs engineers, scientists, and other positions requiring a college degree. Some examples of jobs in this career cluster follow:

➤ automated process technician
➤ machinist
➤ manufacturing engineer
➤ production engineer/technician
➤ quality technician
➤ welding technician

Retail/Wholesale Sales and Service

Careers in this career cluster involve the promoting, buying, and selling of goods and services. Market researchers look for ways to find new customers. Advertisers try to promote products and services by making them appealing. Buyers and purchasing agents get the supplies, equipment, and products their companies need to conduct business. *Wholesalers* are businesses that sell to retailers. Retailers sell to consumers.

Unlike most other career clusters, retail/wholesale sales and service offer many opportunities for unskilled, semi-skilled, and skilled workers. An increasing number of positions, however, require familiarity with a computer.

Warehouse workers and stock clerks are examples of entry-level jobs. Real estate agents must be licensed. Those who provide services such as Web page design need technical training. College degrees are helpful in many jobs and are required for positions in promotion and management. Other examples of jobs in this career cluster follow:

- ➤ buyer
- ➤ customer service representative
- ➤ interior designer
- ➤ marketing director
- ➤ real estate broker
- ➤ sales associate

Scientific Research/Engineering

People working in this career cluster provide basic research as well as laboratory and testing services. Often their work results in a new scientific discovery with the potential for improving life.

Researchers generally specialize in one area of the life or physical sciences. Life sciences involve the study of biology, microbiology, and zoology. The physical sciences involve chemistry, geology, and physics.

Engineers generally specialize in one of more than 20 distinct branches of their profession. They take scientific principles and apply them in new ways. Engineers focus on designing efficient machinery, products, systems, and processes.

Often scientific work goes in unexpected directions. It is common for researchers and engineers to work closely with experts in other disciplines. Computer-aided tools allow scientists and engineers to quickly modify experiments and run tests.

Advanced degrees are common among scientists and engineers. Even entry-level jobs in this cluster require a four-year college degree. Many people can receive training and experience through the Armed Forces. Other examples of jobs in this career cluster follow:

➤ chemical engineer

➤ mathematician

➤ biotechnologist

➤ electrical engineer

➤ biologist

➤ oceanographer

Transportation, Distribution, and Logistics

Transportation involves moving passengers, cargo, and mail on land, at sea, and in the air. Workers are needed to design, operate, and maintain the vehicles used and the systems that track them.

Distribution and logistics are behind-the-scenes activities that make the transportation system run well. Workers in this career area make sure shipments arrive in good condition at the correct destinations on time. They also arrange for adjustments for lost or damaged goods.

Transportation workers on land include school bus drivers, railroad workers, mechanics, and shipping and receiving clerks. Workers at sea include ship captains and deckhands. Airline and helicopter flight engineers and air traffic controllers are needed for air transportation.

Jobs in the transportation industry rely on computers. Even mechanics and shipping clerks now use computerized tools to do their jobs. One such important tool is the GPS system. A *global positioning system (GPS)* is a highly accurate satellite-based tracking system. It signals where specific cargo is in the world at any given time.

Most jobs in this career cluster require technical training at minimum. Drivers need a commercial driving permit called a chauffeur's license or commercial driving license (CDL). Airline pilots and ship captains must have on-the-job experience and a federal license. Other examples of jobs in this career cluster follow:

- automotive technician
- flight attendant
- logistics manager
- truck driver
- warehouse manager

Summary

Learning about different types of careers is interesting. It is also important. The career you eventually choose will be a major factor in your life. You should do all you can to prepare to make a wise choice.

Sixteen career clusters are described in this chapter. Each includes a wide variety of jobs from entry-level to professional positions.

Watch and listen to other people as they work in different careers. Think about how you would feel as a worker in various jobs. The more you do to prepare yourself, the more likely you are to make a satisfying career choice.

Reviewing the Chapter

Match the following job titles (*1* through *12*) with the appropriate career cluster (*A* through *P*).

1. Accountant, entrepreneur, and word processor
2. Actor, journalist, and audio engineer
3. Chef, hotel manager, and travel agent
4. Coach, corporate trainer, and principal
5. Employment specialist, social worker, and psychologist
6. Food scientist, forester, and veterinarian assistant
7. Ironworker, contractor, and plumber
8. Mathematician, biologist, and lab assistant
9. Network administrator, technical writer, and database manager
10. Real estate agent, advertiser, and interior designer
11. Shipping clerk, mechanic, and railroad worker
12. Welder, machinist, and quality technician

    A. Agricultural and natural resources

    B. Architecture and construction

    C. Arts, audiovisual technology, and communications

    D. Business and administration

    E. Education and training

    F. Finance

    G. Government and public administration

    H. Health science

    I. Hospitality and tourism

    J. Human service

K. Information technology

L. Law and public safety

M. Manufacturing

N. Retail/wholesale sales and service

O. Scientific research/engineering

P. Transportation, distribution, and logistics

Building Your Foundation Skills

1. Find a news story about a change in technology. What jobs or career cluster will be affected? Discuss the story in class.

2. Visit your guidance office and obtain three pamphlets describing jobs you think you would like.

3. Interview someone in a career that interests you. Ask questions about the pros and cons of the career. Find out what a typical day at work involves. Prepare an oral report on your findings.

Building Your Workplace Competencies

Work with a team of three or four classmates to create individual posters for six career options within a career cluster. Determine who will do which tasks. Prepare a brief fact sheet for each career that covers the basic job factors discussed in Chapter 4. Use Department of Labor references for your research. Use the computer to conduct your research and create the posters. Determine which facts to display on each poster. Identify the career field and career cluster on each. Present your posters to the class and summarize the key points about each. Attach the appropriate fact sheet to each poster to allow classmates to learn more details later, if they so desire. *(This activity develops competence with resources, interpersonal skills, information, and technology.)*

A Business of Your Own

Objectives

After studying this chapter, you will be able to

- give examples of retail and service businesses.

- decide whether you are the right type of person to own your own business.

- summarize the financial considerations of starting a business.

- name and describe three types of business organizations.

Words to Know

entrepreneurship

retail business

franchise

service business

working capital

wholesale

sole proprietorship

partnership

corporation

stockholder

A Business of Your Own

Does the idea of being your own boss appeal to you? Have you ever thought about starting a business of your own? If so, entrepreneurship may be right for you. See 6-1. *Entrepreneurship* means starting and owning your own business. A person who starts a business is called an entrepreneur. Being an entrepreneur is not easy, but it can be very rewarding.Entrepreneurs need to have good imaginations. They look for business ideas and new and better ways to solve problems. They work to successfully sell their new products and services to others.

Entrepreneurs generally start with small businesses, but their businesses may grow to be quite large. Gas stations, restaurants, and beauty salons are examples of small businesses that are often owned by entrepreneurs. Most small businesses are involved in retail sales or providing services.

Sam's Wash 'N Shine Service

Sixteen-year-old Sam is an entrepreneur. He began last summer when a neighbor asked if he would like to make some money by washing and waxing her car. He agreed and spent a full day working on the car. When he finished, the car looked like new.

Sam's neighbor was so pleased that she told a friend. The friend called Sam to see if Sam would wash and wax his car. Sam agreed and did another excellent job. The word got around, and soon Sam had more cars to wash and wax than he had days left in his summer vacation. Sam called a friend and hired her to help with the work.

Sam now has two people working for him. This summer he and his two employees plan to work full-time washing and waxing cars. Sam has enrolled in an auto body repair program that starts at the local career/technical school next fall. Someday Sam wants to have his own auto body repair shop.

6-1

Some people become entrepreneurs by turning part-time work experiences into full-time businesses.

Retail Businesses

Entrepreneurs who own a *retail business* sell products like food, clothing, and cars to consumers. Many retail businesses are located in shopping malls and business districts.

entrepreneurship
The starting and owning of a person's own business.

retail business
A business that sells products, such as clothing or cars, to consumers.

Some entrepreneurs own one-of-a-kind shops. Others own franchises. A *franchise* is the right to sell a company's products in a specified area. Many of the regionally known chains of stores and restaurants are franchises.

Some entrepreneurs who own retail businesses make the products they sell. Others sell products that are made by others. For example, someone who owns a bakery may make the pastries he or she sells. However, someone who owns a clothing shop probably buys clothes from manufacturers and resells them to the public.

Service Businesses

The service industry makes up a large portion of the businesses in the United States. Entrepreneurs who own **service businesses** perform tasks for their customers. Their businesses may involve such services as cleaning houses, mowing lawns, and dry cleaning. See 6-2.

Do You Want to Be an Entrepreneur?

Entrepreneurs often start their own businesses to achieve certain goals. You may want to become an entrepreneur some day if you have some of the following goals:

- making more money
- developing a new idea
- being their own bosses, setting their own working hours, and making their own decisions
- gaining recognition in the community
- doing a better job than anyone else

6-2

Hairstylists provide the service of washing, cutting, and styling hair for their customers.

Not everyone is the right type of person to start a business. Your answers to the following questions may help you decide if entrepreneurship is for you:

- Do you have unlimited ambition and drive?
- Do you have a good knowledge of the product or service you want to provide?
- Do you make good decisions quickly?
- Can you supervise people well?
- Can you motivate people to do their work well?
- Are you comfortable around strangers?

6-3

Entrepreneurs often spend weekends and late weekday hours doing paperwork for their business.

Starting a business can present some disadvantages. Knowing some of these may help you decide whether you want to become an entrepreneur. One disadvantage is the amount of work to do. Small business owners often work many more hours than people who work for others. See 6-3.

Another disadvantage is the financial risk. Opening a business can be very expensive. Business owners must pay rent, wages, and taxes. They must buy equipment and supplies, too. If a business fails, the owner risks losing the entire financial investment.

For these and other reasons, entrepreneurs must deal with more stress than average workers feel. This is another disadvantage of entrepreneurship.

franchise
The right to sell a company's products in specified areas.
service business
A business that performs tasks for its customers.

Planning a Business

After evaluating your goals and deciding to become an entrepreneur, your first step to entrepreneurship is forming a business plan. What type of business do you want to start? Will you provide a service or a product? Who will your customers be? How will you service them?

Decide what you are capable of doing. It is not wise to start a business doing something you have never done. Most business experts recommend working in a field for a few years before starting your own business. In that way, you will be better prepared to handle problems that arise. See 6-4.

People in the Small Business Administration (SBA) office in your area can help you as you make plans to start a business. They can tell you what legal steps must be followed. They can help you register with the proper state and federal agencies. They can provide detailed information on how to plan your firm, advertise, and manage operations.

The SBA can also help you get *working capital*. This is the money needed to start and maintain a business. Government-funded small-business loans are available to entrepreneurs who qualify.

Financial Considerations

One of the biggest mistakes entrepreneurs make is not planning for business expenses. Some businesses, particularly retail businesses, require a great deal of money to open. To open a clothing shop, for example, you must first buy the clothing.

Service businesses may cost less to start. For instance, you only need yourself and a lawnmower to begin a lawn

6-4
Working in an established business for a few years can prepare a person for starting his or her own business.

maintenance service. The following questions and comments can help would-be entrepreneurs realize what business expenses they may have:

- **Must equipment be purchased?** Equipment may include anything from a computer to many pieces of expensive equipment. See 6-5. Sometimes entrepreneurs can rent equipment instead of buying it. Another alternative might be to lease equipment with the option to buy. This type of lease allows payments to apply toward the purchase price of the item.

6-5
Many small restaurants are owned and operated by entrpreneuers.

- **What kind of supplies are needed?** Paper, pencils, computers, gasoline, and food may be some of the supplies needed for different businesses. Sometimes a business owner can purchase supplies *wholesale*. This is a large quantity of items packaged in bulk with a per-item cost below the retail price.

- **What kind of advertising should be done?** Many businesses cannot survive without advertising. Through advertising, customers learn about businesses and the goods or services they offer. Many small businesses advertise by using direct mail leaflets, newspapers, radio, and cable television. Advertising can be expensive, so it is important to spend advertising dollars wisely. Business owners must reach the people who are most likely to buy their products or services.

> **working capital**
> Money needed to start and maintain a business.
>
> **wholesale**
> A large quantity of items packaged in bulk with a per-item cost below the retail price.

- **At what price should the goods or services be sold?** Business owners must think about many things when setting prices. The cost of providing the goods or services is a chief consideration. Generally, the lower the business owners' costs are, the lower the selling prices can be. Another factor to consider is the price charged by competitors offering similar goods or services.

- **Are employees needed?** Sometimes one or two people are enough to run a small business, particularly when it is just opening. Later, a few employees may need to be hired to help with the work. Each added employee increases the company's expenses. The value of what a new employee produces must be greater than the extra labor costs.

- **What type of work space is needed?** Some people can run their businesses from an apartment or home. This is usually cheaper than renting office or store space. As a business grows, space can be rented as needed. Sometimes the type of work involved requires a particular type of space.

Types of Business Organizations

When you start a business, you will need to decide how you will organize it. The following businesses are the three basic types of organization:

- sole proprietorship
- partnership
- corporation

Sole Proprietorship

One person owns a *sole proprietorship*. It is the easiest type of business to start and dissolve because no other owners are involved. The owner makes all business decisions, does most of the work, and earns all the profits.

Being a sole proprietor also has disadvantages. Being the owner means you are responsible for all bills and expenses. If the business fails, the owner's personal property may be taken to cover any outstanding debts. Many people are good at making a product or providing a service. However, not all of these people have the skills to successfully run a business.

Partnership

Two or more people own a *partnership*. The partners combine their money and energy. They often share the work, responsibilities, debts, and profits.

An advantage of a partnership is having one or more partners with whom to share ideas and discuss problems before making decisions, 6-6. If the business fails, the losses are shared with the partners. Partnerships may have problems, too. One of the partners may feel that he or she is being treated unfairly. Partners may disagree on how to run the business. Such feelings can cause partnerships to fail.

Corporation

A *corporation* can legally act as a single person, even though many people may own it. To *incorporate* means to organize a business as a corporation. People buy a part of the company by purchasing stock. The owners of the stock are called ***stockholders***. Selling stock in a company provides a greater amount of money to the business. Stockholders only risk the amount of their original stock investment if the business fails.

Although they are the owners, stockholders have little responsibility for business decisions. Those decisions are left to the board of directors. The directors, elected by the stockholders, make most of the decisions for the company.

Many corporations are very large and may have thousands of stockholders. A very small company of one or two people may also choose to incorporate. This type of organization offers some different legal and tax advantages than a partnership or sole proprietorship.

6-6
Business partners must consult each other about important decisions.

sole proprietorship
A business owned by one person.

partnership
A business owned by two or more people.

corporation
A business that can legally act as a single person, but may be owned by many people.

stockholder
A person who owns a share of a corporation's stock.

Summary

Entrepreneurs are people who own and operate their own businesses. Most entrepreneurs begin by opening small retail or service businesses. The businesses may stay small, or they may grow.

If you are thinking of starting your own business, you should look at both the pros and cons. You should also take a good look at the type of person you are. Most successful entrepreneurs share certain characteristics.

Once you decide to start a business, plan carefully. You may want to contact the nearest Small Business Administration office for help. Entrepreneurs must decide what type of organization is best for their businesses. They may choose to run their businesses as sole proprietorships, partnerships, or corporations.

Reviewing the Chapter

1. What is the difference between retail businesses and service businesses? Give an example of each.
2. The right to sell a company's products in a specified area is called a _____.
3. List five goals entrepreneurs often have for starting their own business.
4. Name two disadvantages of entrepreneurship.
5. How can the Small Business Administration help entrepreneurs get started?
6. List five financial considerations when planning to open a business.
7. Describe an advantage and a disadvantage of organizing a business as a sole proprietorship.
8. Describe an advantage and a disadvantage of a partnership.
9. True or false. Selling stock in a company provides a greater amount of money for operating a business.
10. True or false. Although stockholders own a corporation, they have little responsibility for business decisions.

Building Your Foundation Skills

1. Design a bulletin board that shows various opportunities for entrepreneurs.
2. Research the success of an entrepreneur. Write a report about how the business was started and how it grew.

3. Interview three entrepreneurs in your community. Ask them what they did to get their businesses started. Find out if they think they should have done anything differently. What advice would they give to a young entrepreneur?

4. Contact the nearest Small Business Administration office. Find out what it takes to qualify for a government loan for working capital.

Building Your Workplace Competencies

Imagine yourself as an entrepreneur and determine the type of business that might interest you. What product or service would you offer? Research who your competitors are by checking library and Internet sources. If you prefer a neighborhood business, learn about your competitors through conversations with friends and family members. What are the strong points of your competitors? What would you do to offer a better product or service than your competitors? Which of the three basic ways to organize a business would you choose? Indicate whether you feel well-suited to entrepreneurship. Give a brief oral report to the class, citing the references you used. *(This activity develops competence with interpersonal skills, information, systems, and technology.)*

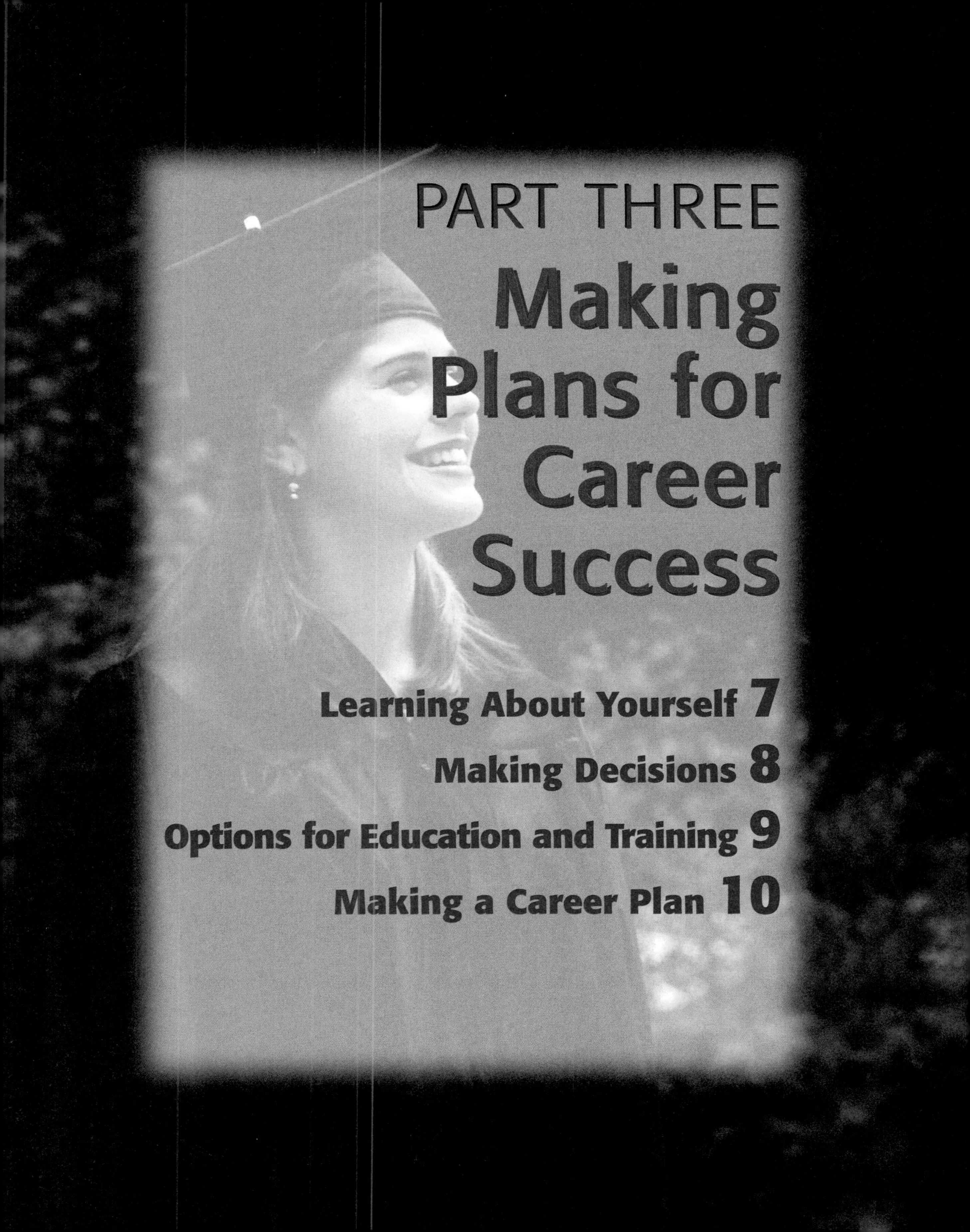

PART THREE

Making Plans for Career Success

7

Learning About Yourself

Objectives

After studying this chapter, you will be able to

- determine how personality, self-concept, interests, attitudes, aptitudes, abilities, and personal priorities affect career decisions.

- analyze how self-concept can affect job performance.

- relate personal priorities to professional priorities.

Words to Know

resource
personality
self-concept
interests
attitude
aptitudes
abilities
personal priorities

The Importance of Knowing Yourself

What career path will you follow? In Chapter 4 of this text, you learned how to explore the various career options available to you. The choices you face may seem overwhelming. Choosing a satisfying career requires knowing about careers, but that's only half the search. The other half is knowing yourself.

In this chapter, you will learn how to better understand yourself. Only then will you be able to choose a career that suits you.

Examining the Real You

Most of us know ourselves better than anyone else does. However, we are not always honest with ourselves. "You are only kidding yourself" is a common saying. Being honest with yourself is important for knowing the real you and choosing a satisfying career path.

Understanding yourself begins by understanding your resources. A *resource* is anything a person can use to help reach his or her goals. Money is a resource you can get. Time is a resource everyone has. The desire to do well is a resource within you. (You will learn more about resources in Chapter 10, "Making a Career Plan.")

The resources within you are important to choosing a career you will like. Your resources include your personality, self-concept, interests, attitude, aptitudes, abilities, and personal priorities. Each of these can affect the career choice you make. Understanding these characteristics about yourself may be as important to career success as your academic preparation.

Your Personality

Everyone has a one-of-a-kind personality. *Personality* is the group of traits that makes each person unique. Some of these traits may be intelligence, enthusiasm, and honesty. Others are listed in Chart 7-1.

Have you ever described someone as having a good personality? You probably meant the person was friendly, happy, pleasant, and kind. Such a person is usually popular. People react in a positive way to someone with a good personality. Your personality is important to your career in the following two ways discussed on the next page.

> **resource**
> Anything a person can use to help reach his or her goals.
> **personality**
> The group of traits that makes each person unique.

Personality Traits

cooperative	greedy	quiet	capable
agreeable	aggressive	confident	lazy
stubborn	assertive	happy	moody
self-disciplined	independent	sad	nervous
friendly	dependent	funny	patient
shy	talkative	witty	kind
intelligent	loyal	boring	religious
thoughtful	honest	dependable	polite
impulsive	dishonest	unreliable	respectful
energetic	pleasant	tolerant	sarcastic
ambitious	enthusiastic	critical	helpful
generous	outgoing	jealous	selfish

7-1

Identifying the personality traits that describe you can help you choose a career that will suit your personality.

- First, understanding your personality helps you choose a career you will like. For example, a talkative person might do well in sales. A supportive person might do well in customer service or health occupations. Your chances for happiness and success are best when your career is suited to your personality. See 7-2.
- Secondly, having a pleasant personality helps you get jobs and do them well. Employers and coworkers react positively to pleasant personalities. They enjoy working with such people. Employers avoid hiring people with poor personalities. Such a person is usually a sign of future problems.

Your Self-Concept

What you know and feel about yourself is your ***self-concept***. Your self-concept affects your personality. When you have a healthy self-concept, you recognize both your strengths and weaknesses. You accept and feel good about your positive qualities. Factors that influence a healthy self-concept include a realistic and complete self-concept and high self-esteem.

You have high self-esteem when you feel good about yourself. You respect yourself and feel that you are a worthwhile person. You recognize what you like and dislike about yourself. You know what to change about yourself to raise your self-esteem.

You develop a realistic self-concept by seeing yourself as you really are, not as you would like to be. As you think seriously about your self-concept, consider your relationships with others.

Your self-concept becomes

7-2

People with friendly, supportive personalities often become teachers.

more complete as you learn more about yourself. New experiences and interactions with a variety of people can help you develop a more complete and healthy self-concept.

Your self-concept can affect your chances of getting and keeping a job. Self-confident employees have a positive attitude. They are able to accept new challenges and responsibilities. People with a healthy self-concept tend to do well in the workplace so employers try to hire them.

Forming and Changing Your Self-Concept

A good self-concept doesn't just happen. What you have learned to believe about yourself forms your self-concept. If you have a good self-concept, you can strengthen it. If you have a poor self-concept, you can change it.

To change your self-concept, you must first be honest with yourself. Often people who brag about what they can do have a poor self-concept. They brag because they want others to think they are able to do more than they really can.

self-concept
Recognition of both your strengths and weaknesses. Acceptance and feeling good about yourself.

How you feel about yourself also affects how others see you. If you feel good about yourself, others will see you in a positive way. If you know your strengths and your weaknesses, and are honest with yourself, others will respect you. Knowing your strengths does not mean always knowing the answer. It means that when you are unsure of something, you aren't afraid to ask. You aren't afraid to make a mistake. You know that you can succeed only by trying.

Your Interests

Everyone has a unique set of interests. **Interests** are the ideas, subjects, or activities a person enjoys. Right now, you may be interested in music and singing. Some of your friends may be interested in the computer, while others enjoy sports and hobbies. No person's interests are better or worse than another's. They simply are different.

Interests play a key role in your career. People who find their work interesting are usually successful and happy. If you like your job, work can be fun and exciting.

Which do you enjoy most? Interacting with people, working with information, or using tools? In other words, do you prefer to work with people, data, or things?

People

Are you a person who prefers to be around others? Do you like to talk with people? Do you make friends easily? Are you outgoing? See 7-3.

Students who are people-oriented prefer socializing to reading a book or watching TV. These students are usually active in many school functions and clubs. They like to assist others. They volunteer to help with community functions. They like to solve conflicts between others.

7-3
Jobs in the service sector need workers who enjoy helping people.

Data

Are you an information seeker? Do you enjoy gathering information from books, magazines, newspapers, TV, or the Internet? Do you know all the football scores and statistics? Do you like to read and research information?

People interested in data like to discover facts. Some enjoy working with figures. They are comfortable spending time alone and often prefer that to socializing with others.

Objects

Do you like to repair broken objects or assemble things? Do you enjoy working on a car, sewing a new outfit, or cooking a special meal?

People who like to work with tools and instruments enjoy making items with their hands, 7-4. They like to take objects apart and put them back together.

7-4

Carpenters and other craftspeople have jobs that focus on tools and the objects that result from using them.

interests
The ideas, subjects, or activities a person enjoys.

Sometimes they enjoy working with others on a hands-on project, but often they enjoy working alone.

Few jobs focus exclusively on people, data, or objects. Most jobs involve all three interest areas. Many careers, like *carpenter, teacher,* and *reporter,* have primary and secondary interests. Knowing your particular interests will help you focus on a good career match.

The Three A's

Attitude, aptitude, and ability are the three A's. You can improve your attitude and abilities, but you have no control over your aptitude.

Your Attitude—Positive or Negative?

Your attitude is very important. *Attitude* is how you react to a situation. Your reaction shapes how other people view you. Is your attitude positive or negative, happy or angry?

You probably know people who are friendly, pleasant, and kind. These are signs of a positive attitude. People with this attitude are very popular. Employers tend to hire these people, and employees like to work with them.

People with a negative attitude are just the opposite. They often complain and are rarely satisfied. They think their ideas are the best and are unwilling to compromise. These people become very difficult coworkers. Employers try to avoid hiring individuals with a negative attitude.

Your Aptitudes and Abilities

Many people have natural talents and can learn to do new things quickly and easily. Natural talents and the potential to learn easily and quickly are *aptitudes*. For instance, some people can play a song on a musical instrument after hearing it only a few times. They have an aptitude for music.

If you have an interest and an aptitude for something, you would probably be very successful in a related career. If you enjoy writing and do it well, you would probably be a good author or journalist.

Some people discover their aptitudes on their own. They may discover their aptitudes when learning something new. Sometimes others can see your aptitudes when you can't. Your friends, family, teachers, and employers can all help you discover your aptitudes.

A school counselor can give you an aptitude test. Such a test does not have right or wrong answers. It just helps you learn about your aptitudes.

Skills you must develop are your *abilities*. Sometimes abilities are aptitudes that you have developed and improved. For instance, an aptitude for quick, coordinated movements could be developed into the ability to type quickly and accurately or play the piano well. Different jobs require different abilities, 7-5.

Sometimes people choose careers for which they have no aptitudes or abilities. This puts them at a disadvantage next to workers who have the natural ability to perform well. For example, an individual may want to be professional singer. Without an aptitude for music or the ability to sing, that person does not have the personal resources for a successful singing career. It is very important to recognize your aptitudes and abilities when considering a career.

7-5

This assembly line task requires skillful finger manipulation. Such coordination is an aptitude, but with practice, a less coordinated person could develop the ability.

The average person has many aptitudes and abilities, but not all lead to a career. For example, one of your favorite pastimes may be repairing cars. This does not mean you should become a full-time auto mechanic. You may simply enjoy fixing cars as a hobby. If so, your other interests would determine the direction of your career.

attitude
How you react to a situation.

aptitudes
The natural talents a person has or the potential to learn certain skills easily and quickly.

abilities
The skills a person has developed.

Your Personal Priorities

Personal priorities are all the beliefs, ideas, and objects that are important to you. People have different personal priorities. Your family, friends, and community influence your priorities. Your life experiences and religious beliefs also influence them. See 7-6.

Each individual has a unique set of personal priorities. Consider yours and be honest with yourself. Try to decide what is most important to you. Then try to act according to your personal priorities. If education is important to you, put your best efforts into your schoolwork. If you appreciate good health, take time to exercise and learn about nutrition.

Besides personal priorities, you also have *professional priorities*. These are related to work that is important to you. Some common professional priorities are listed in 7-7. Take time to think about what you want from your work. Some of your priorities may be the same personally and professionally. People who value honesty with family members and friends also believe it is important with coworkers.

Being able to identify what is important to you will help you make career choices. If you believe time with your family is important, you would not be happy traveling for long periods. If you seek creative outlets, you would not enjoy working on a factory assembly line. If you value high status in the community, you might want to become a doctor or police officer. Consider your personal and professional priorities when you choose a career.

Personal Priorities

Honesty	Are you always sincere and truthful? Do you expect the same in return?
Heath	Do you enjoy practicing good health habits? Do you eat right, exercise, and get enough rest?
Family, Friends	Do you like to be surrounded by the people you love, or do you prefer to see them only at certain times?
Religion	Do you have certain beliefs or rituals that must be maintained?
Education	Do you enjoy gaining knowledge? Do you want to earn an advanced degree?

7-6
Beliefs, ideas, or objects that are important to you are your personal priorities.

Professional Priorities

Ethics	Do you believe in being honest and fair in all business situations?
Independence	Do you like to work as part of a team or on you own?
Variety	Should your workdays be very similar or very different?
Creativity	Do you want a job that involves following directions, or would you prefer a job where no directions exist so you could figure them out for yourself?
Competition	Do you enjoy leading or following your coworkers?
Recognition	How important is it to you that others know what you do?

7-7
Answering these questions honestly will help you identify some of your professional priorities.

How to Evaluate Yourself

There are many ways to evaluate all the characteristics that make *you*. Your school may evaluate you to help you make choices and identify classes. Employers will evaluate you, too. They often use written tests to evaluate your personality, aptitudes, and abilities. They may also use interviews and supervisor reports to assist their evaluation.

You, too, can evaluate yourself. You can recognize your attitude and change it. Simple activities like listing your positive and negative attitudes can be the first step. Deciding which attitude to change and how to do so are the next steps.

Abilities can be changed in the same way. Your ability to play a musical instrument can change with more practice.

Taking an honest look at yourself periodically is the best way to evaluate yourself. Asking your family, teachers, and school counselor what they see in you will also help. When weak points are discovered in you, work to correct them. Then, map your progress.

personal priorities
All the beliefs, ideas, and objects that are important to an individual.

Summary

Being aware of the resources within you can help you choose a satisfying career. Begin with positive personality traits and a healthy self-concept. Employers and coworkers enjoy working with people who possess these resources.

Your interests, attitude, aptitudes, and abilities are other resources you can use to choose a satisfying career. You are likely to be happy and successful if you are interested in your work and able to do it well.

Think about what you want from your personal life and your work. Knowing what is important to you will guide you to satisfying career choices. Work toward knowing yourself better. Change any weaknesses in you that could negatively affect your career choice.

Reviewing the Chapter

1. What are resources?
2. What resources do you have that can help you choose a satisfying career?
3. Name a career and five personality traits that would help a person succeed in it.
4. Describe how you can develop a complete and healthy self-concept.
5. Why should you think about your interests when searching for a career?
6. What are the three basic areas of career interests?
7. How can your attitude affect your career?
8. List three ways people discover their aptitudes.
9. What is the difference between aptitudes and abilities?
10. Which of the following statements is *not* true?

    A. Family, friends, community, life experiences, and religious beliefs influence personal priorities.

    B. Each individual has a unique set of personal priorities.

    C. An individual's professional priorities tend to be very different from his or her personal priorities.

    D. Both personal and professional priorities may affect career choices.

Building Your Foundation Skills

1. Working in a small group, identify and list personality traits you would want your coworkers to have. Compare lists. Which personality traits did everyone in the group list?

2. Research the background of a successful person. Write a one-page report on how the person's interests, aptitudes, and abilities helped him or her succeed.

3. Consider a famous book or popular television show. List the personal and professional priorities displayed by the main character. How do they affect the character's life and career?

4. Design a bulletin board that shows how different interests can lead to various careers.

5. List your positive and negative attitudes. Identify those that you would like to change or improve. Develop a plan that will enable you to change. (Keep this activity private or, if you desire, share it with your teacher.)

Building Your Workplace Competencies

Interview local employers to find out how they try to determine if job candidates have the personality traits, attitudes, and professional priorities they desire in employees. Working with two or three classmates, decide how to divide the following tasks. Interview at least two local employers to obtain the information. Summarize your findings in a one-page report, and create an interesting cover page that focuses on one of the key points you learned. Use a computer to develop both the report and cover page. Present your cover page to the class, briefly describing what inspired your team to create it. *(This activity develops competence with resources, interpersonal skills, information, systems, and technology.)*

Making Decisions

Objectives

After studying this chapter, you will be able to

- distinguish between different types of decisions.

- list the seven steps of the decision-making process.

- apply the decision-making process to real-life situations.

- explain the role trade-offs play in making decisions.

- explain the importance of personal, career, and work decisions.

Words to Know

decision
routine decision
impulse decision
decision-making process
alternatives
implement
trade-off

Decision Making—A Daily Task

When you make a *decision*, you make a specific choice or judgment. You arrive at a conclusion. You make up your mind. You make many decisions every day. Most of them are fairly simple. You make them quickly, without much thought. Some of your recent decisions may have involved the following choices:

- walking to work or riding
- seeing a movie or going to a dance
- studying or watching television
- eating a hamburger or tacos

Other decisions are more difficult to make. You must think about them and plan for them. The following decisions are examples of those requiring thoughtful planning:

- when to get a job
- what courses to take in school
- what to do after graduation
- what career path to follow

As you read this chapter, you will learn more about making both the easy and the difficult decisions. You will also learn ways to make the difficult decisions easier to handle.

Routine Decisions

Routine decisions are decisions you make often. Choosing what time to get up in the morning, what clothes to wear, and what to eat for breakfast are all routine decisions. You make these decisions automatically. At one time, each of these decisions took some thought and planning. By now, they are part of your daily routine. Less and less planning is needed as decisions become automatic or routine. See 8-1.

Impulse Decisions

Impulse decisions are snap decisions. They don't require much thought or planning. Instead, these decisions are made quickly. They are based on feelings or reactions to certain situations. You may grab an umbrella as you leave for school if dark clouds are in sight. You may decide to walk home from

decision
A choice or a judgment.
routine decision
A decision made often.
impulse decision
A decision made quickly, without much thought.

8-1
Wearing a raincoat on a rainy day is a routine decision.

school instead of riding if the sun is brightly shining.

At times, impulse decisions can be fun and exciting. However, important decisions in life should not be made on impulse.

Thoughtful Decisions and the Decision-Making Process

Many of the decisions you will face in life will be difficult decisions. They will be too unfamiliar to treat as impulse or routine decisions. They will be too important to treat as impulse decisions. You will need to take time to think about these important decisions.

The *decision-making process* will help you sort through your thoughts. It is a seven-step guide for making decisions based on careful thinking and planning. See 8-2.

1. Define the Issue

To make a thoughtful decision, you must first define the question or issue. Identify just what it is that you need to choose, judge, or conclude. Sometimes the decision can be stated as a problem that needs to be solved. You must understand a situation before you can make a good decision about it.

The Decision-Making Process

1. Define the issue.

2. Make a self-inventory.

3. List all possible alternatives.

4. Forecast the outcome of each alternative.

5. Choose the best alternative

6. Make a plan of action.

7. Evaluate the results.

8-2

The decision-making process is a tool you will need to use throughout life to make good decisions.

2. Make a Self-Inventory

When facing a question or problem, it is best to review your strengths and weaknesses. What can you do to help solve this problem? Which of your talents and abilities can you use? Knowing what you can do well helps to identify possible alternatives.

3. List Possible Alternatives

Many people fail to think through the many alternatives they have. *Alternatives* are choices or options. As a result, people often never consider the best possible decision. Make a list of all the alternatives you have before you make a decision.

You may not even know what all of your choices are. In that case, do some research. Read books or magazines and talk to people. Get all the information you need. Do not limit yourself. The longer your list of alternatives is, the better your chances are of making a good decision.

decision-making process
A seven-step guide for making decisions based on careful thought and planning.
alternatives
Options a person has when making a decision.

4. Forecast Possible Outcomes

Think through each of your alternatives. Try to predict what would happen as a result of each choice. As you play the "what if?" game, consider both the pros and cons of each choice. Think about short-term and long-term results. Consider how each choice might affect other people as well as yourself.

5. Make a Decision

After carefully considering each alternative, one will probably stand out as the best choice. This is the time to make your decision. If you have followed the first five steps carefully, you will probably be happy with your decision. See 8-3.

8-3
The color, style, and fit of each alternative should be considered when deciding what to buy.

6. Make an Action Plan

After making a decision, you need to put it into action, or **implement** it. When you implement a decision, you are carrying out a plan.

If you aren't sure how to act on your decision, ask the *who, what, when, where, why,* and *how* questions: Who should take action? What should happen? When do you want it to happen? Where should it happen? Why should it happen? How should it happen? The answers to these basic questions will help you implement your plan.

7. Evaluate Results

Finally, look at the results of your decision. This last step is an important one. Take time to judge the outcome of your decision. Good or bad, you must accept responsibility for it. If the outcome turns out as expected and you are pleased, you made a good decision. If not, make an effort to learn from your experience. Determine why you are not pleased. Think again about your alternatives. You may need to alter your decision or make a different decision to get the results you want.

Trade-Offs

Every time you make a decision, you are making a choice. By choosing one alternative, you give up the others. When you choose to get married, you give up being single. When you choose to take a job in a big city, you limit your chances to enjoy the peacefulness of the countryside. There is a ***trade-off*** or exchange for every decision you make. One thing must be given up in return for another. See 8-4.

You may decide to purchase an expensive sweater for the dance next month. To do this, you will need some money. Therefore, you must set up a

8-4   *Bergen County Vocational Technical School*

Not joining the tennis team this year may be a necessary trade-off for choosing to join the archery team and learning a new sport.

savings plan. To reach your goal, you must consider all possible trade-offs. Getting more money to buy a new sweater may mean working more hours at a part-time job. If you don't have a job, buying a new sweater may mean *not* doing some of the following:

- going to a movie
- buying a new tape or CD
- stopping for pizza after a game

Do not make important decisions too quickly. The trade-off principle is always at work. Keep this in mind when you make decisions.

implement
To put a plan into action.
trade-off
The giving up of one thing for another.

Personal Decisions

Personal decisions are choices that affect you personally. They are influenced by your likes and dislikes. Your personal decisions will determine such areas as the following:

- your hairstyle
- the clothes you wear
- your friends
- the lifestyle you lead

Your personal decisions may affect your career decisions. If you choose to dress in a trendy style, you may be rejected by the business world. If you choose friends that have questionable character or a bad reputation, you may have trouble getting a good job. Personal and career decisions are often interwoven.

8-5

If you can think clearly and speak persuasively, you have some of the important traits needed for becoming a lawyer.

Career Decisions

Many people spend more time planning their vacations than they do planning their careers. Explore many career paths to find one or more that you might like to pursue. Then match your traits with the requirements of the career paths you are considering. See 8-5.

Gather as much information as you can to assist you in making a wise career choice. Discuss your career plans with your teachers and guidance counselors. Talk to friends, family members, and neighbors. They can help you explore career paths. Do additional research in libraries, if necessary. Do not limit yourself.

Analyze your career alternatives so you can choose a career path that suits you. Once you decide on a career, draw up a plan of action that will help you reach your career goal. As you make career decisions, consider the following factors:

- What courses and programs will you take in high school?
- How much effort will you put into your studies?
- What skills will you develop?
- What schooling and training beyond high school are you willing to pursue?
- What careers will you explore?

Work Decisions

In the work place, you will face many decisions. These decisions may affect your job. They may also affect other people. See 8-6. Remember, decisions are choices. As a worker, you will make decisions every day. The following decisions are some that you might face:

- Should I complete this order or go on break?
- Should I work overtime?
- Should I tell my boss about a faulty product?
- Should I take this promotion or wait for another?

Often the answers are obvious, but sometimes they are not. In some cases, you may face two or more choices that seem good. Simply follow the seven steps of the decision-making process.

Remember, *making no decision* is actually a decision. It is choosing to take no action. It is deciding to accept whatever happens or whatever other people choose for you. It is giving up a chance to manage your own life.

8-6
A customer service agent frequently must decide how to deal with impatient customers.

Summary

You make many decisions every day. You make most of them quickly and easily, without much thought. Important decisions that will affect your future deserve careful consideration. The decision-making process is a seven-step guide based on careful thinking and planning. It can be applied to any situation.

All decisions involve trade-offs. Be sure to consider the trade-offs involved in your decisions. The results of personal decisions sometimes affect more than just your personal life. They may influence your career.

Career questions and work issues are often difficult. Use the decision-making process to help sort through your thoughts. If you follow each step, you are likely to make good decisions and get the results you want.

Reviewing the Chapter

1. Give five examples of routine decisions.
2. On what are impulse decisions based?
3. List and explain the seven steps of the decision-making process.
4. What should you consider when forecasting the possible outcome of each alternative to a decision?
5. When people implement plans, what are they doing?
6. Why is the last step of the decision-making process an important one?
7. What is the relationship between decisions and trade-offs?
8. Which of the following is an example of the results of personal decisions?

   A. classes offered by your school

   B. the friends you have

   C. your football team's opponents

   D. businesses that offer entry-level jobs

9. True or false. Personal decisions are not related to career decisions.
10. What happens when you do *not* make a decision?

Building Your Foundation Skills

1. Write a short story in which the main character makes both routine and impulse decisions.
2. In class, discuss ways in which personal decisions may influence career decisions. Also discuss ways in which career decisions may influence personal decisions.
3. As a class, make a list of common work-related matters that require decision making.

Building Your Workplace Competencies

Apply the seven steps of the decision-making process to a real or imaginary career-related example. Work with two or three classmates and determine as a team who will do which tasks. Use the example to explain the decision-making process in a class presentation. Include posters and/or handouts designed with the help of a computer. *(This activity develops competence with interpersonal skills, information, systems, and technology.)*

Options for Education and Training

Objectives

After studying this chapter, you will be able to

- explain the importance of basic skills in any career choice.

- determine the impact of technology on the job market.

- list the opportunities that are available for job training and higher education.

Words to Know

career/technical program

cooperative education

apprenticeship

associate degree

bachelor's degree

graduate degree

master's degree

doctoral degree

internship

The Need for Further Training and Education

Jobs are changing quickly, primarily because of technology. Before the computer revolution, a high school diploma often was adequate preparation for the workplace—but no longer. High school graduates without special training are rarely considered for good-paying jobs today. The higher-paying jobs go to workers with more education and training.

Further training and education is very likely to be a part of your future. Prepare yourself for that step by perfecting your foundation skills *now*.

The Importance of Foundation Skills

Any career you choose will require you to have good *foundation skills*. These involve the following basic skills and thinking skills:

- *Basic skills* include reading, writing, math, speaking, and listening abilities.
- *Thinking skills* include thinking creatively, making decisions, solving problems, visualizing ideas, knowing how to learn, and reasoning.

Suppose you plan to apply for work in a grocery store as a cashier. You would need to be able to read and write in order to fill the job application form. As a cashier, good math skills would be crucial, 9-1. You would also need good reasoning skills to be able to handle customer questions and unexpected events.

The best way to perfect your foundation skills is to work on them now while in school. Study as much as possible to get ahead. Take advantage of your schooling and gain as much knowledge and experience as possible. Perfecting these skills now will pay off in the future. Employers appreciate a

9-1
People who work with money must have good math skills.

job applicant who has performed well in school. Employers realize that a good student is likely to be a good employee.

Preparing for a Career

As you learn about different types of jobs, check the education and training needs. What is required by the career you seek? Is prior work experience necessary? Once you know all the requirements of a career field, you can begin preparing for it.

For some careers, you can enter training programs while in high school. A career/technical school is one example.

Most of the advanced training and education programs, however, are available after high school. Some of the options are private trade schools, business schools, colleges, and universities. Most higher education programs are at least one year in length. Often day and evening classes are available.

Career/Technical Training

Many schools throughout the country offer a *career/technical program*. In these programs, you learn and develop the skills necessary for entry-level employment. You also learn the technical information required for earning a living. These programs are offered in the areas of health, business, agriculture, skilled trades, and marketing.

Some career/technical programs are offered to students who are still in high school. See 9-2. These programs are often called *Tech-Prep programs*. Tech-Prep programs begin in the junior year and usually involve two years of additional schooling after high school. They allow students to receive college credit for work done in high school.

For information about technical or career programs in your area, talk with your teacher or school counselor.

9-2
Career/technical schools teach high school students entry-level skills in areas such as carpentry.

Cooperative Education

Many schools offer cooperative education programs, also called co-op programs. *Cooperative education* is an arrangement between schools and places of employment. The program allows students to receive on-the-job training through part-time work. At the same time, students attend classes part-time.

In co-op programs, students earn money for their work. They also earn credits toward graduation. Their grades are based on their performance at work and on class assignments. Often their class assignments relate to their jobs. For instance, students may be asked to do the following projects:

- Research a career ladder for their occupation.
- Write reports about the occupations in the companies for which they worked.
- Research their career fields
- Write about their cooperative education job experiences.

Apprenticeships

Another kind of training for an occupation is an *apprenticeship*. It involves learning a trade by working under the direction and guidance of a skilled worker. Most apprenticeships are for adults who have already graduated from high school. However, anyone who is at least 16 years old can apply for an apprentice program.

In an apprenticeship, beginners can learn a trade or skill by working very closely with a master craftsperson. While working and learning, the apprentice is paid entry-level wages for a beginner in that field.

Apprenticeships can lead to over 900 different careers. The following are some examples:

- automotive mechanic
- carpentry
- commercial foods
- jewelry making
- photography
- tailoring
- upholstering

career/technical program. A program that teaches students skills necessary for entry-level employment.

cooperative education A program between schools and places of employment that allows students to receive on-the-job training through part-time work.

apprenticeship Occupational training involving learning a trade by working under the direction of a skilled worker.

Company Training Programs

Some large companies offer their own training programs. These programs are designed to prepare employees to do specialized jobs. The programs may train employees to operate certain types of equipment or teach them specific skills.

The length and quality of training programs vary. A short-term program may involve up to one month of on-the-job training. Long-term training involves more than one year of on-the-job training or a combination of training and classroom instruction. Most people who take part in company training programs consider them very helpful, 9-3.

Community and Junior Colleges

Community colleges and junior colleges usually offer programs that are two years in length. When you complete a two-year program, you usually receive an *associate degree*. After completing an associate degree, it is very common to transfer to a four-year college for additional studies.

Many high schools link their course offerings to community or junior college programs in the area.

9-3

Company training programs focus on teaching information or skills needed by employees to do their jobs better.

Colleges and Universities

When you complete a four-year program at a college or university, you receive a *bachelor's degree*. Hundreds of majors are offered at thousands of colleges around the world. A major is an area of study in which you specialize while in school.

Information about programs of higher education is available in many places. Start with the guidance department at your school. Guidance counselors have books that list programs and give information about schools. These books can also be found in libraries.

Write to the schools you might want to attend and schedule appointments to visit the campuses. During your visits, talk to administrators and teachers as well as students. Doing so will help you determine if a particular school is right for you.

Jobs requiring an advanced degree require schooling beyond a bachelor's degree. An advanced degree is also called a ***graduate degree***. Basically, there are two levels of graduate degrees.

- A ***master's degree*** involves one to two years of study beyond a bachelor's degree.
- A ***doctoral degree***, the most advanced degree, often requires three years of study beyond a bachelor's degree. This degree is also called a *doctorate*.

Try not to make quick decisions when choosing a program or school. Higher education is quite expensive and time-consuming. A poor decision may result in wasted time and tuition on courses that may not be accepted by another school.

Internships

An internship is another type of occupational training program. An ***internship*** is usually an unpaid period when a college student or graduate gains practical experience under supervision. Teachers, doctors, nurses, dentists, dietitians, and other professionals must successfully complete an internship before they can work in their career fields. A classroom, a hospital, and a television newsroom are just some of the sites of an internship.

Military Training

Another way to gain experience is through military training. Many military duties are the same as those done by civilian workers. The

associate degree
The award granted after completing a two-year college program.

bachelor's degree
The award granted after completing a four-year college or university program.

graduate degree
An advanced degree requiring education beyond a bachelor's degree.

master's degree
An advanced degree involving one to two years of study beyond a bachelor's degree.

doctoral degree
The most advanced degree, often requiring three years of study beyond a bachelor's degree; also called a doctorate.

internship
An occupational training program, usually unpaid, a college student or graduate gains practical experience

military offers a variety of jobs that are similar to those in nonmilitary communities. Many workers start their career training while serving in the military.

The branches of the U.S. military are the Army, Navy, Air Force, Marines, and Coast Guard. After basic training and a series of aptitude tests, a person is usually sent for further training. In the military, you can begin to prepare for such careers as *mechanic*, *chef*, or *electronics technician*. See 9-4. Some branches of the service also offer apprenticeships and college degree programs.

Financing Further Training

Many young people have career goals that require education beyond high school. If you choose this path, you will need to consider how to pay for the training.

Higher education can be costly. Suppose you decide to enroll in a one-year program at a trade school. If the school is far from home, you will have daily living expenses to pay in addition to tuition. You will need money to cover items such as room and board, school supplies, clothing, and health care. You should know how much money you have available for education. You also need to know how much your education will cost.

The costs of attending school may be high, but you may be able to lower these costs. Perhaps you could get a loan or scholarship to help pay for the tuition. Maybe you could live with a relative in a nearby town. Maybe you could work part-time while going to school or attend a school nearby.

9-4

Military training can prepare people for careers in many technical fields.

You may be able to get financial help in the form of loans, grants, or scholarships. The government offers a variety of loans and grants. The school you will attend probably offers various forms of financial assistance, too. Private sources provide a variety of loans and scholarships. Your guidance counselor will be able to tell you more about the options available to you. See 9-5 for more tips on financing further training.

Tips for Financing Further Training

- Know how much money you have to spend and how much your education will cost. Then plan for ways to make up the difference.

- Plan ahead. Save the money you earn from part-time and summer jobs. Apply that money toward your education.

- Work while in school to help cover your costs. You may want to work part-time or get involved in a work-study program. You may prefer to work full-time and be a part-time student.

- Choose an education option you can afford. Local community colleges are a fairly low-cost option. State colleges and universities are less costly than private colleges and universities. Tuition is less if you attend school in your state than if you attend school in another state.

- Live at home or with a relative while attending school.

- Apply for government funded loans, grants, and scholarships. This is done by filling out forms describing your family's financial status. Aid is given to those who show financial need.

- Apply for any other scholarships for which you might qualify. These might be based on need, athletics, or academics. They are available from many sources.

- Consider borrowing money from a person or a financial institution.

- Join the military and arrange to have all or part of your education costs paid through military funding.

- Talk with your guidance counselor and do library research to learn more about financing further training.

9-5

Many resources are available to help meet the high costs of career training.

Summary

Education plays a key role in a person's career. The basic skills of reading, writing, math, speaking, and listening, together with the thinking skills, are needed for success in any job. Further education is often necessary due to technological change. The more education a person has, the better his or her chances are of moving up the career ladder.

Training is available in different forms to prepare people for various careers. Options include career/technical training, cooperative education programs, and apprenticeships. Other options are company training programs, colleges, universities, internships, and military training.

Financing higher education can be costly. Students can lower this cost by planning ahead and seeking financial assistance from other sources.

Reviewing the Chapter

1. For which jobs are foundation skills needed?
2. Why do employers appreciate a job applicant who performs well in school?
3. What is the single most important reason for the rapid changes in the job market?
4. Name three subject areas in which career/technical programs are offered.
5. What is the basis for grades in cooperative education programs?
6. What kind of training involves learning a trade by working under the direction and guidance of a skilled worker?
7. What is the difference between an associate degree and a bachelor's degree?
8. Name three jobs that require internships.
9. Why should you think carefully before choosing a program or school of higher education?
10. Name two nonmilitary careers for which military training can help you prepare.

Building Your Foundation Skills

1. Design a poster that depicts the benefits of education.
2. Interview someone in a career field that interests you. Find out what education and training he or she would recommend for a person entering that field today.
3. Contact the Bureau of Apprenticeship and Training within the U.S. Department of Labor. Request materials describing the U.S. apprenticeship system. Ask for an area training representative to speak to your class.

Building Your Workplace Competencies

Research a career field that interests you. Identify the education and training required and the time and costs associated. Talk with your school counselor to learn which schools offer this training. Then write to two schools for information about program specifics and costs. Obtain as much information as possible through the Internet. If your schooling would force you to live away from home, find out costs for room, board, and travel. Summarize your findings in a written report. Indicate the career researched, the education and training needed, and the schools selected. Also report all related costs, itemized per school year, and your ideas about how to pay for them. Based on what you have learned, which school would you choose? Share your decision and the facts that led to your decision in a brief written report. *(This activity develops competence with interpersonal skills, information, systems, and technology.)*

Making a Career Plan

Objectives

After studying this chapter, you will be able to

- explain the importance of setting goals.

- identify your resources.

- list your personal and professional goals.

- develop a career plan.

Words to Know

human resources
nonhuman resources
goals
career plan

The Importance of Planning

What do you want to achieve by planning your career? You might answer, "to get a job." However, would you really accept any job? If you are honest with yourself, you can name some jobs that you would not accept under any condition.

Like everyone else, you want a job that you will enjoy. A satisfying job doesn't just happen. You must plan for it. Without plans, you're likely to have no direction in life. See 10-1. People without direction often end up with whatever jobs are left, or no job at all.

The actions you take and decisions you make today lay the groundwork for your future career. This may sound overwhelming at first, but it really isn't. Choosing a career involves several steps. Planning helps you take those steps in an orderly way. Planning keeps you organized and on track.

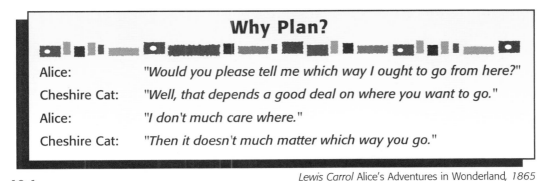

Why Plan?

Alice:	*"Would you please tell me which way I ought to go from here?"*
Cheshire Cat:	*"Well, that depends a good deal on where you want to go."*
Alice:	*"I don't much care where."*
Cheshire Cat:	*"Then it doesn't much matter which way you go."*

Lewis Carrol Alice's Adventures in Wonderland*, 1865*

10-1
Without a plan, you will lose your way and wander, just as Alice in Wonderland did.

Exploring Your Resources

One of the first steps of the career planning process is to identify your resources. A resource is anything a person can use to reach his or her goals. Chapter 7 discussed the resources within you, such as your interests and aptitudes. The resources within you are ***human resources***.

human resources
The resources that people have within themselves.

Some other human resources available to you are your teachers, counselors, and family members. They know you almost as well as you know yourself. Talk with them to help sort through your interests and explore career questions.

Other resources that can help you reach your goals are nonhuman resources. *Nonhuman resources* include time—24 hours every day—and the material resources around you. A car to travel to school and money for career training are examples of material resources.

Other material resources that will help you prepare for your career are your school and community. Within these material resources are people, human resources who can help you. See 10-2. Explore all that your school and community have to offer.

Your School

The library contains reference material relating to jobs and careers for you to explore. More importantly, your guidance counselor has a wealth of information on careers, their educational requirements, and schools for further training.

The school counselor will also help you choose classes related to your career interests. If college is required, he or she will help you select the courses needed for college acceptance. Extracurricular activities can provide opportunities for developing your special skills as well as learning teamwork skills.

10-2
Your teacher is a human resource, but your school is an example of a nonhuman resource.

Your Community

A wide variety of volunteer activities are available to help you experience job duties firsthand. You can learn about employers in the area and possibly tour their facilities. You can make contacts with various people who can give you inside tips about their careers. They can provide job leads for you when you search for part-time or full-time work. Also, when you need job references, community contacts are usually very willing to serve that role.

Examining Career Interests

When you imagine yourself in a career, you try to picture what you would like about the job. Your likes and dislikes help you sort through potential careers to one that will satisfy you. Often, your likes are identical to your interests. By making a list of your likes and dislikes, you will see a pattern develop. From that pattern, you can conclude which career areas might interest you and which will not.

For example, the person whose interests are listed in Figure 10-3 might enjoy the following careers:

- child care worker
- teacher
- exercise instructor

Figure 10-3 also lists that person's dislikes. Based on those dislikes, he or she probably would not enjoy the following careers:

- data processor
- landscaper
- wallpaper hanger

Exploring Interests

Dislikes
Traveling and driving for long distances
Reading technical material
Painting or working from a ladder
Cutting grass and doing yardwork

Likes
Talking and being with people
Working out and exercising
Leading a group or teaching
Planning activities for children

10-3
A simple list of your likes and dislikes will help you discover your career interests.

nonhuman resources
All the material resources around you.

Your list of likes and dislikes will be much longer than the example shown here. If you have difficulty with creating a list, talk with your school counselor. He or she will help you determine your interests.

Sometimes interests are determined through aptitude tests. These tests are fun to take because there are no right or wrong answers. The tests match your interests with jobs that involve tasks you enjoy. Your answers to these tests paint a clearer picture of which career areas are best for you.

Setting Career-Related Goals

Have you ever seen people at work and imagined yourself in their shoes? Have you read about someone's interesting life and thought about yourself in a similar role? Without knowing it, you were considering those careers as goals for yourself. *Goals* are aims or targets a person tries to reach or achieve.

Successful people plan for their success. They set goals for themselves and then work to reach them. To succeed in life, you cannot just wait for things to happen to you. You must make them happen. The best way to make things happen is to set goals.

Your goals may be grouped into two categories—long-term or short-term. Generally, *long-term goals* are those that will take more than six months to accomplish. *Short-term goals* can usually be accomplished within several days or weeks. See 10-4.

10-4

Catching a fish is a short-term goal. Becoming a fish and game warden is a long-term goal.

The goals you want to achieve for yourself are your personal goals. As a student, many of your personal goals may be tied to your education. Some will also be related to your career. Wanting to achieve good grades and to graduate on time are two examples. Other examples of personal goals include the following:

- to talk to the school counselor about taking an aptitude test next week (short-term)
- to practice your math skills during the summer break (short-term)
- to join the debate club next season (long-term)

As you think about a career, you should also consider your professional goals. Any target you want to reach in your career is a professional goal. The following are some examples:

- to begin a college program in accounting next month (short-term)
- to obtain an entry-level accounting job in a large company after graduating from college (long-term)
- to have a management position within three years of working for the company (long-term)

Often personal goals are closely related to professional goals. For example, the personal goal of living in a big city may be due to your professional goal of working downtown. Writing your goals down is a good way to keep them foremost in your mind.

Taking Steps to Achieve Career Goals

After setting your goals, you must decide how you will achieve them. Be specific about what steps you will need to take to reach each goal. Writing the steps down on paper will help you think clearly. An example is shown in 10-5.

Sometimes people set goals without knowing how to achieve them. If you don't know what to do, ask your friends, family members, and teachers. Perhaps they can share experiences with you that will help you plan for your future.

When you complete a step toward reaching your goal, cross that step off your list. It will make you feel a great sense of accomplishment. When you finally reach your goal, you will have reason to celebrate.

goals
The aims a person tries to achieve.

How to Reach a Goal

The goal: to get a part-time job in a department store within the next two months *(short-term)*

Steps to reach the goal:
1. Look for a job in the classified section of the newspaper.
2. Stop at local department stores and fill out applications in their personnel departments.
3. Set up interview times.
4. Prepare for the interviews.

10-5

Writing down the steps needed to reach a goal can help you see what actions are needed.

Questions to Consider

Sometimes you may find that one of your goals is unrealistic or can't be achieved in the time period set. If this happens, you may need to change your goal or timeframe. Don't be afraid to adjust your goals so you can reach them. You may be better able to work toward a goal if you modify it. There are three questions to consider when setting career-related goals.

What Do You Want to Achieve?

This may be the most difficult question of all to answer. Rarely do people know their exact career goal at an early age. Even after reaching the career of their dreams, some people go on to explore other careers.

You should try to narrow your search to one career area that most interests you. However, staying alert to other interesting career areas is important in today's fast-changing workplace.

What Can You Realistically Achieve?

As you investigate the job that interests you, you need to learn what is required to get the job. For example, some employers in the trades require their employees to have their own tools, 10-6. If you cannot afford to buy tools immediately, you may need to look at an alternative job until you can afford them.

Sometimes special training or education is required for a job. If your career goal is to be an engineer, you will need a bachelor's degree. This may not be a realistic choice for you if your family is unable to pay for college. You may not have the grades necessary to get into college.

While the goal of *engineer* is a good one, you may have to start at a different level. For example, you might start as a draftsperson or a clerk in an engineering office. You may also look at other related careers, such as an engineering technician or a land surveyor. It may take a little longer to reach your goal, but the additional work experience will greatly benefit you.

10-6
Often construction workers and other trades people must provide their own tools.

What Is a Realistic Period to Accomplish What You Want?

Your level of motivation will help to determine what you can accomplish in a given period. If you are willing to give up other activities and concentrate on reaching your goal, you may reach it in a relatively short period. The less time you spend working toward your goal, the longer it will take to achieve it.

Developing a Career Plan

Knowing your resources and understanding what you want to do in life prepares you for the next step—creating a career plan. A ***career plan*** is a list of steps you need to take to reach your career goal. It should include the following:

- extracurricular and volunteer activities that help prepare you
- entry-level jobs that provide experience
- education and training requirements

A career plan is simply a guide. It helps to focus your attention on your career target and how you plan to achieve it. A career plan can be developed for any career. If your goals should change, your plan can be changed to reflect them.

One possible career plan is shown in 10-7. It shows the steps that one person might take to achieve the dream of becoming a landscape architect. Landscape architects design public outdoor areas so they are beautiful and useful. Notice the career plan focuses on successive stages in life. It also lists the activities—ranging from easy to advanced—that can be handled in each.

In developing your career plan, it is important that you are true to yourself. You may know people that entered a career path because their friends were planning to do so. Sometimes people follow a certain path because they want to fulfill their parents' wishes. If you feel pressured by a similar situation, it is important that you talk about how you picture your future. Explain that you appreciate their concern for your well-being. Let them know that you hope they will support you and your career choice.

It may take several conversations before they understand your view. However, they may never agree with your decision. Still, you must address the issue with them so they know that you have thought carefully about your future.

Career Plan for a Landscape Architect

Junior High School
- Mow neighborhood lawns for the experience and extra money.
- Grow ornamental plants for state fair competition.
- Volunteer to help cleanup events for neighborhood parks and highways.

High School
- Join the local horticulture club.
- Start a neighborhood lawn care service.
- Work at a garden and nursery center part-time.
- Take classes in drawing and a college preparatory program emphasizing art, botany, and mathematics.

College
- Earn a bachelor's degree in landscape architecture.
- Work during summers at a golf course to help maintain the greens.
- Intern in the senior year with a respected landscape firm.

After college
- Work for the local landscape firm for two or three years before opening a new landscaping business.
- Consider obtaining a master's degree.

10-7

As you accomplish each step of a career play, your activities move you closer to your goal.

career plan
A list of steps a person takes to reach his or her career goals.

Summary

Choosing a career is an important step in your life. If you have a plan, you will stay focused on your goals and reach them sooner than you would without a plan.

Use the resources that are available to you. In addition to those within you, teachers, counselors, family members, your school, and your community are other resources to use. Resources help you achieve goals.

Setting goals for yourself is a way to make things happen. Goals help you achieve success. You may have both long-term and short-term goals. Some of your goals may be personal, and some may be professional.

Once you have set your career goals, decide how to achieve them in a career plan. Then work toward your goals, making changes to the plan if and when they are necessary. There is more than one way to arrive at your goal. Consider all possibilities and create a plan that best suits you.

Reviewing the Chapter

1. Why is career planning important?
2. What two basic types of resources are available to you?
3. Why should you examine your likes and dislikes?
4. How do long-term goals differ from short-term goals?
5. Are personal goals related to professional goals?
6. What three questions should you consider when setting goals?
7. Name two reasons why a person might need to enter a career later than planned.
8. What is a career plan?
9. When should a person first write a career plan?
10. What three types of activities are included in a career plan?

Building Your Foundation Skills

1. Write a report on a career that interests you.
2. List all your likes and dislikes in separate columns.
3. List one short-term goal and one long-term goal you want to achieve. They can be personal or professional. List the steps you will take to achieve each goal. Put this list in a place where you will see it often. Record your progress and cross out each step as you achieve it.

Building Your Workplace Competencies

Map the steps of a career plan for the career that interests you most. Make your career plan cover at least the next 10 years. Be sure to list community and school activities plus volunteer or paid positions that will be helpful. Also identify any special training or education that is required. Give separate copies of your career plan to your teacher and school counselor for their review. Consider their recommendations and incorporate them in your plan if you desire. File your plan in a safe place for reference and update it when necessary. *(This activity develops competence with resources, information, and systems.)*

PART FOUR

Acquiring Workplace Skills

Job Search Skills

Objectives

After studying this chapter, you will be able to

- use want ads, the Internet, and other job search tools.

- prepare a personalized resumé and list of references.

- develop a list of potential employers.

- complete a job application form.

Words to Know

want ads
open ad
closed ad
private employment agency
public employment service
resumé
references
job application form

Sources of Information About Jobs

The job search is one of the most important steps in your career. Knowing how and where to find a job is a valuable skill. As a new worker, you should be careful in your choice of employment. The job you choose may last for many years.

Think carefully before making a career choice. Study the companies in your area. Ask questions about the kinds of jobs they offer. Think about your hobbies and other interests. These can help you select a job you might enjoy. When looking for a job, use as many sources of information as you can.

Want Ads

Want ads appear in the classified section of the newspaper. See 11-1. Want ads are also called *classified ads*. They are a common source of information about available jobs. Some want ads are easy to read and understand. Other ads are more difficult to read because they include many abbreviations. Common abbreviations are listed and explained in 11-2.

Classified ads may be either open or closed. An **open ad** gives you specific information about the job, pay range, and company. A **closed ad** gives general information about the job. The company's name and a salary figure are rarely given. Instead, you are directed to send your resumé to a post office box, or a fax or e-mail number.

Friends

One of the best ways to find job openings is by checking with family and friends. Ask if their employers are hiring. Perhaps they know someone who works for a company that is looking for help. Generally, family and friends will be eager to help you in your job search.

Internet

Searching the Internet is a good way to find information and leads for a job. The Internet provides information on jobs in your area and across the country. Sometimes the information resembles newspaper want ads. When you use such search words as *job opportunities* or *careers*, hundreds of information sources appear.

want ad
A source of information about available jobs, found in the classified section of the newspaper.

open ad
A classified ad providing specific information about a job.

closed ad
A classified ad giving general information about a job.

Classified Section		
Employment Opportunities		
Help Wanted	**Help Wanted**	**Help Wanted**
BOOKKEEPER Expd. bookkeeper for expanding law firm. Require independent workers with word processing skills. Previous law office exp. a plus. Resumes to: Personnel, 135 S. LaSalle, Cleveland, OH 45204	COOK Seeking full-time cook. Call 555-1433 bet. 1&3 p.m.	MACHINISTS Expd. machinists needed to repair and rebuild all plant equipment. First shift. Good salary and benefits. Apply at: ACE MFG. CO. 5716 W. Roosevelt Rd. EOE M/F
CABINET MAKER Position open for expd. furniture maker. Good opportunity for advancement. Call Mike 555-8066.	DRIVER West side electrical contractor has opening for driver. Will train. Some overnight travel required. EOE. Send resume to MHX 288, Journal 45211	WORD PROCESSING Immediate opening for experienced operator. Some desktop publishing exp. helpful. Excellent opportunity for advancement. Competitive salary. For additional information and a personal interview, please call: Ms. Hamond, 555-5508 bet. 9-4.
CLERK/SECRETARY Order processing dept. of south suburban book publisher needs versatile clerk. Some clerical duties. Excellent salary and benefits. Good phone skills. EOE. Send resume to: Box MHX 409, Journal 45211	EDITOR Editor needed to review manuscripts for textbooks. Strong writing skills req. Teaching exp. a plus. Send resume, recent writing samples, and salary requirements to: Box MHX 592, Journal 45211	

11-1

Check the want ads in the classified section of your local newspaper for leads to jobs.

You can use the Internet as a job search tool in two ways. First, you can search the Internet for specific jobs. Also, you can post your resumé on job-search bulletin boards. These electronic bulletin boards are sites that many employers review to find employees. When you post a resumé on the Internet, many employers know you are available for work.

A resumé posted on the Internet becomes public information. It is wise to take precautions to safeguard your privacy. Omit your home address and the address of your current employer. You can provide that information later at an interview.

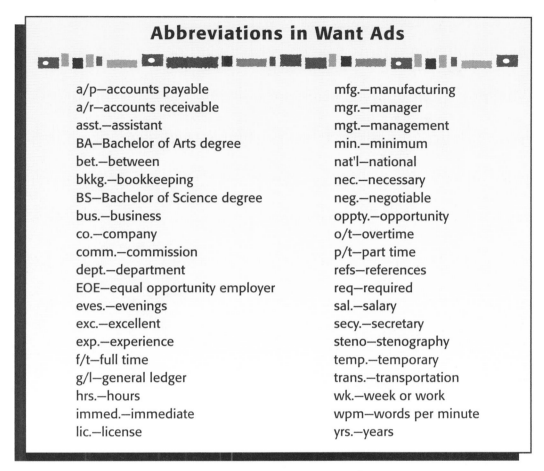

Abbreviations in Want Ads

a/p—accounts payable	mfg.—manufacturing
a/r—accounts receivable	mgr.—manager
asst.—assistant	mgt.—management
BA—Bachelor of Arts degree	min.—minimum
bet.—between	nat'l—national
bkkg.—bookkeeping	nec.—necessary
BS—Bachelor of Science degree	neg.—negotiable
bus.—business	oppty.—opportunity
co.—company	o/t—overtime
comm.—commission	p/t—part time
dept.—department	refs—references
EOE—equal opportunity employer	req—required
eves.—evenings	sal.—salary
exc.—excellent	secy.—secretary
exp.—experience	steno—stenography
f/t—full time	temp.—temporary
g/l—general ledger	trans.—transportation
hrs.—hours	wk.—week or work
immed.—immediate	wpm—words per minute
lic.—license	yrs.—years

11-2
Knowing these abbreviations will help you understand the want ads.

The Internet is becoming one of the primary sources of job leads. To access these leads, take some time and plan. You should first organize your search materials to prevent becoming overwhelmed with responses. If you do not organize your search, you could receive information on countless jobs that do not interest you.

When you use the Internet to search for a job, you will need an electronic resumé. This will be discussed in more detail later in the chapter. See 11-3.

11-3

The Internet puts information about thousands of jobs at your fingertips. Focus on those that match your interests.

Employment Agencies

Employment agencies fall into two categories, private and public. ***Private employment agencies*** are businesses that help people find jobs. This type of employment agency receives a fee from either the employer or the applicant. Find out the exact cost and who is responsible for paying it before using the service.

The fees charged by private employment agencies vary. Some are only as much as the applicant earns in one week on the new job. Others are thousands of dollars.

The government supports ***public employment services***. They receive no fees. They help people find jobs in government, industry, and other areas. Most large cities have public employment services. To find the office nearest you, look in the "State government" telephone listings under *Job Service* or *Employment*.

The Yellow Pages

The Yellow Pages give information about businesses in your community. It is another source to check when looking for a job. The Yellow Pages can help you select employers based on your areas of interest. To use the Yellow Pages, look up a topic of interest, perhaps *computers*. Then look below that heading to find companies you would like to contact.

Community Bulletin Boards

People often place ads on community bulletin boards. These can be found in places like supermarkets, bus stations, and drugstores.

You may wish to place your own ad on a bulletin board. It might read as follows:

> **Wanted—Lawn care position**
> **Have experience and my own car**
> **Call 555-7272.**

Resumés

Suppose you decide what kind of work you want and where to apply for a job. The next step is to get your paperwork in order. Many employers will ask for a copy of your resume. A ***resumé*** describes your education, work experience, and other qualifications for work.

private employment agency
A business that helps people find jobs for a fee.

public employment service
A government-supported group that helps people find jobs for free.

resumé
A formal written summary of a person's education, work experience, and other qualifications for a job.

Preparing Your Resumé

The employer's first impression of you may come from your resumé. It is important that the information be correct and neatly organized. Your resumé should include the following information:

- name
- address
- telephone number
- current employer and date of employment
- past employers and dates of employment
- schools attended, dates of attendance, and general course of study
- school and community activities and honors
- special skills
- the availability of references

Each section of the resumé is important. You should keep your resumé current, updating it as changes take place. See the example in 11-4.

A good resumé contains facts about you that are important to the job you seek. Employers will want to know about your experience and education. Facts about activities and honors are important, too.

People with little or no work experience will want to report extracurricular activities that demonstrate the qualities employers seek. These qualities include dedication, a willingness to cooperate, and originality.

People with special skills may list them in a separate category. This helps to highlight a person's specialty area.

Personal information, on the other hand, should never be included. Examples of such information involve your age, height, or marital status. Including this information may convince some employers that you have no further job-related facts to provide.

Many students are finding they need two forms of resumé. The traditional form is used to take to interviews and to respond to newspaper ads. The electronic form is used for job searches on the Internet.

JOYCE Q. HENRY
123 South River Street
Trenton, NJ 07864
609-555-1141
jqhenry@serviceprovider.com

EMPLOYMENT
- J.B. Van Buran, Inc.
  13 West End Avenue
  Trenton, NJ

- Retail Sales Person
  2/03 to present

- Speedy Serve
  Route #31
  Trenton, NJ

- Counter help/cashier
  11/02 to2/03

EDUCATION
- Trenton High School
  Chambers Street
  Trenton, NJ
  Graduated June, 2004

- Major: Office Occupations Program,
  including classes in Microsoft Office,
  WordPerfect, Microsoft Word,
  Excel, and PowerPoint

- Junior High School No. 2
  Olden Avenue
  Trenton, NJ
  Graduated June 2001

- Major: General Studies

ACTIVITIES AND HONORS
- President, Business Professionals
  of America local chapter – 2004
- Vice President, Student Council – 2004
- Member, Ski Club
- Member, Mercer County 4-H Club

SPECIAL SKILLS
- Keyboarding, word processing,
  microcomputer applications,
  and business mathematics
- Fluent in Spanish

REFERENCES
- Available on request

11-4

A good resumé is neat and accurate.

Sample Electronic Resumé

```
JOYCE Q. HENRY
123 South River Street
Trenton, NJ 07864
609-555-1141
jqhenry@serviceprovider.com

EMPLOYMENT
*Retail Sales Person, 2/03 — present
 J.B. Van Buran, Inc.
 13 West End Avenue, Trenton, NJ

*Counter help/cashier, 11/02 to 2/03
 Speedy Serve
 Route #31, Trenton, NJ

EDUCATION
*Trenton High School, graduated June, 2004
 Chambers Street, Trenton, NJ
*Major: Office Occupations Program, including classes in
 Microsoft Office, WordPerfect, Microsoft Word, Excel,
 and PowerPoint

*Junior High School No.2, graduated June, 2001
 Olden Avenue, Trenton, NJ
 Major: General Studies

ACTIVITIES AND HONORS
President, Business Professionals of America
 local chapter — 2004
Vice President, Student Council — 2004
Member, Ski Club
Member, Mercer County 4-H Club

SPECIAL SKILLS
*Keyboarding, word processing, microcomputer applications,
 and business mathematics

*Fluent in Spanish

REFERENCES
Available on request
```

11-5
An electronic resumé is simple and plain.

Electronic Resumés

Your job search on the Internet will require a different style of a resumé. A resumé used on the Internet is often referred to as an *electronic resumé*. Electronic resumés use simplified formats because they must be readable to many different types of computers. The simplified format is often called *plain text* or *text only*. The example in 11-5 is a plain text resumé.

Create an electronic version by opening your existing resumé document and saving a copy as a text file. (Be sure to preserve the original formatted document.) Saving a copy as a text file eliminates formatting codes. Electronic resumés do not contain columns, indents, bullets, or bold or italic type.

Although electronic resumés eliminate normal formatting, some attention-getting devices can be used. Notice the use of capitalization and asterisks in the example. See 11-5. When you develop your electronic resumé, follow certain rules.

- Use an 11-point, standard-width typeface, not a condensed style.
- Make sure no line exceeds 65 characters. Hit the *enter* key to force additional words to another line.
- Include every keyword that applies to you. For example, do not simply write *word processing*. Instead, list all the specific computer programs you use.
- Never e-mail an attachment. Send your cover letter and resumé as text in a single message.
- Close your e-mail message stating that a fully formatted hard copy is available.

Before e-mailing your resumé to an employer, send it to yourself and a friend. Check whether the document appears as planned upon arrival. If not, adjust the format before using it.

References

References are people who know you. They can comment on your character and skills.

When choosing references, choose people who will be respected by an employer. Such individuals include coaches, teachers, school counselors, and former employers. Choose three or four individuals who know you well enough to answer an employer's questions.

> **references**
> People who can speak about a person's character and skills.

Do not choose a friend, parent, or relative as a reference. Employers will probably not trust the accuracy of any reports they give about you.

Always ask for permission to use a reference's name. Get permission *before* you give that person's name to an employer.

In your resumé, say that references are available on request. When an employer asks for your references, provide a separate page that lists them. Do not guess about names, job titles, addresses, or phone numbers. Be sure everything is accurate.

Job Application Forms

Many companies will ask you to complete their ***job application form***. This form asks for information about you and your background. It helps employers compare your job qualifications to those of other job candidates.

Whenever you apply for a job, be prepared to complete a job application form. If you have your resumé and a pen, you will be ready. You will have the information you need.

Read through the entire application before starting it. If you do not understand a question on the application, ask someone to explain it to you.

It is important that you complete the application neatly and correctly. Look at the two applications in 11-6. If you were the employer, which person would you hire?

First, read the directions carefully. Take your time and print the information requested. Always use a pen, never a pencil.

Respond to all questions. If a question does not apply to you, draw a short line in the space. If you leave a space empty, the employer may think you overlooked it or forgot to answer it. Sign your full name. Do not use a nickname.

If you can take the unanswered application form home with you, do so. This allows you to be very careful as you complete it. Remember to return the application promptly. Usually, though, you will be asked to complete the application form in the company's office.

Remember, the employer forms an opinion of you from your application. If the form is sloppy, incomplete, or inaccurate, you may never get a chance to be interviewed.

11-6
Always complete job application forms neatly and correctly.

job application form
A form completed by a job applicant to provide an employer with information about the applicant's background.

Summary

During a job search, use as many sources of information as you can. Talk to friends and others. Read the want ads. Check the Internet. Visit employment agencies. Use the Yellow Pages. Read ads and place your own ad on community bulletin boards. The more you learn about job openings, the more likely you are to get a job.

Prepare a resumé that will help you make a good impression. Present your qualifications in an honest, positive way. Be sure to include all the information that employers need.

Be ready to complete job application forms during your job search. Use a pen to fill them out neatly and correctly. Respond to all questions.

Reviewing the Chapter

1. Where should you look to find want ads?
2. Which kind of want ad gives you more information?
3. Who pays a fee to a private employment agency?
4. How can you use the Yellow Pages in your job search?
5. What information should a resumé include?
6. What information should *not* be included in a resumé?
7. Why should you *not* choose a friend, parent, or relative as a reference?
8. True or false. You should ask your references for permission to use their names before giving them to an employer.
9. Why should you have your resumé handy when you complete a job application form?
10. If a question on a job application form does *not* apply to you, what should you do?

Building Your Foundation Skills

1. Find a want ad with many abbreviations. Rewrite the ad without abbreviations. Discuss your ad in class.
2. Contact the nearest public employment service. Request pamphlets that explain the services offered.

3. Look in the Yellow Pages for places where you would like to work. List your top five employers.

4. Following the guidelines presented in this chapter, prepare two forms of a resumé for your preferred career area and a list of references.

5. Obtain a job application form from a local company. Complete it neatly and correctly.

6. Using a computer, search for an occupation of your choice. Make a printed copy of the results.

Building Your Workplace Competencies

Search three sites on the Internet for a job that interests you. One site to explore is *http://www.ajb.org.* (The U.S. Department of Labor provides the information on this site.) Search two other sites for the same job title and note which sites you search. Print copies of all three. Compare and contrast the information you obtained and report your findings to the class. *(This activity develops competence with information, systems, and technology.)*

Interviewing Skills

Objectives

After studying this chapter, you will be able to

- prepare for an interview.
- describe what to do and what not to do during an interview.
- write a follow-up letter.
- evaluate a job offer.

Words to Know

interview
interviewer
interviewee
telephone interview
personal interview
job description
follow-up letter

The Most Important Step

The interview is the most important step in a job search. It can be a good experience if you are prepared and know just what to expect.

An *interview* is a talk between an employer and a job applicant. It may also be described as a talk between an interviewer and an interviewee. An *interviewer* is an employer. In large companies, an interviewer may be a company representative who has the task of talking with job applicants. An *interviewee* is a person who is looking for a job. This person is also called a *job applicant.*

In large companies, the personnel department or the human resources department often conducts interviews. The function of these departments (or departments with similar names) is to find the right people to fill available positions.

An interview is usually your first chance to meet with an employer. Remember that first impressions are lasting impressions. Your interview is your chance to make a good first impression. See 12-1.

Preparing for Interviews

Do a little homework to learn about the company. You should know what the company does. Does it make a product or provide a service? Does the company participate in civic and community projects? Have you ever used the company's product or service? Were you satisfied? Be prepared to say something positive about the company. For example, if you have used its product and are pleased with it, say so. Above all else, be truthful in whatever you say. *Never* tell a lie to get a job.

Be prepared to tell the interviewer about the skills you have that fit the job. If you are applying for a clerical job, for instance, be prepared to talk about your clerical skills. Think about the questions that the interviewer might ask and be ready to answer them. You may be asked, "Do you type?" Your answer may be, "Yes, I learned that three years ago and type all my school reports and papers. I also do my church's weekly announcements."

Think of ways to let the interviewer know you are dependable. Be prepared to talk about anything you have done in the past that would help you do the company's job well.

---

interview
A talk between an employer and a job applicant.

interviewer
An employer who talks with a job applicant.

interviewee
A job applicant who receives an interview.

12-1

An interview gives a job applicant and an employer a chance to find out how well they might work together.

Telephone Interviews

A want ad may list only a telephone number. To answer the ad, a job applicant must have a ***telephone interview.*** This is a telephone conversation between a company representative and a job applicant. Usually, if a telephone interview goes well, the job applicant is invited for a personal interview.

When you call for a telephone interview, introduce yourself and state your purpose. For instance, say, "My name is John Wright, and I'm calling about your ad in Sunday's paper for a stock clerk. I'm a senior at Franklin High School. I can work in the afternoons and on weekends. I am very interested in working as a stock clerk and coming in for an interview."

12-2
A business suit or something similar is appropriate attire when interviewing for an office position.

When you make the call, be ready to accept a specific day and time for a personal interview. Try to fit your schedule around the interviewer's time schedule. If you can't meet when the interviewer suggests, explain why and offer another time and date. Whenever possible, change your schedule to be available for the interview.

Personal Interviews

A *personal interview* is a face-to-face meeting between an employer and a job applicant. It usually determines whether or not the applicant will be hired.

Plan what you will wear to the personal interview. You must look clean, neat, and dressed for the type of job you seek. You should wear businesslike attire for an office or sales position, 12-2. You may wear casual clothes when applying for a construction job. Observe how the employees holding the job you seek are dressed and arrive looking as good or better.

Your shoes should be spotless and polished. Your hair should be styled in a businesslike fashion and neatly combed. Male job applicants should be clean-shaven or have a neatly trimmed beard. Female applicants should have a proper style and size handbag, if they carry one at all. Also, they should not wear heavy makeup or lots of jewelry.

telephone interview
A telephone conversation between a company representative and a job applicant.

personal interview
A face-to-face meeting between an employer and a job applicant.

Be Well Groomed

Proper grooming tells people you care about yourself. A major part of the interview is convincing the interviewer that you're the best person for the job. Take a bath or shower, and brush your teeth before going to an interview. Use a deodorant. Your hair, hands, and fingernails must be clean. Don't let poor grooming spoil your chances for getting a job.

Be on Time

Get a good night's sleep. You want to be at your best for the interview. If you are tired, it will show. Go to bed early if you have an early morning interview.

Too many times a job is lost because an applicant is late for the interview. Arriving late gives the interviewer the impression that you believe tardiness is okay. If you must depend on public transportation, make sure you know the schedule and the time needed for the full trip. Plan to be at least a few minutes early.

You should know the exact time and place of your interview. If you aren't sure of the time or place, telephone the company. Identify yourself and say, "I am checking about my interview. Where should I arrive and at what time?" See 12-3.

12-3
Always arrive at the interviewer's office at least five minutes before your appointment.

Plan to Go Alone

The interview is an important step in getting a job. It is something you must do by yourself. Do not bring a friend to the interview. An interviewer expects you to speak for yourself. If your friend wants a job in the same place, it would be better to let your friend set up a separate appointment. An applicant who rushes through the interview for a waiting friend is not likely to get the job.

Interviewing Tips

The interview is a chance for the company to meet you. It is also a chance for you to learn more about the company. The interviewer is looking for a person who can do the job and work well with other people.

It is natural to be nervous during an interview. However, remember that the interviewer is interested in you. Try to relax and answer all questions honestly. You know your good points and an experienced interviewer will learn them through your answers. Be yourself!

What to Do

Knowing what to do will make the interview easier. By knowing how to behave, you will also appear confident. For each interview, prepare to do the following:

- Introduce yourself when you meet the interviewer and smile. Use the interviewer's name. For example, say, "Good morning, Mr. Brown. I'm Josephine Smith."
- Shake hands firmly if the interviewer extends a hand.
- Remain standing until you are offered a seat. Be relaxed, but sit straight in your chair. If you slouch in your chair, you probably won't get the job. Look at the interviewer.
- Don't stare at the wall, ceiling, or your lap. Making eye contact with the interviewer says you are interested in the job and the company.
- Keep a pleasant smile. Speak clearly and loud enough to be heard. Let the interviewer lead the discussion.
- Talk freely. Give more than just *yes* and *no* answers. The interviewer needs information to make a hiring decision.
- "Sell" yourself. Tell the interviewer why you are interested in the company and the job. Talk about your skills and why you're the best person for the job.
- Be polite and have a positive attitude.

What Not to Do

Serious job applicants display their best behavior during an interview. Consequently, they avoid the following behaviors, listed here and on the next page:

- being late
- chewing gum or smoking

- laying things on the interviewer's desk
- acting like a know-it-all
- saying, "I'll take anything" instead of describing the kind of work you want to do
- trying to run the interview by talking too much
- discussing personal problems
- trying to read the material on the interviewer's desk
- answering questions with lies
- arguing or displaying a negative attitude. See 12-4.

Interview Pluses	Interview Minuses
Some people are hired because they	Some people are not hired because they
■ show interest in the company and the job	■ show no interest in the company or the job
■ know about the company's products or services	■ know nothing about the company
■ have clearly defined career goals	■ have no career goals
■ are qualified for the job	■ do not have the knowledge and skills needed for the job
■ express themselves clearly	■ communicate poorly
■ have a record of past accomplishments	■ appear lazy
■ are mature	■ are immature
■ get along well with others	■ do not get along with others
■ have a positive attitude toward life and work	■ have a bad attitude
■ are well groomed	■ are poorly groomed
■ have good manners	■ have poor manners

12-4
Showing positive characteristics can help you get a job. Showing negative charactersitics will encourage the interviewer to end the interview early.

Questions to Answer

An interviewer gets to know you by asking questions. You will be rated on your answers throughout the interview. Simple *yes* and *no* answers are not enough. Answer the questions completely. How you answer the questions will help to determine whether or not you get the job. Be ready to answer questions such as the following:

- What are your goals for the future?
- What were your favorite and least favorite subjects in school?
- In what school activities have you participated?
- How has hard work helped you to get ahead?
- How well can you follow instructions?
- How dependable are you?
- What is your major weakness?
- What salary do you expect?
- Why do you think you might like this particular job?
- What kind of work do you eventually hope to do?

Before you are asked any questions, the interviewer may say, "Tell me about yourself." This is your opportunity to summarize your best points and emphasize their benefits to the job. Be ready with a brief reply, just in case.

Questions to Ask

The interviewer is not the only one who can ask questions. You can and should ask questions. Your questions should show the interviewer that you are interested in the job.

At some point during the interview, you should learn more about the job than the brief description provided in the want ad. You will have an opportunity to read (or hear the interviewer read) the job description. A ***job description*** details the tasks you are to perform. Make sure you completely understand what the job involves.

Don't ask questions unrelated to the job. Do not ask questions just to have something to say. Above all, do not ask questions that the interviewer has already answered in earlier remarks. Some common questions asked by job applicants follow:

- What are the work hours?
- Is much overtime work involved?
- Is there room for promotion?
- Was the last person who held this job promoted?
- What are the job duties?

- What is a typical day like?
- What skills does an employee need to succeed in this job?
- What training does the company provide for employees?

Your questions tell the interviewer that you are interested in the job. Your questions and the interviewer's answers also help you decide if you would like to have the job. See 12-5.

After the Interview

Soon after the interview, find a quiet place and go over the interview in your mind. Write down any questions that gave you trouble. This will help you develop answers if you are asked back for a second interview. It will also help you in future interviews with other companies.

Evaluate the Job and the Company

You should be ready to accept or reject a job if it is offered to you. In order to make your decision, you need to honestly evaluate the job and the company. The time to do this is right after the interview while the experience is still fresh in your mind.

How can you tell if a job is right for you? Make a list of what is important to you. Consider your needs, career goals, and the type of work you want to do. Compare your list with the opportunities and working conditions offered by the employer. Do you like the results?

Your list of positive and negative feelings will help you make a final decision about the job. The following sample questions provide a starting point in making your own list:

12-5   *Bristol-Myers Squibb Co.*
By asking relevant questions, you show the interviewer that you are interested in the job.

- Do you feel you can do this job?
- Would you enjoy doing this job?
- Does the job seem right for you?
- Are the working conditions comfortable?
- Did the other employees seem to like their work?
- Does the company offer training and opportunities for promotions?
- Is the salary right?
- Would this job help you in your long-range career goals?
- Do you have enough information to make a decision?

Write a Follow-Up Letter

Shortly after the interview, write a follow-up letter to the interviewer. A *follow-up letter* is a brief letter written in business form to thank the interviewer for the interview, 12-6. Your letter should include the following points:

- a short thank-you for the interview
- a statement about your interest in the job
- additional points that are important but were not discussed, such as job qualifications you possess and failed to mention
- a request to hear from the interviewer about the company's decision

If your evaluation has made you realize that you would be interested in the job, state this in your letter. Likewise, if your evaluation has shown that you would not be interested, you should politely indicate this. A follow-up telephone call can be made within a week if you have not heard from the interviewer.

Receiving a Job Offer

You may be offered a job at the end of an interview. However, do not be upset if the interviewer does not offer you a job on the spot. The interviewer may want to check your references or interview others. You should be told when to expect an answer. If you have not been told, ask if you can call back in a few days.

job description
An explanation of tasks to be performed by an employee in a specified position.
follow-up letter
A brief letter written in business form to thank an interviewer for an interview.

32 Ashland Avenue
Mountain View, CA 94043
August 10, 2003

Ms. Judith Samson
Goodright Company
117 Main Street
Oceanport, CA 94702

Dear Ms. Samson:

Thank you for taking the time yesterday to talk with me about the maintenance job with the Goodright Company. The information you provided was very helpful.

During my interview, we discussed my experience as a carpenter's assistant with the Build-It Construction Company last summer. However, I didn't have an opportunity to mention the plumbing and electrical systems classes I've taken at the Mountain County Area Vocational School. I believe the skills I've learned in these classes have prepared me for many of the maintenance tasks I would perform if employed by your company.

I am excited about the possibility of joining your company and, if offered the job, I will do my best to be a good employee. I look forward to hearing from you soon.

Sincerely,

Michael King
Michael King

12-6

Sending a follow-up letter shows an interviewer that you are a serious job candidate.

When a job offer is extended to you, you may wish to ask for a day to think about it. The interviewer will usually say yes, but you might be asked to decide right away. The job may need to be filled quickly, and more interviews may be necessary.

If you still want the job, tell the interviewer you are pleased to accept. Be sure to ask *where, when,* and *to whom* you should report for work. Find out if you will need to bring anything with you to the work site. If you will need a uniform, ask where and when you should get it.

Find out everything you need to know to feel ready for your first day at work. If the interviewer doesn't know the answers to your questions, he or she will refer you to your supervisor. Your supervisor will be able to tell you anything else about the job you may need to know.

If you decide not to accept a job offer, thank the interviewer. Be polite. The interviewer will appreciate your honesty. Remember, the company wants employees who want to work there. They know that every job does not appeal to everyone, and they are looking for the right person for the job.

Steps to Follow if You Do Not Get the Job

It is rare to get a job after only one interview. You may have many interviews before you get a job. This is true for most people throughout their careers.

You should learn from each interview, especially if you do not get the job. Think about what happened during the interview. Did you have a specific job in mind when you applied? Did you know about the company's business? Were you able to give good answers to all the interview questions? Would you have hired yourself for the job?

If the answer to any of these questions is *no,* then perhaps you already know why you did not get the job. Sometimes the reasons are not so simple. You could politely ask the interviewer to tell you why you did not get the job. This information might help you on your next interview.

Another question you might ask yourself is, "Do my skills need improvement?" If so, you may want to talk to your vocational counselor or teacher. Most importantly, do not get discouraged. There is a job out there for you. You just need more time to find it.

Summary

The interview is the most important step in getting a job. You need to prepare for it carefully. Find out about the company's products or services. Be ready to discuss your skills and other job qualifications.

Pay attention to your clothes and grooming when you get ready for an interview. Plan to go alone and arrive on time. Be positive, pleasant, polite, and truthful. Be prepared not only to answer questions, but also to ask them.

After the interview, take time to review what happened. Be sure to write a follow-up letter. If you are offered a job, evaluate the offer carefully. Think about your needs and career goals before you make a decision. If you are not offered a job, do not be discouraged. Learn from the experience and try again.

Reviewing the Chapter

1. What usually happens if a telephone interview goes well?
2. True or false. A personal interview usually determines whether or not the job applicant will be hired.
3. Why is it important to be on time for an interview?
4. True or false. If both you and your friend are applying for jobs at the same place, you should go to your interviews together.
5. List five behaviors you should demonstrate during an interview.
6. List five behaviors you should *not* demonstrate during an interview.
7. List five questions to ask an interviewer during an interview.
8. If you accept a job offer, what should you be sure to ask?
9. What four points should be included in a follow-up letter?
10. List five questions you would ask yourself when evaluating a job offer.

Building Your Foundation Skills

1. Write an article for your school newspaper about what you should and should *not* do during interviews.
2. Discuss how you would prepare for interviews for the following jobs: gas station manager, file clerk, and salesperson in a fashion shop. (Remember that dressing appropriately is part of the preparation process.)

3. Work with a partner to practice telephone interviews.

4. Prepare a list of questions that an interviewer might ask you in an interview.

5. Write a sample follow-up letter to an interviewer.

Building Your Workplace Competencies

Practice your job interview skills with two classmates. Plan to have each person of the team interviewed jointly by the other two in separate sessions. Together, schedule appointment times for the three interviews. Also, determine what type of position you seek as "interviewee" and let the interviewers know. (This will allow the two interviewers enough time to develop questions related to the position you seek.) Carefully record the job positions your teammates plan to seek so you can develop appropriate questions when you interview them. Interviewers should take notes during the interviews and, after each interview, discuss the strengths and weaknesses observed. As a team, share your reactions to the interview process with the class. *(This activity develops competence with resources, interpersonal skills, information, and systems.)*

Good Employee Skills

Objectives

After studying this chapter, you will be able to

- determine what you may gain as an employee if you succeed in winning at work.

- identify expectations of employers.

- describe how you can do your best as an employee.

Words to Know

work ethic
penalty
reprimand
termination
punctual
dependable
privilege

Winning at Work

"Winning at work" means that you gain something from your job. You may feel you have won just by getting a job. That is an accomplishment. As you work, however, you will have many more chances to win. You will be able to win respect if your work pleases your employer. You also win self-esteem when your work meets your personal standards.

In order for you to win at work, it is not necessary for someone else to lose. When you win, you will be a contented employee. This will allow your company to win through your contributions of effort and ideas. See 13-1.

**Employee of the
Month Award
given to**

**Bill
Martinez**

**In recognition of outstanding
performance during the
month of April**

Cardinal Engineering Services

13-1
Employees gain self-esteem when they excel and companies gain profits.

Consider Your Employer's Expectations

To give an honest day's work for an honest day's pay is a common work ethic. A **work ethic** is a standard of conduct and values for job performance. Having a good work ethic will help you win your employer's approval.

work ethic
A standard of conduct and values for job performance.

When you win with your employer, you may be rewarded with job security, raises, and promotions. The best way to win with your employer is to meet his or her expectations.

Imagine yourself as an employer. What traits would you want your employees to have? How would you expect them to behave? What kind of employees would you reward with raises and promotions? Your answers to these questions should help you understand how employers think and act. Your answers are probably similar to the list of employer expectations in 13-2.

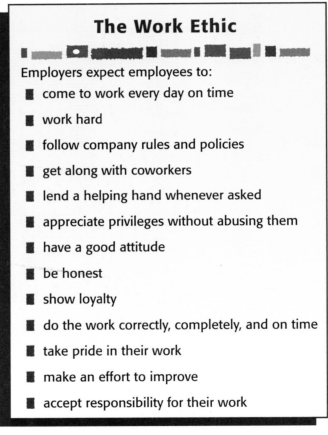

The Work Ethic

Employers expect employees to:
- come to work every day on time
- work hard
- follow company rules and policies
- get along with coworkers
- lend a helping hand whenever asked
- appreciate privileges without abusing them
- have a good attitude
- be honest
- show loyalty
- do the work correctly, completely, and on time
- take pride in their work
- make an effort to improve
- accept responsibility for their work

13-2
Considering your employer's expectations will help you become a winning employee.

Employers want what you want. They want to be treated fairly and with respect. They want employees who can get along with others and make the company a success.

Getting Along with Others

You will be expected to get along with your employer. Getting promoted is not likely if you can't get along with your employer. You might even be fired in such a case.

All employers are different so their personalities differ. Their styles of supervision also vary. The best way to get along with your employer is to do your job well.

As a new employee, don't try to tell your employer how to change the operation. You should get to know your employer and the operation before making suggestions for change. If you don't know how to handle a task, ask questions and be willing to learn. Let your employer know that you want to do a good job.

Your employer will expect you to get along with your coworkers. If you are unable to cooperate with others, you will reduce the productivity of your department. Employers cannot afford to keep employees who interfere with the company's ability to get a job done.

Your employer will also expect you to get along with customers and business contacts, 13-3. You need to deal with people outside the company in a helpful, friendly, professional way. If you fail to treat these people with respect, they are likely to get a bad impression of your company. They may even stop doing business with your company. If your attitude or actions hurt your company's business, they will hurt your chances of keeping your job.

13-3
Smiling and being courteous to customers are requirements for service-oriented jobs.

Obedience

Obeying company rules and policies is another employer expectation. As a new employee, you may be told these rules and policies, or you may receive a written copy. It is your responsibility to learn the rules and policies and follow them. Ask your employer to explain any company rule or policy that you do not understand.

Breaking company rules and policies usually results in a penalty. A ***penalty*** is a loss or hardship due to some action. The specific penalties that apply to different cases are detailed in a company's rules and policies manual. For instance, a construction company may require you to wear a hard hat at all times when on the job. If you failed to obey this company policy, you could be penalized in the following way:

- First offense is a verbal reprimand. A ***reprimand*** is a severe expression of disapproval.
- Second offense is a written reprimand and a fine. The written reprimand goes into your personnel file. It affects future decisions about your pay level and job opportunities.
- Third offense is termination. ***Termination*** is the end of employment or the loss of a job.

Punctuality

One company policy is likely to involve your working hours. Employers expect their employees to put in a full day's work. To do so, you must be ***punctual***. This means being on time. You should try to be at your workstation at least five to ten minutes early. You should not leave before the official quitting time.

Employers have many ways of checking on the starting and quitting times of employees. Some companies use time clocks. You punch your time card when arriving and when leaving work, as well as when taking your breaks. See 13-4. Many offices use sign in/sign out sheets. Employees are required to sign a logbook when entering or leaving the building.

No matter what system is used at your place of employment, you should get into the habit of being early. Then, you will not need to worry about being late.

Dependability

Employers, coworkers, family, and friends expect you to be dependable. Being ***dependable*** means being reliable. This means workers expect you to be a person of your word. Not only must you be punctual, you must also stay busy at doing your assignments. Being dependable means not taking time off for nonessential purposes.

13-4

Some employers record employees' punctuality by using time cards punched by a time clock.

Many people depend on you to do the job you were hired to do. This means accomplishing the tasks you were expected to complete, as outlined in your job description. It also means doing tasks according to your supervisor's directions.

Employers and coworkers appreciate dependable people. Dependable workers are usually the first to be considered for job advancements and raises.

penalty
A loss or hardship due to some action, such as breaking company rules or policies.

reprimand
A severe expression of disapproval.

termination
The end of employment or the loss of a job.

punctual
On time.

dependable
Being reliable.

Do Not Abuse Privileges

Some company policies may concern certain privileges for employees. A *privilege* is a right that is given as a benefit or favor. Most employees have several privileges at work. Two examples are breaks and the use of office equipment. Do not abuse or take advantage of such privileges.

Breaks from work allow employees to relax and return to work refreshed. If you are given a 15-minute break, do not stretch it into a 20-minute break. Your supervisor depends on you to return to work promptly.

Your company may allow you to use the telephone to make some important local telephone calls. Don't abuse this privilege. Keep your personal calls to a minimum. Use this privilege to call home when you'll be late or to take care of an urgent personal matter. Don't chat with family members and friends, and don't allow them to call you at work just to chat.

Likewise, do not send personal faxes or e-mails on company equipment. To prevent this from occurring, many companies have strict rules regarding the use of office equipment. Abusing these privileges robs your employer of your work time. It also creates unfair expenses for your employer. More importantly, your activities may tie up communication channels and prevent customers from easily reaching the company. This could result in lost sales and customers.

Honesty

Your employer expects you to be an honest employee. One type of dishonesty that is a problem in some workplaces is stealing. Stealing does not always involve taking money from your employer. Stealing also includes taking company supplies, tools, or equipment for personal use.

Stealing *any* amount of your employer's property is dishonest. Even taking something as minor as a package of pencils is considered stealing. This is just like taking money from the cash register. Your employer must replace the stolen pencils at a cost to the company.

Another form of dishonesty is taking too much time for breaks. Doing so cheats the employer out of time that workers should be devoting to work. It also cheats the employer out of wages that are not earned. All companies have a definite starting and quitting time. Don't arrive at work late, and don't quit work early. Coming in late or sneaking out early is unfair to the company. Also, it will cause discontent among coworkers and could be grounds for dismissal.

You should be honest in all your dealings with your employer. An employer is likely to go to great lengths to keep an employee who is honest. See 13-5.

Loyalty

Would you remain friends with a person who always tells others about your faults and secrets? Would you continue to like a person who always "puts you down?" You probably wouldn't. You want friends who are loyal. You want friends who talk about your strengths, not your weaknesses.

Employers are very much like you. Employers expect their employees to be loyal. They want employees who speak highly of the company. They want employees who will not give away company secrets or grumble about decisions the employer makes.

13-5

Honest employees do not stretch their breaks beyond the specified time allowed.

privilege
A right that is given as a benefit or favor.

Being loyal to your employer, however, means keeping company business within the company. It does not mean you must ignore those things that should be improved. Instead, loyalty means always working to make the company better. As a loyal employee, you earn the respect of your employer.

Do Your Best as an Employee

To win at work, you must do your very best as an employee. This means doing your job to the best of your ability. It means looking for ways to improve and being willing to learn new skills. Doing your best as an employee involves accepting responsibility for your work and having a good attitude. If you make a true effort at this, you will win. You'll win self-esteem by knowing you're doing the best job you can do.

Use All Your Abilities

Your first challenge is getting a job. Your next challenge is keeping the job. Many people spend a lot of time working to get a job. Once they have the job, they relax. Don't let this happen to you. You should put your best foot forward at all times. "Do an honest day's work for an honest day's pay" is an old saying that still applies. Your employers and your coworkers expect you to do the job you were hired to do. Doing your job to the best of your ability has another benefit, too. It allows you to feel good about yourself and build your self-esteem.

Some employees do only what they are told to do and no more. Employees who work to the best of their abilities, however, notice other tasks that need to be done. These employees do extra tasks without being asked. For instance, your assigned task may be to dust the shelves. While dusting, you may find items like rubber bands and paper clips lying on the shelves. If these items do not belong there, remove them. To simply dust around these items is not doing the job to the best of your ability.

Don't simply ignore other tasks that need to be done while doing an assigned task. On the other hand, if the extra tasks require considerably more time or expertise, first check with your employer. Always make sure you are using your time on the job in the way your employer wants.

Take pride in what you do. If you are sweeping floors, sweep them as clean as you can. If you are baking pastries, try to make them perfect in shape, texture, and taste. If you are writing a report, try to write it without a single error. Treat each task like the most important task the company could give you. See 13-6.

There is truth in the old saying "practice makes perfect." Visualize each step of your job. Work at perfecting whatever you do. Go over each detail until the steps become automatic. Be patient. Developing skill takes determination and practice.

Watch for Ways to Improve

Your first obligation to your employer is to do the job you were hired to do. When your end result does not meet your employer's standards, seek your employer's help. Try to improve your skills. A positive attitude, training, and practice will help you improve.

After you master your job, look for new skills to develop. This will help you become more valuable to your employer. Watch the more experienced workers do their jobs. Ask them to show you how to do some advanced tasks. Don't be afraid to try new assignments.

Let your employer know that you want to handle additional responsibilities. Volunteer for extra training and other job assignments. Take self-improvement courses that help you advance on the job. The more you learn and do on the job, the more valuable you become to your employer.

13-6
Take pride in your work to do the best job you can do.

Be Willing to Learn

You must be willing to learn your company's way of operating. Every company operates somewhat differently. For instance, the style of typing a letter for one company may differ from the style used by another company.

Your willingness to learn and keep your skills updated is important to your company. Your company will provide you with on-the-job training. It might even send you to seminars or school to improve your skills. Skilled workers help the company earn higher profits. Higher profits help pay for more jobs and higher wages. See 13-7.

13-7

Be willing to learn the skills needed to keep up with your company's changing needs.

Accept Responsibility for Your Work

There will be times when you make mistakes on the job. Don't be afraid to admit your mistakes. Everyone makes mistakes at one time or another. Learn from your mistakes. Try not to make the same mistake twice. Whatever you do, don't blame others for your errors. Rather, accept responsibility for them. You will get more respect from your employer and your coworkers when you do.

Have a Good Attitude

A positive attitude will help you accomplish your tasks to the best of your ability. Try to develop a "can do" attitude. This attitude shows you are willing to try any task. It also shows your belief in your own ability to succeed.

Having a good attitude ranks high with most employers. Many prefer workers with positive attitudes to workers with perfect skills. Employers can teach workers the skills they need. The workers themselves, on the other hand, must develop a positive attitude. See 13-8.

Signs of a Good Attitude

- Listen to others' suggestions.
- Avoid making excuses for mistakes or blaming others for them.
- Live up to supervisors' and coworkers' expectations.
- Try to see things from the other person's point of view.
- Respect the opinions of others.
- Give a day's work for a day's pay willingly.

13-8

An employee with a good attitude will win an employer's respect.

 ## Summary

Winning at work means benefiting from your job. You do this by meeting your employer's expectations and doing your best as an employee. It means having a good work ethic.

Employers seek employees who will obey company rules and policies. They also seek employees who will be honest, dependable, and loyal. Employers know that employees who meet these expectations will help the company be successful.

You should always excel in your role as an employee. Living up to your personal standards will allow you to develop pride in your work. Your self-esteem and self-confidence will grow. You will be a winner at work!

 ## Reviewing the Chapter

1. List 10 expectations employers have regarding their employees.
2. Why is it important to obey company rules and policies?
3. Why must an employee be punctual?
4. Give two examples of abusing company privileges.
5. Describe honesty on the job.
6. Explain how an employee can show loyalty at work.
7. Explain why it is important to do your job to the best of your ability.
8. Describe two ways you can improve on the job.
9. What should you do when you make a mistake on the job?
10. List five characteristics of a person with a good attitude.

 ## Building Your Foundation Skills

1. Interview three workers from different companies. Ask them about the workplace importance of dependability, honesty, and getting along with others. Summarize your findings in a brief report.
2. Interview an employer to learn his or her idea of a good employee. Report your findings to the class.
3. Obtain a company's rules and policies manual. Make a list of all actions that lead to penalties. Beside each action, describe its penalty. Put a check mark beside actions that can lead to termination.

Building Your Workplace Competencies

Working with three or four classmates, develop two short skits depicting "good" and "bad" employer/employee interactions over an employer expectation discussed in this chapter. (Two examples are honesty and obedience.) Develop a two-minute script for each skit. Decide as a team what the performers should say and do to deliver a memorable message. Together determine who should do which tasks. Present the skits to the class live or videotape the skits and play them back during class. Summarize the point of the message at the end of the skits. *(This activity develops competence with resources, interpersonal skills, information, systems, and—if videotaping is used—technology.)*

Being a Team Player

Objectives

After studying this chapter, you will be able to

- explain the importance of being a team player at work.

- list several tips for new workers.

- describe how to accept criticism positively.

- distinguish between a good sense of humor and the poor use of humor.

- state the importance of avoiding arguments, rumors, and comparisons to coworkers.

Words to Know

teamwork

criticism

ridicule

sarcasm

conflict

argumentative

rumor

grapevine

gossip

Teamwork Leads to Success

Being hired by a business as an employee is only the first step. You need to work well as a member of the team in order to achieve success.

Consider how a high school drill team functions. It can function only if every member cooperates. It is important for all members to be team players. When one member "fouls up" or fails to cooperate, the entire team looks bad.

Companies depend on teamwork in the same way. *Teamwork* is two or more people working toward a common goal. If one employee fails to cooperate, the entire company can look bad. Without cooperation, the company cannot produce products as quickly or provide services of the highest quality. If customers feel they are not getting the best a company can offer for the price, they shop elsewhere. A company that disappoints its customers will lose business as a result.

Becoming an Effective Team Member

No single employee, no matter how good he or she is, can make a company successful. Employees must work as a team to achieve that goal. As a new employee, make it your business to be a team player at your company. Don't focus on what great work *you* can do. Focus on what great work *your company* can do because you are part of the team.

Employers are looking for individuals who can work together harmoniously. They are looking for individuals who can share ideas and solve problems. Strong interpersonal skills are workplace skills workers need to be effective. (Refer to Figure 1-7 on page 30.)

No single characteristic or trait makes a team member effective. It requires a combination of interpersonal skills. This chapter discusses several interpersonal skills important in the workplace and ways to develop them.

Developing an Effective Team

A capable team can accomplish more than one person left to do a job alone. Forming such a team is not easy. It requires the skills, talents, trust, and cooperation of all members.

teamwork
Two or more people working toward a common goal.

Teams must learn to work together before they can be successful. Consider a successful sports team, chorale group, or planning committee. Members must get to know each other's strengths and weaknesses. They must develop a plan and an organized way to accomplish it. Most importantly, they must learn to trust each other and function as a team. The following behaviors are signs of an effective team.

Sharing Ideas

Every member of an effective team is encouraged to participate. No one feels that his or her input is not valued. All ideas are considered important.

Being Open to New Ideas

Keeping an open mind is most important to team planning. Predetermining that an idea won't work without first discussing it often discourages members from making suggestions. Not allowing all members to get involved can doom the team to failure. See 14-1.

14-1
Companies want employees to recommend new ideas that could improve the company.

Sharing Leadership

The person with the most expertise should serve as team leader. That person has the responsibility to encourage everyone to participate. However, no single person is likely to have strengths in all the areas needed. For that reason, the leader of an effective team welcomes seeing others contribute to the group's effort.

Creating an Action Plan

After much thought and discussion, the members decide a course of action. Goals, objectives and timetables are developed.

Working Toward a Common Goal

All members of an effective team have a clear understanding of the task at hand. Each individual knows what he or she must do to accomplish the group's goal. The plan of action is followed carefully, but modified if the team considers it necessary.

Showing Trust

Every member shows support for his or her fellow team members. Each speaks freely, without fear of being criticized or ridiculed for their input. Everyone tries to do his or her assigned tasks as well as possible and on time.

Staying Focused

The hardest part of teamwork is keeping everyone focused on the task at hand. It is easy to get sidetracked and lose focus, especially if the task takes a long time. Periodically, the members of an effective team remind each other of the importance of their mission.

Teams become effective after going through several stages. Experts who study group behavior identified the four stages of team development. Recognizing and understanding these stages will help you succeed as a team player. These stages are summarized in 14-2.

Tips for New Employees

On your first day of work, your main concern should be learning to do the job. However, even at this early date, devoting some of your attention to your coworkers is important. Your early dealings with them may have long-term effects. You are the new person on the job. You need to be accepted by your supervisors and coworkers. Being a friendly, respectful, likable person will help you gain the acceptance of your fellow employees.

Stages of Team Development

1. Forming
Team members share personal information as they try to get to know and accept one another. It is an exciting new adventure, but not everyone is comfortable.

2. Storming
Team members usually compete for status and often question why the team was formed. Tensions arise as members jockey for control. Leadership from members may not be evident.

3. Norming
The team begins to work as a unit. A leader emerges and members begin to listen to one another. Trust forms.

4. Performing
This is the highest level of team performance. The team accomplishes complex challenges. Tasks are handled efficiently.

14-2
Before a team becomes effective, members must know, accept, and trust one another.

Be Friendly

When you start a new job, introduce yourself to other employees with a smile and a firm handshake. Get to know your coworkers by name. Greet them when you arrive, and say good-bye to them when you leave.

Don't overdo it. Trying too hard to be friends with your new boss can be a mistake. You might be labeled an "apple polisher."

In short, be friendly and pleasant. However, do not expect everyone at work to be your friend. Attaining the friendship of your coworkers is nice, but receiving their cooperation is your main goal.

Respect Your Coworkers

As you meet your coworkers, remember they deserve your respect as workers and as people. As workers, respect your coworkers for their knowledge and skills. They would not be working for the company if they did not have useful talents to offer.

Respect your coworkers for their positive qualities. Like all people, your coworkers have good and bad traits. Don't focus on their bad traits. Instead, look for their good traits.

Present Yourself as a Likable Person

Your new coworkers will start to form impressions of you from your very first meeting. Consequently, you want to present yourself as a likable person who gets along with everyone.

Avoid appearing self-centered. Your coworkers will quickly tire of hearing you talk about yourself endlessly. You will bore them by always talking about your own problems and interests. Listen to what they have to say. Talk about your common interests.

Also avoid acting like a know-it-all. Don't assume a superior attitude and pretend to know all the answers. Listen to instructions and follow them. Ask questions when necessary. See 14-3.

As a new employee, do not tell your boss or experienced workers how to do their jobs. There will be plenty of time to offer suggestions after you get to know the job and your coworkers better.

14-3
Successful companies rely on employees who have good interpersonal skills with coworkers and customers.

14-4

Your supervisor may use criticism to help you improve your work. Learn to accept it positively.

Accept Criticism Positively

When you start a new job, you should be prepared to accept instructions and some criticism. A *criticism* is a judgmental remark about your work. As you work, your supervisor may show you a better way to do a job. A coworker or your boss may tell you when you have done something wrong. See 14-4.

No one likes to be criticized. Being told that you have done something wrong is not fun. However, when employees make mistakes, their supervisors must tell them what they did wrong. This helps the employees learn. If employees were not told what they did wrong, they would continue to make the same mistakes. Your supervisor understands that new employees may make some mistakes. You must understand that mistakes can cause a company to lose business and money.

The way you react to criticism shows how willing you are to be a team player. You can react to criticism in two ways: negatively or positively. Being defensive is a negative response to criticism. You defend yourself by blaming others or making excuses. Another negative response is getting angry with yourself. Staying upset about the criticism for a long time is also negative. None of these responses will help you or your coworkers achieve the team goal of getting a job done.

To respond in a positive way, try to keep a good attitude. Listen to what is said. Accept it as a suggestion for a better way to do your job. Think of it as a learning experience. Do not overreact and assume that you are a failure. Remind yourself that you are a valued employee. Tell yourself that you can and will do better next time. Then apologize and express your desire to improve.

A positive reaction to criticism will help you be a better team player. You will save yourself from being too upset. Your supervisors and coworkers will be impressed with your willingness to improve. If you improve enough, you may be promoted!

Have a Positive Attitude

People like to be with coworkers who have a *positive attitude.* Those with a positive attitude see the optimistic side of everything. They are upbeat, cheerful, and eager to find solutions to problems. On the other hand, people with a *negative attitude* only see the problems. They look at the gloomy side of everything. They are grumpy and full of complaints.

Negative attitudes do not help team members achieve goals at work. Positive attitudes do, 14-5. Try to develop behaviors that reflect a positive attitude. Try to be a worker who does the following:

- smiles often
- shows enthusiasm
- seldom complains
- makes changes willingly
- tries to understand others' views
- seldom criticizes others
- volunteers help
- avoids making excuses
- accepts responsibility for mistakes
- always tries to perform at a high level

A positive attitude can be reflected in what you say. Saying something positive about someone is just as easy as saying something negative. Your coworkers are more likely to accept you as a team player if you speak kindly of them.

14-5
Working cooperatively is a sign of the positive attitude needed to achieve goals at work.

criticism
Judgmental comments about your work.

Keep a Good Sense of Humor

A good sense of humor can help your team get through difficult situations at work. Having a sense of humor is being able to laugh at yourself when you do something foolish or silly. When this happens, try not to get angry at yourself or at others. Try to laugh it off and avoid repeating the mistake. No one likes a person who acts too seriously. Don't take yourself so seriously that you forget how to laugh.

Avoid the Poor Use of Humor

Knowing how to use your sense of humor in the workplace is important. However, you must not get carried away.

Most people like to hear and tell jokes. Jokes make people laugh. Jokes are fine to tell as long as they do not deliberately offend anyone. Crude jokes should be avoided. Crude jokes are vulgar and in bad taste. They are offensive to most people. A person who tells crude jokes is seldom held in high regard by coworkers.

Having a sense of humor does not mean spending a lot of time at work telling jokes or acting silly. You may get a laugh or two, but your coworkers might begin to see you as a clown. Your supervisor may consider you a *slacker.* That is a person who avoids work or responsibility. You might put your job or your chances for promotion in danger.

You should not cause laughter at the expense of someone else's feelings. Ridiculing another person is never funny. To **ridicule** a person is to make fun of him or her. A person who ridicules another person is cruel and insensitive. You should always try to respect other people's feelings.

Like ridicule, sarcasm is not funny, nor does it contribute to the team effort. *Sarcasm* is the use of cutting remarks. The intention is to put another person down. Words can often hurt as much as, if not more than, physical force.

Do Not Cause Conflict

Being a team player means cooperating with your coworkers to do the best job your company can do. Most of your adult life will be spent working. A good portion of your time will be spent with coworkers. If you don't get along with them, you may not be able to advance in your job, 14-6. In fact, you stand a good chance of losing your job altogether.

You Must Be a Team Player Before You Can Be a Coach

Tom had recently been transferred into Sally's department. Sally was asked to help Tom in his new assignment. Tom made a minor error and Sally became upset. A great deal of friction developed between them. Sally told everyone of Tom's mistake. As the weeks went by, she continued to be highly critical of Tom. The entire department began to feel sorry for Tom because of the treatment he received from Sally.

When an opening for the position of department supervisor became available, Sally applied for it. She knew her skills were excellent. She felt that she was qualified to do the job. However, Sally did not get the promotion.

Sally observed her new supervisor, Kathy, to figure out why Kathy got the job. Like Sally, Kathy had very good skills. She also got along well with other employees. Kathy did her work and helped others when needed.

Sally realized that her attitude toward others had caused her to lose the promotion. She realized that she must learn to get along better with her coworkers. She made up her mind to make an effort to do so.

14-6
This case study illustrates how your ability to work well with coworkers can affect your chances of getting a promotion.

People have to work together to get most jobs done. Friction on the job creates unpleasant working conditions. You cannot work at peak performance when you, or those around you, cause conflict. ***Conflict*** is a hostile situation resulting from opposing views. It can become a destructive force if not resolved. Starting arguments, spreading rumors, and gossiping are three ways to cause conflict.

ridicule
To tease or belittle
sarcasm
The use of cutting remarks.
conflict
Hostile situation resulting from opposing views.

Do Not Cause Arguments

Being a team player at work means avoiding arguments. There are two sides to most situations. Try to see the other person's side.

Some people seem to look for arguments. They disagree with just about everything. If you say it's nice outside, they'll say it isn't. These people are described as being *argumentative*. Don't become this type of person. Most people tend to stay away from people who are argumentative.

If you have frequent and major disagreements with your coworkers, they will shun you. You may lose not only their friendship and cooperation, but also your job or a promotion.

Another situation to avoid is taking sides in other people's arguments. Often the arguing parties eventually make up and you become the bad guy. It is best not to get involved in the first place. See 14-7.

14-7
Being able to avoid arguments with your coworkers will help you become a more valuable team player at work.

Do Not Spread Rumors

Rumors can interfere with your ability to work with your coworkers as a team. *Rumors* are bits of information that pass from one person to another without proof of accuracy. At work, rumors pass swiftly along the *grapevine*, an informal and unofficial flow of information.

Rumors are usually only half-truths. Perhaps someone hears part of a conversation. This person then tells another person what was heard. The person who starts the rumor usually does not have all the facts. The person either invents or adds facts to make sense of the message. As the rumor passes through the grapevine, others add or delete information.

Gossip is part of the rumor mill or grapevine. When you *gossip*, you tell personal information about another person. Sometimes this information is true. Often it is not true. Gossip, like rumors, is usually information that should not be told to others.

Do not gossip or spread rumors. Your employer and coworkers consider people who gossip and spread rumors as people who can't be trusted. You will lose everyone's respect if you talk about others.

Also avoid letting others spread gossip to you. Some people may try to use gossip to influence your impressions about your fellow workers. Form your own opinions without listening to gossip. Rumors and gossip can deeply hurt your coworkers.

Avoid Comparisons

As a new worker, you may see some of your coworkers enjoying benefits that are greater than yours. Do not compare your work or benefits with theirs. Although you are players on the same team, senior employees are often entitled to more benefits. They may have worked for the company for many years. Perhaps they have positions that require more responsibility.

argumentative
Easily creating arguments.

rumor
Information passed from one person to another without proof of accuracy.

grapevine
An informal and unofficial flow of information.

gossip
To tell personal information about someone.

14-8
Employers expect workers to stay focused and not waste time by comparing their assignments to their coworkers.

Avoid comparing workloads, salaries, and the treatment of coworkers. Senior employees will not appreciate questions about their benefits. See 14-8.

Don't Compare Workloads

Your first obligation to your employer and your coworkers is to do the work described in your job description. It is your responsibility to perform those tasks to the best of your ability.

Always ask your supervisor for more responsibilities when you have completed your assigned duties. You should also be willing to give your coworkers a helping hand when you have extra time. However, do not show off by trying to take on more than you can handle. You do not want your coworkers to think you are trying to put them down.

Never compare your workload to a coworker's workload. Another employee may appear to have a light workload. However, you may not realize how complex his or her tasks are. Let your employer judge the work you do.

Don't Compare Salaries

Employers set different salary levels for different jobs. Employees with more experience usually earn more than workers with little or no experience. Employees with special knowledge may also receive higher wages. As you gain experience and knowledge, your salary will increase.

Don't Compare the Treatment of Coworkers

Senior employees usually receive more benefits than beginning workers. Extra benefits are earned by having more years of experience with the company, 14-9. They may also be earned by holding jobs in the company that involve greater responsibilities. The employees are rewarded with benefits such as the following:

- preferred parking spaces
- longer vacations
- first choice on vacation schedules
- preferred working schedules
- bigger bonuses
- stock options

If these benefits appeal to you, don't just envy those who have them. Work as hard as they did to earn them.

14-9

Employees often receive special recognition for many years of service to a company.

Summary

Being a team player at work is necessary if you want to get along with your coworkers and succeed at your job. If you are not a team player, friction with your coworkers will cause unpleasant working conditions. Neither you nor your coworkers will be able to perform to the best of your abilities. The company could suffer losses. You could lose a chance for a promotion. You might even lose your job.

When you are a team player, everyone wins. The work site becomes a pleasant place. All jobs are done well and on time. The employees and the company enjoy success.

You can develop skills and behaviors that will help you become a team player. No one characteristic or trait makes you a team member. It is a combination of effective interpersonal skills. Put forth your best efforts right away, from the very first day at a new job. Be friendly and respect your coworkers. Accept criticism positively and have a positive attitude. Keep a good sense of humor, but avoid the poor use of humor. Do not cause arguments or spread rumors. Finally, avoid comparing your work situation with your coworkers' work situations. Your efforts to be a team player will be rewarded.

Reviewing the Chapter

1. Why should you, as a new employee, make it your business to be a team player at your company?

2. Which of the following statements are true?

    A. You should always be a team player.

    B. You should *not* expect everyone at work to be your friend.

    C. As a new employee, you should tell experienced workers how they could do their jobs better.

    D. It is easier to be accepted by others if you speak kindly of them.

    E. When coworkers have a dispute, you should get involved right away and help them settle it.

3. Describe a positive way to respond to criticism.

4. List five behaviors that reflect an employee's positive work attitude.

5. How does having a good sense of humor help you when you do something foolish or silly at work?

6. Name three types of humor that should be avoided.

7. Describe an argumentative person.

8. Why should you avoid spreading gossip and rumors?

9. Why should you avoid comparing your workload to your coworker's workload?

10. Why do senior employees usually receive more benefits than beginning workers?

Building Your Foundation Skills

1. Write a two-page fictional story about an employee's interactions with coworkers. Then exchange stories with a classmate. What behavior improvements would you recommend for the employee in your classmate's story?

2. Watch a television show in which the main characters are at work together. Make a list of the scenes in which they cooperate with each other.

3. Give a one-minute oral report on why the workplace needs team players.

4. Invite an employer to class to talk about the importance of teamwork. Be prepared to ask questions.

Building Your Workplace Competencies

With two classmates, visit a local store, library, or government office to observe how coworkers interact with supervisors, customers, and each other. (First talk with the manager and ask permission to observe examples of teamwork and take notes, otherwise people will wonder what you are doing.) Note and record what is said and done when employees work together. Decide with your classmates how to divide the following tasks. Make an oral report to the class summarizing the best example of teamwork skills you saw as well as the worst example. Identify how the second situation should have been handled. *(This activity develops competence with resources, interpersonal skills, information, and systems.)*

Keeping Safety First

Objectives

After studying this chapter, you will be able to

- identify proper office safety procedures.

- explain proper safety procedures when working with machinery and tools.

- describe safety procedures related to lifting, housekeeping, and using ladders.

- apply fire safety procedures.

- list five lifesaving steps in first aid.

- describe responsibilities of employers and employees under OSHA.

Words to Know

dismissal

grounded

flammable liquid

fire triangle

evacuate

first aid

OSHA

workers' compensation

disability

Thinking and Acting Safely

Accidents on the job cost companies money. Medical bills must be paid. Production goes down. New or part-time workers may need to be hired to take the place of injured workers. Fines and lawsuits are also possible.

Preventing accidents is everyone's business. It is important to always think and act safely. You must know the safety rules, but simply knowing them will not stop accidents. More importantly, you must follow safety rules to prevent accidents.

The first rule of safety is to learn the right way to do your job. That will always be the safe way. Never operate equipment or use tools unless you have been shown the proper and safe method. If you are not sure about any part of your job, ask your supervisor for further instruction. Don't guess! A mistake could cost your life or someone else's.

Ten general safety rules are listed in 15-1. Following them will help keep you safe on the job.

Ten General Safety Rules

1. Comply with all company safety rules and signs.
2. Follow all instructions. Do not take chances. If you don't know the rule or procedure, ask!
3. Correct or report all unsafe conditions.
4. Use the correct protective equipment. Wear properly fitted clothes.
5. Report all accidents. Get first aid promptly.
6. Use, adjust, and repair equipment only when authorized. Report safety hazards immediately.
7. Use the right tool for the job. Use it correctly and safely.
8. When lifting, bend your knees. Get help for lifting heavy loads.
9. Don't goof off.
10. Keep your work area clean.

15-1
Following these general safety rules will help you avoid accidents and injuries on the job.

Unsafe Acts

Do you always act safely? At least 95 percent of all accidents are caused by unsafe acts or unsafe conditions. Most of these accidents could be avoided by using common sense.

People cause unsafe acts. No one really wants an accident to happen, but sometimes people act before thinking. For instance, some people feel that wearing safety glasses around moving machinery is unnecessary. However, a chip of wood or a tool hitting a person in the eyes could cause injury or blindness. Knowing that, is taking off your safety glasses worth the risk? Beware of the following unsafe acts:

- wiping or cleaning moving machinery
- failing to wear proper protective clothing
- smoking in a nonsmoking area
- failing to follow safety rules and signs
- goofing off
- lifting a load too heavy
- removing or not using machine guards
- taking chances

You have to act safely to protect yourself. You must also act safely to protect others. Being careless can hurt not only you, but others as well.

Unsafe Conditions

Unsafe conditions cause accidents. Whenever possible, you should correct unsafe conditions, even if you didn't cause them. For example, clean up spills so no one will slip and fall. Pick up objects left on steps so no one will trip or fall. Do not be responsible for some other person's accident.

You cannot correct all unsafe conditions. Those that can't be corrected should be reported. Your supervisor will thank you for it. Be on the lookout for the following unsafe conditions:

- poor housekeeping
- dim lighting
- blocked fire exits
- high stacks of boxes
- overused electrical extension cords
- opened drawers left unattended

- dangerous objects overhead
- tools left lying around
- oily rags in paper boxes

Can you think of other unsafe conditions that might occur at work? If so, how would you correct them? See 15-2.

Proper Safety Attitude

Your actions speak louder than words. The way you act on the job reflects your safety attitude. In order to practice safety, you must think about safety. Thinking about and practicing safety requires a proper safety attitude.

Certain attitudes can lead to accidents. Try to avoid these and develop safety-conscious attitudes.

15-2
Correcting unsafe conditions can help prevent accidents in the workplace.

Forgetfulness

Forgetting safety details can cause you and others serious injury. Make it a habit to follow all the safety steps associated with your job.

Disobedience

Disobeying company safety rules and signs can be the first step toward an accident. Follow instructions. Do not violate orders.

Carelessness

Your job requires your full attention. Daydreaming on the job can result in a mistake that causes someone pain and injury. Keep your mind on what you are doing.

Bad Temper

You are a prime target for an accident if you are not in full control of your emotions. Hotheads react without thinking. It's too late to be sorry after an accident has occurred. Learn to control your temper and think clearly.

Uncertainty

If you are not sure how to perform a task, ask for instructions or a demonstration. A wrong decision can lead to an injury.

Fatigue

You cannot operate at your best when you are tired. Alert people have fewer accidents. Get plenty of rest and pay attention to what you do on the job.

Laziness

People who don't want to make the effort to follow good safety practices are asking for an accident to happen. Ignoring safety rules is a serious matter that could cause your *dismissal*. That is another term for being fired.

Showing Off

A show-off is a danger to everyone. That person is more interested in gaining attention than in promoting safety. A show-off usually takes unnecessary chances, 15-3.

Office Safety

Many office workers do not consider their work areas unsafe. Because they feel safe, they often forget to follow simple safety precautions. Accidents, however, do occur in offices.

Most office accidents are caused by a combination of an unsafe act and an unsafe condition. Office workers need to recognize safety hazards and correct them. Workers should adhere to the following safety practices:

15-3

Racing machines or showing off in other ways can cause extensive property damage and serious injury to you and your coworkers.

- Close all desk and file drawers when they are unattended or not in use. Make sure drawers do not open into aisles or walkways where people could bump into or trip over them.

- Be careful when using manual paper-cutting machines. Pay attention to what you and those around you are doing. Use extreme caution with blades of any type.

- Turn off all office machines before cleaning, adjusting, or adding fluid or cartridges. Office machines can be as harmful to people as factory machines.

- Make sure all electrical machines and electrical cords are kept in good repair and grounded. A plug that is *grounded* has an electrical connection with the earth. It prevents shock by causing electricity to flow to the ground rather than into your body.

- Do not touch electrical machines or connections with wet hands. Water is a good conductor of electricity. An electrical shock could cause serious injury or even death.

dismissal
Another term for being fired.
grounded
Connected to the earth to avoid electrical shock.

- Don't lean too far back in a chair or sit on the edge of the seat. It could slip from beneath you. See 15-4.
- Replace worn electrical cords or plugs. Frayed cords and bad connectors can create sparks and cause fires.
- Unplug electrical connections by pulling the plug, not by pulling the cord. Pulling the cord could damage the protective covering and cause a shock or start a fire.
- Do not overload electrical circuits with too many machines or appliances. Overloading can cause wires to heat and start a fire.
- Use the handrails on stairs to prevent falls.
- Keep the floors clean and dry to prevent slips and falls. Keep telephone wires and extension cords away from places where people could trip on them.
- Never stand on movable office furniture to reach high bookshelves or to replace lightbulbs. Use sturdy ladders or step stools with nonslip treads.
- Read and follow all directions on storing and using chemicals for office machines.
- Be extremely careful of dangling hair, jewelry, scarves, and neckties when working with office machines. Anything that could be caught in machinery should be held back or removed before working with the equipment.

15-4
Sitting properly in a chair can help to prevent office accidents.

Safely Using Machinery, Tools, and Workplace Items

Factory and construction workers need to be especially aware of safety hazards. Many of the machines and tools used by these workers can be dangerous if not handled properly. See 15-5. A few general guidelines should be followed when working with machinery and tools.

- Work at a safe speed. Rushing and taking short-cuts could cause accidents. Never take a chance. Trying to save a minute or two could cost you a finger or even your life.
- Wear the right clothes. Clothes should fit snugly. Loose clothing can get caught in moving machinery. Keep your outer clothes buttoned. Don't take a chance on getting pulled into moving machinery.
- Protect your feet. Do not wear sneakers or sandals on industrial or construction work sites. You should wear hard-toed safety shoes. They protect your feet from falling tools and equipment. Safety shoes can save you pain and serious injury.

15-5

People who work with machinery and tools must take extra precautions to stay safe at work.

Working with Power Tools and Equipment

The first rule of personal safety is *always think first*. This rule applies to all operations. The second rule is *never operate any power tools or equipment without first receiving proper operating instructions*. Power tools should be used correctly and safely. Adhere to the following safety rules with electrical tools and equipment:

- Never operate unfamiliar equipment until you receive specific instructions on its operation.
- Make sure your hands are dry before using an electrical cord. To unplug a cord, grip the plug itself. Do not pull on the cord.
- Keep the starting switch in the off position when plugging in equipment.

- Examine the equipment before turning it on. If an electrical cord is cut or has exposed strands of wire, do not use it.
- Never operate defective equipment.
- Wear the proper protective clothing. Also remember to wear safety goggles to protect your eyes from dust and flying objects, 15-6.
- Report defective tools and equipment to your supervisor.
- Keep all safety guards and shields in place.
- Do not oil, clean, or adjust equipment when the power is on.
- Disconnect electrical equipment when not in use.

Proper Use and Care of Hand Tools

Many accidents are caused by improper use and maintenance of hand tools. You should learn to use each tool the correct way. Choosing and using the right tool for the job gets it done faster and more safely.

Tools should be kept clean and in good condition. Dull tools should be sharpened. Broken handles should be replaced.

15-6
Workers in many areas need to wear safety goggles or other types of eye protection.

Each tool should be stored in its own place when not in use. It will be easier to find when needed. Also, properly stored tools will not fall on you or cause you to trip.

Carry sharp or pointed tools in kits or tool belts. Never carry them in your pockets. Always cover points or sharp edges with shields.

Lifting

Improper lifting is a common cause of accidents on the job and at home. Thousands of people injure themselves each year because of improper lifting. Lifting too much at one time or lifting objects incorrectly can cause hernias or back injuries.

A smart worker learns to lift properly. This includes knowing how much, how often, how far, and how high you can lift. You should also know how much help you need and what mechanical aids are available to help you.

The first step is learning how to lift. Always remember that your legs are much stronger than your back. The key to lifting, then, is to use your leg muscles. When lifting an object from the floor, keep your arms and back straight. Bend your knees and lift with the powerful muscles in your legs.

Know your limitations. Know how much you can safely lift. Seek help with loads in excess of your limit. Play it safe. Do not handle more than you can lift.

Use mechanical aids to save time and energy. Learn the proper procedures for using cranes, hoists, elevators, conveyors, and hand trucks. Failure to learn the safe operating procedures of mechanical aids can be more dangerous than manual lifting. Keep the following safety guidelines in mind when lifting:

- Lift with your leg and arm muscles.
- Keep your back as straight as possible.
- Always carry the load close to your body.
- Be sure you have good footing.
- Be sure you can see where you are going.
- Ask for help when necessary.
- Use mechanical aids to save your energy.
- Keep your work area free from tripping hazards.
- Work smart, not hard. See 15-7.

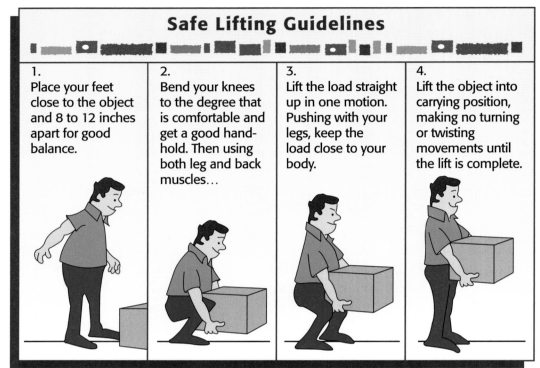

Safe Lifting Guidelines

1.	2.	3.	4.
Place your feet close to the object and 8 to 12 inches apart for good balance.	Bend your knees to the degree that is comfortable and get a good hand-hold. Then using both leg and back muscles…	Lift the load straight up in one motion. Pushing with your legs, keep the load close to your body.	Lift the object into carrying position, making no turning or twisting movements until the lift is complete.

15-7   *National Institute for Occupational Safety and Health*

Following proper lifting procedures can help prevent strains and back injuries.

Housekeeping

Good housekeeping reduces hazards. A clean work area is a safe work area. Cluttered and messy areas can lead to accidents such as tripping, slipping, or being struck by falling objects.

Keep your work area clean. Always put your tools away after use. A tool on a ledge or overhang could slip and hit someone walking or working beneath.

You should clean the floors regularly to remove any hazards that might cause slipping. Pick up scraps and wipe up spilled liquids. When mopping floors, always use safety cones or caution signs to warn of slippery conditions. Place the signs so they can be seen from all directions of approach.

Using Ladders Safely

Many jobs require the use of ladders. Ladders are useful aids, but they must be used with care. See 15-8. Choosing the right ladder for the job is important. Metal ladders should not be used near electrical equipment or high-voltage wires. Metal conducts electricity. Someone standing on or touching a metal ladder could be seriously injured or killed if electrical contact is made with the ladder.

Always check a ladder before using it. Check to see that all the rungs are in place. Make sure the ladder is steady and strong enough to support you. Never use crates, boxes, or machinery as makeshift ladders. The chances of slipping and falling are too great.

Many people fall off ladders because they overreach. You should never stretch on a ladder. Instead, safely move the ladder within an arm's length of your work. Some other safety guidelines for using ladders are listed in the chart in 15-9.

15-8
To safely access high places, use a sturdy, securely positioned ladder and work within an arm's reach.

Safety Guidelines for Using Ladders

■ Be sure the ladder is in good condition.

■ Make sure the ladder has firm footing and is correctly placed.

■ Open a ladder to its fullest width and lock it in position before you climb.

■ Do not work from a ladder placed in front of a door that could be opened. Lock or block the door first.

■ Always face the ladder when climbing up or down.

■ Always take one step at a time and use both hands.

■ Do not lean off-balance to reach the work. Instead, move the ladder.

■ Never stand on the top two steps of a ladder.

■ Do not use objects to create a makeshift ladder.

■ When working outdoors on a home, make sure an extension ladder extends three feet above the roofline.

15-9

Ignoring any of these guidelines could result in a serious injury.

Fire Protection

Fire is a threat to life and property. You must be on guard at all times to prevent fires. A fire at your workplace could put you out of a job. Even worse, someone could get seriously injured.

Each year, careless smoking and faulty electrical wiring and appliances account for nearly half of all fires. Other major causes include the following:

- faulty heating equipment
- grease buildup in kitchen ventilation hoods
- unattended open flames in kitchens and labs
- careless use of flammable liquids

A *flammable liquid* is one that can easily ignite and burn rapidly. Gasoline and solvents are flammable liquids.

Fire takes place when three elements are present—oxygen, fuel, and heat. If you remove any one of these three factors, you will extinguish the fire. Figure 15-10 illustrates the classic *fire triangle*. The triangle symbol represents the three elements required to provide the necessary condition for a fire.

Fire Triangle

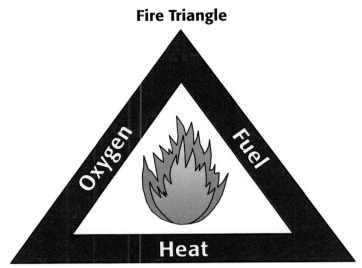

15-10

Fire cannot result unless all three sides of the fire triangle—oxygen, fuel, and heat—are present.

By removing a factor, the triangle opens and you extinguish the fire. If you keep any one factor from joining the other two, you prevent a fire from starting. In the event of a fire, you need to know the following:

- the location of all fire alarms, fire extinguishers, and exits
- how to use a fire alarm pull-box
- how to use the telephone to report a fire—Many regions of the country use *911* for emergency police and fire calls. Familiarize yourself with how to contact that outside line from a workplace phone. In the case of a fire, you would give your name and say, "I want to report a fire at XZY Company." Give the building's address and the exact location of the fire or smoke within the building.
- how to evacuate the building—To *evacuate* means to empty or vacate a place in an organized manner for protection. Fire drills are a must at work and at home.

flammable liquid
A liquid that can easily ignite and burn rapidly.

fire triangle
A symbol representing the three elements that provide the necessary condition for a fire: oxygen, fuel, and heat.

evacuate
To empty or vacate a place in an organized manner for protection.

■ how to use a fire extinguisher on a small fire—The purpose of a fire extinguisher is to put out a small fire or keep a fire from spreading. For the most part, firefighting should be left to trained firefighters.

Additional fire prevention tips are listed in 15-11.

Health and First Aid

Your health affects your performance at work. The food you eat and the amount of sleep you get could affect your work. Fatigue on the job often leads to carelessness and accidents. The same holds true for lack of proper food. A simple rule to follow is *get plenty of rest and proper nourishment.*

Observe simple hygiene rules. Always wash your hands after working with chemicals or before eating. Workers have transmitted harmful substances into their bodies because they failed to wash their hands before eating or smoking.

Where you eat on the job is important. Observe no-eating and no-smoking signs. Never eat where germs can infect your food and drink. Washrooms are not sanitary eating places, nor are most work areas.

Fire Prevention Tips

■ Make sure smokers smoke only in designated areas.
■ Keep your work area clean.
■ Don't overload electrical wires. They can short-circuit and cause a fire.
■ Never store oily rags and paper in open containers. They can build up heat and ignite.
■ Keep containers of flammable liquids tightly closed and stored in cool areas.
■ Always obey all safety rules. When in doubt, ask!

15-11
The best way to assure fire safety is to prevent one from ever starting.

It is best to stop working if you become ill on the job. You will not be working at top performance. Further, your illness may cause you to be careless and injure yourself or someone else. When ill, report to your supervisor. Your supervisor will make sure that you get proper medical assistance.

All injuries should be reported immediately. Get help fast. Report immediately for first aid, regardless of how slight the injury. If a coworker is injured, call for help. Remain calm and wait for proper medical assistance to arrive.

First aid is immediate, temporary treatment given in the event of an accident or illness before proper medical help arrives. Everyone should receive some formal first aid training. Essential lifesaving steps are listed in 15-12.

First Aid

When someone is injured, follow these basic first aid steps until proper medical help arrives.

1. Make sure the injured person has nothing in his or her mouth or throat. Food or gum could prevent the injured person from breathing.

2. Stop any bleeding. Apply pressure over the wound. A tourniquet should be used only as a last resort.

3. Prevent shock. Keep the injured person flat on his or her back with the head low. Keep the person warm.

4. Call for medical help. Stay with the injured person until help arrives.

5. Remain calm. Move the injured person only when there is an immediate threat of further injury if he or she is *not* moved.

15-12
Knowing how to give basic first aid could help save a person's life.

first aid
Immediate, temporary treatment given in the event of an accident or illness before proper medical help arrives.

OSHA

The Occupational Safety and Health Act is a federal law that calls for safe and healthy working conditions. The law and the government agency that enforces it are both called *OSHA*. The Occupational Safety and Health Administration is the name of the enforcement agency.

As an employee, you should know what OSHA requires of employers and employees. The law was passed to reduce hazards in the workplace. Both employers and employees have obligations under the law.

Employers' Responsibilities

OSHA requires employers to provide workplaces free from safety and health hazards. It also requires them to know and follow the standards set forth in the law. Employers' responsibilities include the following:

- providing a safe place to work
- examining conditions in the workplace to make sure they meet safety and health standards
- making sure employees use safe tools and equipment
- requiring employees to use personal protective gear
- using color codes, posters, labels, or signs to warn employees of potential hazards
- keeping OSHA records of work-related injuries and illnesses
- placing the OSHA poster in the workplace so employees know their rights and responsibilities
- allowing employee representatives to participate in safety inspections

Employees' Responsibilities

OSHA regulations also require employees to follow all rules, regulations, and orders issued under the law. Employees' responsibilities include the following:

- reading the OSHA poster at your job site
- knowing and following OSHA standards that apply to your work
- adhering to all of your employer's safety and health standards and rules
- reporting hazardous conditions to your supervisor
- reporting any job-related injuries or illnesses to your employer and seeking treatment quickly

■ cooperating with OSHA compliance officers when they inspect conditions at your job site

■ using your rights under the OSHA law responsibly

■ wearing and/or using prescribed protective equipment (See 15-13.)

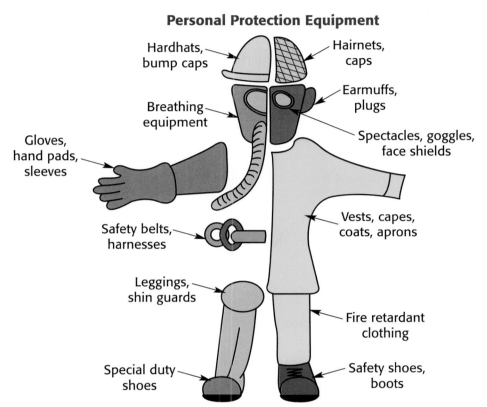

Personal Protection Equipment

Hardhats, bump caps

Hairnets, caps

Earmuffs, plugs

Breathing equipment

Spectacles, goggles, face shields

Gloves, hand pads, sleeves

Vests, capes, coats, aprons

Safety belts, harnesses

Leggings, shin guards

Fire retardant clothing

Special duty shoes

Safety shoes, boots

15-13

OSHA requires workers to wear specific kinds of protective equipment based on the potential hazards of their jobs.

OSHA
A government agency and a federal law that calls for safe and healthy working conditions. The Occupational Safety and Health Administration is the agency, while the Occupational Safety and Health Act is the law.

Workers' Compensation

As a worker, a workers' compensation law probably covers you. ***Workers' compensation*** is insurance against work-related accidents. Most American workers are covered by workers' compensation.

All 50 states have workers' compensation laws. These laws fall into two categories: compulsory and elective. Employers in the *compulsory* category must participate in the plan. Employers in the *elective* category may decide for themselves whether to participate. In the states where participation is elective, most employers provide coverage to limit their risk of negligence suits.

Unlike other forms of worker insurance, workers' compensation does not cost you any money through payroll deductions. Employers pay the premiums for workers' compensation. If you are injured on the job, your workers' compensation will cover the following:

- cost of unlimited medical treatment, including doctors, hospital fees, and rehabilitation services
- payment of lost wages (in the form of a percentage of your regular wage)
- death benefits to your family (in the form of a fixed amount of income)
- insurance against occupational diseases caused by working conditions, such as lung diseases
- income benefits for disability

A ***disability*** is a temporary or permanent physical or mental condition that prevents an employee from working. Sometimes a temporary disability is called *short-term,* and a permanent disability is called *long-term.* If permanently disabled, you will receive payments for the rest of your life.

The specifics of workers' compensation laws differ from state to state. You can find out about your state's law by contacting your state labor department.

Disability Insurance

If you suffer a long-term disability, social security will pay you monthly benefits. See 15-14. Disability benefits from social security begin after a six-month waiting period. They are payable at any time before age 65, if you've worked long enough. To qualify for disability benefits, you must have worked at least 20 of the last 40 quarters.

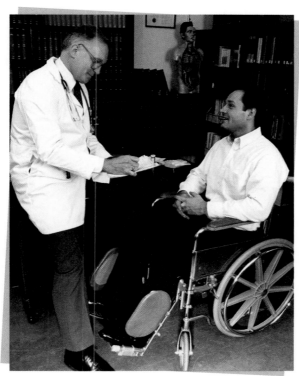

15-14
Disability benefits are paid to workers who cannot work for long periods of time due to job-related injuries.

Young workers who are disabled can also collect. Young workers may not have worked the entire 20 quarters, but they are still eligible in the event of long-term disability. Young workers' benefits are figured using a different scale. Young workers are eligible for disability benefits 18 months after they begin working.

If you become disabled and can't work, you should contact your local social security office. It will assist you with the needed information and forms.

workers' compensation
An insurance against loss of income from work-related accidents.
disability
A temporary or permanent physical or mental condition that prevents an employee from working.

Summary

Safety is everyone's concern. You must avoid unsafe acts and correct unsafe conditions. You also must develop a proper safety attitude. Whether you work in an office or a factory, you must always practice safety when working with tools and equipment. Job safety also includes proper lifting, good housekeeping, and correct use of ladders.

Fire is a threat to life and property. Do all you can to prevent fires. If a fire does occur, you need to be prepared. You should know what to do and how to report the fire by phone.

You must be alert and healthy to do a job well and safely. Follow good health and hygiene practices. Immediately report any injury you suffer. If you have a chance to take first aid training, do so.

OSHA is a federal law and a federal agency. Both promote safe and healthy working conditions. OSHA places responsibilities on both employers and employees. Insurance against workplace injuries is covered by workers' compensation.

Reviewing the Chapter

1. Describe five unsafe acts and five unsafe conditions that lead to accidents.
2. List five safety practices that should be followed by office workers.
3. Describe five proper safety procedures to follow when working with machinery and tools.
4. Name five safety hints to keep in mind when lifting.
5. Give five safety rules to follow when using ladders.
6. Name the three sides of a fire triangle and explain the principle illustrated by it.
7. Explain how you would use the telephone to report a fire in your classroom.
8. List five steps in first aid.
9. Name five employer responsibilities and five employee responsibilities as a result of OSHA.
10. Of what importance is workers' compensation to employees?

Building Your Foundation Skills

1. Read a newspaper story about a work-related accident. Write a paragraph summarizing the accident. Write a second paragraph summarizing what, if anything, could have been done to prevent the accident.

2. Research one aspect of first aid. Present your findings to the class in an oral report.

3. Write a report about the history of the OSHA agency, the workers' compensation program, or the social security program.

4. Demonstrate a safety tip to the class.

5. Invite a firefighter to speak to your class about fire protection. Be prepared to ask questions.

Building Your Workplace Competencies

Participate in a Safety Awareness campaign at school. Working with two or three classmates, examine the school premises and determine what safety tips need to be emphasized to students. Decide as a team how to divide the work. Using a computer software program, create posters highlighting the safety message. Post them in appropriate locations around the school. Research the frequency of accidents—locally, statewide, or nationally—caused by the situation your posters address. Prepare a two-page report and briefly summarize your findings to the class. *(This activity develops competence with resources, interpersonal skills, information, systems, and technology.)*

Handling Changes in Job Status

Objectives

After studying this chapter, you will be able to

- determine factors to consider when changing from part-time to full-time work.

- identify reasons why workers are fired from their jobs.

- explain what positive action people should take after losing their jobs.

- describe ways to prepare for a promotion.

- list reasons why people change jobs.

Words to Know

wages

overtime pay

salary

commission

laid off

fired

letter of resignation

Changing from Part-Time to Full-Time Work

Throughout your career, you are likely to experience several changes in job status. One change in job status might occur when you change from part-time to full-time work. See 16-1.

Many people begin working on a part-time basis. Some work part-time because they cannot find full-time jobs. Others choose to work only a certain number of hours each week. Students often have part-time jobs while going to school.

Changing from part-time to full-time work is a big step. It requires some careful thinking. Full-time work will bring changes in income, fringe benefits, and lifestyle.

Income

Income is the money a person receives for doing a job. Most part-time and many full-time workers earn hourly *wages*. They earn a set amount of money for every hour of work. An example is $6.50 per hour.

A full-time worker may be able to earn *overtime pay*. This is usually one-and-a-half times the regular wage. It is usually paid for hours worked beyond the normal 40-hour week. For instance, a worker may earn $6.50 per hour for 40 hours and $9.75 for each extra hour of work thereafter. ($6.50 + $3.25 = $9.75)

A full-time worker may earn an annual *salary*. This is a set amount of money for a full year of work. The amount is divided into equal payments. As an example, a worker with an annual salary of $26,000 earns $2,000 a month or about $500 every week. The same amount is earned each pay period regardless of the number of hours worked. For example, some weeks may require more than 40 hours of work.

Some full-time workers, especially those in sales, earn commissions. A *commission* is a percentage of the dollar amount of sales made. Therefore, a salesperson who sells more will earn more. For instance, a 10% commission on sales of $100 is $10. The same rate of commission on sales of $200 is $20.

wages
The money earned for doing hourly work.

overtime pay
The wages earned, usually one-and-a-half times the regular wage, for working additional hours beyond the normal 40-hour week.

salary
A set amount of money paid to an employee for a full year of work.

commission
A percentage of the money received from a sale.

16-1

Many people get early work experience with a part-time job in food service. Some people go on to full-time food service careers.

Some people do not feel secure working for a commission because they do not receive a stable income. A good salesperson can achieve high earnings by working for commission. However, if a salesperson makes very few sales, he or she will not have much income.

When changing to a full-time job, think about the income you want to earn. Do you want a job where you would earn hourly wages? Would you want to receive overtime pay for extra work? Would you enjoy the steady pay of a job with a salary, or would you prefer the flexibility of commissions?

Fringe Benefits

Fringe benefits are extra financial rewards beyond regular paychecks. Examples include medical, dental, life, and disability insurance, 16-2. Others are paid holidays, vacations, and sick leave. Some companies also offer bonuses, pension plans, tuition aid, and child care assistance.

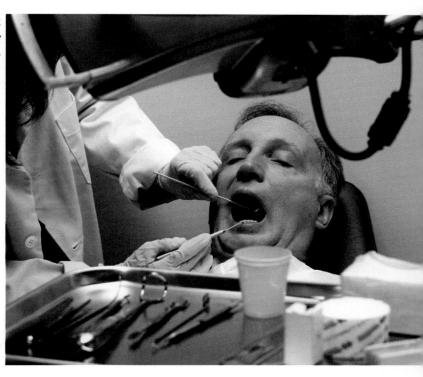

16-2
Dental insurance is just one of many fringe benefits companies often provide for full-time employees.

Part-time workers receive few, if any, fringe benefits. The fringe benefits offered to full-time workers vary widely from company to company. When you look for a full-time job, consider fringe benefits as well as income.

Lifestyle

Taking a full-time job will affect your lifestyle. A full-time job usually involves at least 8 hours of work a day for a total of 40 hours per week. When you accept such a job, your employer expects you to be there full time. You should not arrive late or leave early. You should show up every day. You should not take time off unless you are truly ill.

Your time at work should be devoted to your job. You must arrange to take care of personal and family matters after work or on your days off. This means that you will not have as much free time as you did as a student or part-time worker.

Getting accustomed to working 40 hours a week may take some time. You may feel tired at the end of the workday or workweek. After a while, you will adjust to the longer hours. Until you do, you may have to give up some of your activities.

Losing a Job

No one wants to think about losing a job. It is an unpleasant experience. However, the fact remains that people do lose their jobs for various reasons. Some are laid off and others are fired.

The reason for being *laid off* is beyond a worker's control. A worker may be laid off because the company is failing and short of money. The company may be reorganizing or cutting back on production. In such cases, the last person hired is usually the first one to be laid off. Being laid off is not the worker's fault. It does not mean the person was not a good worker.

Being *fired* from a job is different. A worker is usually fired because of poor performance. The person's work may be unsatisfactory. The person may not be able to get along with others. Common reasons why people are fired are listed in 16-3.

Take Positive Action

If you lose a job, try to maintain a positive attitude. Brooding about a job loss is useless. The sensible thing to do is to take a good, long look at yourself. List your personality traits, interests, aptitudes, and abilities. Think about your values and goals. Decide what kind of work you want to do. Find out if you need more education. If you need retraining to enter another field, get it. When you are ready, go out and seek another job.

Common Reasons for Firing Employees

- Disregarding orders and being disrespectful
- Failing to follow rules and policies
- Abusing drugs or alcohol
- Being dishonest
- Making costly mistakes and failing to do the work properly
- Being lazy
- Often arriving late or being absent
- Failing to get along with supervisors, coworkers, and/or customers
- Causing trouble and acting carelessly
- Behaving rudely and using abusive language
- Always acting dissatisfied
- Making fun of coworkers
- Acting superior and bossing others around

16-3
Employers consider any of these behaviors to be a "just cause" for firing employees.

If you were fired from your job, learn from the experience. Look at the situation from your employer's point of view. Think about what went wrong. Correct your faults and move ahead. Be determined not to make the same mistakes again. Think positively and begin a new job search.

Being Promoted

At some point, you may feel that you have achieved all the goals you set for yourself in a job. You want new challenges. When this happens, it is time to seek a promotion. A promotion is a move up to a higher position within a company.

You may need to be patient to get a promotion. Generally a higher position becomes available in two ways. In some cases, an employer creates a new position to be filled. More often, a position becomes available when a worker leaves it. That worker quits, is fired, retires, or is promoted to a different job.

If you want a promotion, start preparing for it early. Do your best to be ready when a higher position becomes available. The following tips will help you prepare:

- Always strive to do your job well.
- Maintain a good attendance record.
- Have a positive attitude about work.
- Get along with everyone.
- Volunteer to do extra work.
- Look for ways to learn on the job.
- Take additional training or further education.
- Be willing to accept more responsibility.
- Express your desire for new challenges.
- Be able to accept change and use it constructively.

Changing Jobs

The average person changes jobs at least five times during a career. Because employers do not expect workers to stay in the same jobs forever, they try to promote them into new positions. This is not always possible. Therefore, people change companies and sometimes careers. Common reasons for changing jobs are listed in 16-4.

laid off
To lose a job because the employer must release the employee for financial reasons.

fired
To lose a job because of unacceptable work or behavior.

Common Reasons for Changing Jobs

- Problems with supervisors and/or coworkers
- Problems with health that dictate a job or environment change
- Transportation problems
- Desire to have one's own business
- A company closing or relocation
- Elimination of one's job (because of technological changes, company restructuring, or other reasons)
- Desire for better pay and/or fringe benefits
- Desire for more opportunities for advancement
- Desire for better working conditions or hours
- Desire for a job that better uses one's knowledge, skills, and abilities

16-4

People change jobs for many reasons during their careers.

Some people change jobs for a good reason. Others change jobs without thinking through their decisions. Before you make a decision to change jobs, you should ask yourself the following questions and answer them honestly and thoughtfully:

- What are my real reasons for leaving this job? Am I leaving to accept something better? (If not, maybe you shouldn't be considering a change at this time.)

- Am I getting along with my boss and my fellow employees? (If not, why not? Is there something you can do to change a bad situation into a good one? Have you discussed your feelings with your employer? Many problems can be solved through employer-employee discussions. Perhaps you just need a change in job assignment or a transfer to a different department.)

- Have I given myself and the job a chance? (Employers do not want an employee who seems to hop from one job to another. Employers don't expect employees to stay with them forever, but they do expect a stay of a year or more.)

If you aren't sure you want to change jobs, don't rush. Take time to think about both the pros and cons of changing jobs, as listed in 16-5. Close friends or family members can help you explore your reasons for seeking a new job.

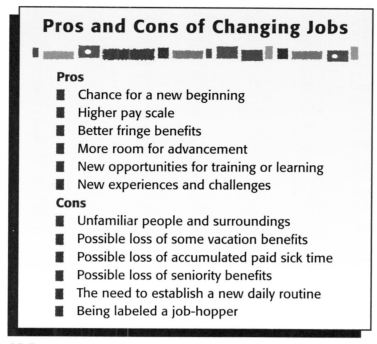

Pros and Cons of Changing Jobs

Pros
- Chance for a new beginning
- Higher pay scale
- Better fringe benefits
- More room for advancement
- New opportunities for training or learning
- New experiences and challenges

Cons
- Unfamiliar people and surroundings
- Possible loss of some vacation benefits
- Possible loss of accumulated paid sick time
- Possible loss of seniority benefits
- The need to establish a new daily routine
- Being labeled a job-hopper

16-5
Consider the advantages and disadvantages carefully before making a job change.

Leaving a Job

Once you decide to change jobs, resist the urge to quit your current job right away. Instead, start looking for a new one while working at your current job. Employment is not always easy to find. Unless you have enough money set aside, consider keeping your current job until you find a better one.

When you are ready to quit your job, do so in a professional manner. Tell your employer before you tell any of your coworkers. Give at least two weeks' notice, preferably three. Your employer needs that time to find a replacement for you.

The most polite and professional way to exit a job is to put your plan to quit or resign in writing. A sample letter of resignation is shown in 16-6. Your *letter of resignation* should include the following points:

- your last day of work
- a positive reason for your resignation
- a few nice words about your present employment

letter of resignation
A formal letter stating plans to quit or resign from a job.

3 Park Avenue
Perth Amboy, NJ 07728
August 10, 2004

Ms. Arlene Banks
First Bank and Trust Company
33 Main Street
Perth Amboy, NJ 07728

Dear Ms. Banks:

Please accept my resignation from the position of bank teller as of
August 24, 2004.

My decision to resign is based on my desire to further my business
education. I recently enrolled as a part-time business student at Taft
Community College. Therefore, I have accepted a teller position with
the Union Bank, located across the street from the Taft campus.
This will allow me more flexibility in scheduling my business
classes.

My position with First Bank and Trust Company has been rewarding
both personally and professionally. I wish to thank you for providing
me with the opportunity to enhance my skills in the banking field.

Sincerely,

Terry Smith
Terry Smith

16-6
*Leaving a job in a professional manner involves giving your employer a letter
of resignation.*

It is wise to personally give notice to your employer. You can do this just before you hand in your letter of resignation. Take time to tell your employer about your new job. Also tell your employer how much you have gained from working in your current job. You can also use this time to ask your employer for a letter of recommendation. It could help you the next time you search for a job.

Make every effort to be on friendly terms with everyone when you leave. During your last days at work, continue to do your job to the best of your ability. Do not complain about your current job. Do not brag about your new job. Be as pleasant as possible to your supervisor and coworkers. You may need their help sometime in the future. You may need to use their names as references in future job hunts. You may even find your career paths crossing again. It is better to have friends than enemies. See 16-7.

16-7
Use a positive, friendly attitude when giving your employer notice that you are quitting your job.

Summary

Throughout your career, your job status is likely to change many times. One change may be from part-time to full-time work. Taking that step will create other changes in income, fringe benefits, and lifestyle.

You will want to avoid losing a job. If you are laid off or fired, you will need to take positive action to find another job.

A change for the better in job status is a promotion. Start preparing for a promotion early. Then you will be ready if a higher position becomes available.

If you are like the average worker, you will change jobs at least five times during your career. Think carefully before you decide to change jobs. Consider both the pros and cons. Once you decide to leave, do so in a professional manner. Give your employer at least two weeks' notice. Submit a letter of resignation. Do your best to leave on friendly terms.

Reviewing the Chapter

1. When a person's income is stated as $30,000 a year, that person is earning _____.
   A. hourly wages
   B. overtime pay
   C. an annual salary
   D. a commission
2. List five examples of fringe benefits.
3. Describe one way in which changing from part-time to full-time work might affect a person's lifestyle.
4. Differentiate between being laid off and being fired.
5. List five reasons why people are fired.
6. What positive action should a fired employee take?
7. Name five ways to prepare for a promotion.
8. List five reasons why people change jobs.
9. Why should workers give their employers at least two weeks' notice when they decide to change jobs?
10. What three points should a letter of resignation contain?

Building Your Foundation Skills

1. Read the want ads in a newspaper. Find two jobs that offer hourly wages, two that offer annual salaries, and two that offer commissions. Identify which jobs mention fringe benefits and what they are.

2. Find a news story about a company that laid off workers. Prepare an oral report about the story. In it, explain why the workers were laid off. If the news story includes interviews with the workers, describe how they felt and what actions they planned to take to find new jobs.

3. Interview someone who has changed jobs. Find out why the person decided to change jobs. Ask what the pros and cons of the decision were. Find out what steps the person took in leaving the old job. Prepare a written report.

4. Write a letter of resignation for a fictitious job.

Building Your Workplace Competencies

Suppose you own a small flower shop with three full-time employees. All three do the same job: they create floral arrangements for most of the day and interact with customers as needed. You have $7,000 to divide among the three for bonuses and/or pay raises next year, but first you must decide how to determine which worker qualities or accomplishments deserve a bonus or more pay. First, list the outstanding characteristics and/or behaviors that should be considered. Then, with a computer, develop a chart or table to analyze whether employees rate *average, above average,* or *super* in each category. Present your conclusions to the class with a brief explanation. *(This activity develops competence with resources, interpersonal skills, information, systems, and technology.)*

PART FIVE

Developing Personal Skills for Job Success

Basic Skills for Job Success

Objectives

After studying this chapter, you will be able to

- state the importance of the basic skills: reading, writing, and math.

- count change correctly.

- describe the conventional and metric systems of measurement.

Words to Know

vocabulary

illiterate

proofread

metric system

meter

gram

liter

degrees Celsius (°C)

The Starting Point—Basic Skills

Basic skills are taught throughout your years in school because they are so important in your life. The three basic skills are reading, writing, and math. Why are these skills called basic? It is not because they are simple. Reading, writing, and math are called basic skills because they are the foundation for the development of more advanced skills. Basic skills also are keys to success.

Reading Skills

As you read this sentence, you are practicing the basic skill of reading. Imagine not being able to read. How would you find your way to a new place if you could not read a map or street signs? How would you know where to apply for a job if you could not read the newspaper want ads?

Most jobs involve reading in some way. At work, you may need to read the following:

- business letters
- customer orders to fill
- directions for operating pieces of equipment
- instructions from your supervisor
- the policies and procedures of your workplace

Once you have learned the basic skill of reading, you will need to continue practicing. The more you read, the better your reading skills will become. Reading for pleasure is a good way to improve your reading skills. *Reading for pleasure* means taking time to read about any subject that interests you. You can choose books, magazines, or newspapers. Reading newspapers is also a great way to keep up with events that are occurring around you.

Reading helps you to increase your vocabulary. Your ***vocabulary*** is the group of words you know and use. Likewise, increasing your vocabulary helps to improve reading skills. If you do not understand a word you read, take time to look it up in a dictionary. You will learn a new word, which increases your vocabulary. You will get more enjoyment from what you are reading because you will understand it. Reading is a routine part of many jobs in the workplace, 17-1.

vocabulary
The group of words known and used by an individual.

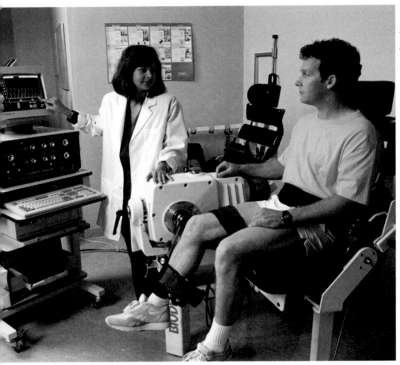

17-1
Health professionals need to be able to read instruments and patients' records.

Writing Skills

A number of work tasks involve writing. Your job may require you to write the following:

- telephone messages
- memos to your coworkers
- business letters to customers
- orders from customers
- reports of your job activities
- reports of your research

Writing skills are closely related to reading skills. People who enjoy reading are likely to be good writers. Good writers use their vocabularies to express themselves on paper.

Your writing skills include your ability to spell and use proper grammar. Writing skills also involve your ability to construct clear sentences and organize paragraphs, 17-2.

Like reading, writing is a basic skill needed to perform most jobs. A person who does not know how to read or write is *illiterate*. Thousands of people in the United States are illiterate. This handicap often interferes with their ability to get or keep a job.

The quality of your writing says a lot about you. Whenever people read something another person has written, they form an impression of that person. If there are many errors, they may assume that the person lacks writing skills. On the other hand, they may think the person is too careless or lazy to check what they have written and correct the errors. It is important to be a good writer. You do not want people to think you do not care about your work.

17-2
Workers are expected to have the skills necessary to take complete, accurate messages.

Whenever you write something for someone else to read, be sure to proofread it carefully. To ***proofread*** means to read something and mark any errors. As you read, think carefully about what your words say. Do they make sense? Are your ideas stated in an orderly manner? Use a dictionary to check your spelling. Use a language reference book to check your grammar and punctuation. Be sure to correct your errors as you rewrite or retype what you have written.

Practicing your writing skills can help you to improve. Try to write something every day. Writing can be in the form of a letter to a friend, an essay for school, or a personal journal or diary. When you are in school, much of your writing is done for homework. On days when you are not in school, try writing a short letter or e-mail message to a friend or family member. If you are creative, try writing a short story. You might want to keep a journal. This is a good way to record your thoughts on paper in a casual style. Whether you are writing for pleasure, for a job, or for school, always try to use good grammar and proper punctuation.

illiterate
Being unable to read or write.
proofread
To read something, check for mistakes, and mark any errors found.

17-3
The ability to use a computer to communicate is a requirement for many jobs.

Using the Computer

One way to practice writing is with a computer. Some people write more easily with a computer than with a pen and paper. This requires basic keystroking skills that are perfected with practice. Using the computer for writing will strengthen your writing skills and prepare you for the workplace, 17-3.

When using a computer, the words are visible on the monitor's screen before they are actually printed. This allows the writer to *edit,* or change words easily. Often a better way to express a thought comes to mind. This also allows the writer to proofread the message and correct all errors before printing it.

The computer software programs that specialize in creating written communications are *word processing programs.* They usually include a feature that checks spelling, grammar, and punctuation. This feature does not, however, help you with *synonyms*, such as *sail* and *sale.* These are words that sound alike but are spelled differently. This is one example of the need for proofreading even when using a computer.

Many types of software programs are available to do just about anything you wish. Some of the most popular programs used at home are math and accounting programs. These help people balance their checkbooks and keep their finances in order. The computer handles math calculations with lightening speed.

Math Skills

Jobs that require high-level math skills often have special computer programs for workers to use. Most jobs require basic math ability. This involves adding, subtracting, multiplying, and dividing.

Many people use these basic math skills every day in their job. They count money, count items to fill an order, and add prices to get totals. Accountants, cashiers, and bank tellers continually work with numbers. Many other workers need a good working knowledge of numbers, too.

- Bakers and chefs measure ingredients, 17-4.
- Nurses must give patients the correct doses of medicine.
- Architects use precise measurements when drawing plans.
- Salespeople add totals and subtract discounts.
- Carpenters take frequent measurements when building houses.

17-4 *Hershey Entertainment and Resort Company*

Determining portion size and ordering the right amount of ingredients are some of the food service tasks that require good math skills.

Even if a job does not require math ability, employers expect workers to be able to make basic calculations when needed. To prepare yourself for a variety of jobs, you should be able to work with whole numbers and mixed numbers. You should also know how to figure percentages, decimals, and fractions.

You have probably learned and reviewed each of these math skills. Identify the areas that give you trouble and practice solving math problems that address them. If you practice now, you will develop confidence and become better at math. Your efforts now in perfecting these skills may help you avoid job problems in the future.

Counting Change

Many jobs involve accepting money and counting change. Examples are the jobs of bank tellers, store clerks, food servers, and cashiers. People in these jobs must account for every penny of each transaction. Knowing how to count change is an important skill in your personal life, too. If you cannot accurately count your own money, you may cheat yourself or someone else.

Some basic guidelines will help you count change accurately.

- Count from the amount of the purchase. For example, suppose a purchase totals $2.57 and someone gives you a $5 bill.
- Begin with three pennies to make $2.60.
- Add one dime and one nickel to make $2.75.
- Add one quarter to make $3.00.
- Add two one-dollar bills to make $5.00.
- You give the customer $2.43 in change.

Do not rush! Take your time and count clearly. This may be difficult when there are 10 people in a cashier's line. Just stay calm and steady. The customer will appreciate your taking the time to assure accuracy. See 17-5.

17-5

Businesses require their employees to count change out loud in front of the customer.

Measurements

Many jobs involve taking and using measurements. Fashion designers need to take body measurements and measure fabric. Chemists need to measure chemicals. Engineers need to measure distances. If measurements are not made precisely, work may not be completed accurately.

In the United States, most measurements are made using the *conventional system*. However, many other countries use the **metric system** of measurements. It is a decimal system of weights and measures.

Many products used in the United States are imported from countries that use the metric system. Therefore, being familiar with both systems will help you in many jobs. For instance, mechanics often use tools sized to fit metric parts.

The conventional system measures distance in inches, feet, yards, and miles. In the metric system, the basic unit of measuring distance is a **meter**. One meter (m) is slightly longer than one yard.

Weight is measured in ounces, pounds, and tons in the conventional system. In the metric system, the basic unit of measuring weight is a **gram**. One gram (g) is much smaller than an ounce.

Volume has been conventionally measured in cups, pints, quarts, and gallons. In the metric system, the basic unit of measuring volume is a **liter**. One liter (l) is somewhat more than a quart.

Meters, grams, and liters are the basic units of measurement in the metric system. The size of the units are increased or decreased in multiples of 10. Six prefixes are added to the basic units to increase or decrease the size of the units. They are *kilo-, hecto-, deka-, deci-, centi-,* and *milli-*. See 17-6.

Temperature under the conventional system is measured by degrees Fahrenheit (°F). Water freezes at 32°F, and it boils at 212°F. In the metric system, the basic unit of measuring temperature is measured in **degrees Celsius (°C).** Water freezes at 0°C and boils at 100°C. One degree Celsius is somewhat more than two degrees Fahrenheit.

metric system
A decimal system of weights and measures.

meter
The basic unit of measuring distance in the metric system.

gram
The basic unit of measuring weight in the metric system.

liter
The basic unit of measuring volume in the metric system.

degrees Celsius (°C)
The basic unit of measuring temperature in the metric system.

Metric Prefixes

Prefix	Meaning	Distance	Weight	Volume
kilo-	one thousand	kilometer (km) 1000 meters	kilogram (kg) 1000 grams	kiloliter (kl) 1000 liters
hecto-	one hundred	hectometer (hm) 100 meters	hectogram (hg) 100 grams	hectoliter (hl) 100 liters
deka-	ten	dekameter (dam) 10 meters	dekagram (dag) 10 grams	dekaliter (dal) 10 liter
deci-	one-tenth	decimeter (dm) .1 meter	decigram (dg) .1 gram	deciliter (dl) .1 liter
centi-	one-hundreth	centimeter (cm) .01 meter	centigram (cg) .01 gram	centiliter (cl) .01 liter
milli-	one-thousandth	millimeter (mm) .001 meter	milligram (mg) .001 gram	milliliter (ml) .001 liter

17-6

The metric system uses these prefixes to increase or decrease the size of meters, grams, and liters by multiples of 10.

Changing from one unit to another in the conventional system can be confusing. All the units are in different proportions. For instance, to change inches to feet, you must divide by 12. However, to change feet to yards, you must divide by 3.

Changing from one unit to another is easier in the metric system. All the units are multiples of 10. To change centimeters to decimeters, you divide by 10. To change decimeters to meters, you also divide by 10. (Simply moving the decimal point left one place is an easy way to divide by 10.)

Formulas can be used to convert measurements from the conventional system to the metric system and vice versa. See chart 17-7. Normally you will work with one system rather than converting between the two.

Measurement Conversions

Conventional to Metric

Known		Multiplied by		Equals
Distance				
inches	x	25.40	=	millimeters
inches	x	2.54	=	centimeters
feet	x	0.3048	=	meters
yards	x	0.9144	=	meters
miles	x	1.6093	=	kilometers
Weight				
ounces	x	28.350	=	grams
pounds	x	454.00	=	grams
pounds	x	0.454	=	kilograms
Volume				
ounces	x	29.573	=	milliliters
pints	x	0.473	=	liters
quarts	x	0.946	=	liters
gallons	x	3.785	=	liters
Temperature				
Fahrenheit	x	0.555 (after subtracting 32)	=	Celsius

Metric to Conventional

Known		Multiplied by		Equals
Distance				
millimeters	x	0.039	=	inches
centimeters	x	0.394	=	inches
meters	x	3.2808	=	feet
meters	x	1.0936	=	yards
kilometers	x	0.6214	=	miles
Weight				
grams	x	0.035	=	ounces
grams	x	0.002	=	pounds
kilograms	x	2.2	=	pounds
Volume				
millimeters	x	0.034	=	ounces
liters	x	2.1	=	pints
liters	x	1.056	=	quarts
liters	x	0.264	=	gallons
Temperature				
Celsius	x	1.80 (then add 32)	=	Fahrenheit

17-7

These equations can help you convert measures between the metric and conventional systems.

Summary

Basic skills are needed in school, at work, and in your personal life. You should do all you can to develop good reading, writing, and math skills.

Knowing how to write messages correctly is a skill needed by people in all types of careers. Writing well requires expressive language and accurate spelling, grammar, and punctuation. All the writing you do improves your writing skill, even writing for pleasure.

Computers can be used to sharpen your reading, writing, and math skills. You will most likely use a computer of some sort on your job.

Math skills, like the other basic skills, are needed to succeed both personally and professionally. You should be able to add, subtract, multiply, and divide. These skills will allow you to perform basic job functions like counting change and using measurements.

Reviewing the Chapter

1. Identify the three basic skills and why they are important.
2. Describe two work tasks that involve reading.
3. How can you improve your reading skills?
4. Why is illiteracy a job handicap?
5. What kinds of impressions might people form about a writer whose material is full of errors?
6. How can you improve your writing skills?
7. Name three careers in which basic math skills are used every day.
8. Suppose a cashier is given a $10 bill for a $7.28 purchase. What coins and bills should be returned to the customer?
9. What is the basic unit of distance in the metric system?
10. Why is changing from one unit to another easier in the metric system than the conventional system?

Building Your Foundation Skills

1. Read a book, magazine article, or newspaper story about a topic that interests you. Make a list of any words you do not understand. Use a dictionary to look up the words and write their definitions. Share your new vocabulary words in class.

2. Write a brief report summarizing what you read in Activity 1. Read your report and circle in ink any errors you find. Rewrite the report making any necessary corrections.

3. Correspond with a pen pal. Share information with each other about yourselves, your families, and your goals for the future. Remember to use good grammar and proper punctuation.

4. Using play money, work with a partner and practice counting change.

5. Visit a supermarket and find 20 different items. Develop a chart, and list each item's conventional and metric measures.

6. Write a report explaining how a word processing program can check spelling.

Building Your Workplace Competencies

Imagine you are in charge of determining work schedules for a small clothing store. Your doors open at 9:00 a.m. and stay open until 9:00 p.m. Your busiest hours are from 4:00 p.m. to 8:00 p.m. on weekdays and all day Saturday. During these busy hours, at least two people are needed on duty. Your store closes at 6:00 p.m. Saturday. You have one full-time employee who works five 8-hour days each week at $8.00 per hour. She knows the store well enough to take care of it when you are gone. You can get part-time helpers who work less than 30 hours per week for $6.00 per hour. Using a computer, develop a chart showing who works when—including yourself—for every hour the store is open. Total the cost of your helpers. Summarize your plan and report it to the class. *(This activity develops competence with resources, interpersonal skills, information, systems, and technology.)*

Time Management and Study Skills

Objectives

After studying this chapter, you will be able to

- examine how you spend your time by keeping a daily time log.

- list five suggestions for making the best use of your time.

- take notes that will help you review what you study.

- identify helpful tips related to preparing for, taking, and learning from tests.

- compare good and poor study habits.

Words to Know

time management

time log

IRS time

priorities

procrastination

concentrate

Why Is Time Management Important?

Time management is a skill that is needed throughout life. Adults need to manage the time they spend at work and at home. As a student, you need to manage the time you spend at school as well as studying after school. You need to manage the time you spend with your family and the time you have for other activities, too. This chapter will help you plan and manage your time. It will also help you identify good study habits to help you make the best use of your study time.

Time Management

Time can be a valuable ally or your worst enemy. Time only moves forward, never backward. You can never recapture misused time or undo what has already happened. Learn to use time as a valuable resource. The way you manage this resource can make the difference between success and failure.

Planning how to use your time is *time management*. It is a key element in your study habits. No one can plan or manage your time but you. Too many people fail to control their use of time. Some people even allow others to use up their time. The key to success, however, is to make wise use of time.

If you are in the habit of wasting time, you can work to break the habit. Managing your time is not a difficult or unpleasant task. Much of your time is planned for you, such as your school and work hours. Your teachers and school officials set the hours you are in school. Your employer determines the time you are assigned to work. It is your job to manage the rest of your time. You might plan for the following activities:

- uninterrupted periods for study
- personal duties and chores
- relaxation and fun

Most people don't know how they spend their time. They are often surprised to find out how much time they waste. If you are in the habit of wasting time, you should work to break the habit. Do you know how you spend your time? A good way to find out is to keep a daily time log for two weeks. A *time log* is a written record of a person's use of time. A sample time log is shown in 18-1. At the end of two weeks, you may be surprised to see how you spent your time.

time management
The planning and using of time.

time log
A written record of a person's use of time.

Sample Time Log

	Sun	Mon	Tues	Wed	Thurs	Fri	Sat	Total
Sleeping	9	8	8	7.5	8.5	7	8	56
Eating	1.5	.75	1	.75	.75	1.25	1.25	7.25
Grooming	1	.5	.75	.75	.75	1	1.25	7.25
Going to school	0	7	7	7	7	7	0	35
Studying/doing homework	2	1.25	2	1	2.5	0	1	9.75
Working	6	3.5	0	3.5	0	0	6	19
Doing chores	.75	.5	0	.25	.25	.25	.75	2.75
Participating in extracurricular activities	0	0	2	0	2	0	0	4
Watching TV/ listening to music	.5	1.25	.5	1	0	2	1.25	6.5
Talking on the phone	1.25	.5	1.5	.5	.25	.75	.5	5.25
Visiting friends	0	0	.75	0	1.5	3	3	8.25
Reading and relaxing	0	0	0	.25	0	.25	.5	1
Doing other activities	2	.75	.5	1.5	.5	1.5	.5	7.25

18-1

A time log shows the number of hours used for different activities. It can help you see how much time you are wasting.

IRS Time

You know that you cannot create more time. The earth's timetable is fixed at 365 days a year, 24 hours a day, 60 minutes an hour, and 60 seconds a minute. How can you get more time to do everything you want to do? The answer is to be a better manager of time. One suggestion is to place yourself on IRS Time. *IRS time* is defined as Individual Responsibility for Saving Time. You take whatever steps are needed to make the best use of your time. The following suggestions may help you:

- Make a to-do list each day. Don't rely on your memory to recall what is important. Get into the habit of writing it down.

- Organize your time according to your priorities. ***Priorities*** are everything that you consider highly important. Tasks that are most important have the highest priority. You should do those first. Using your to-do list, rank each of your tasks. Write A beside each task that you must do. Write B next to the tasks you should do. Use C to mark the tasks you want to do if you have time. Then follow your list. After you finish the A-list, do your Bs and, if time permits, work on your Cs.

- Avoid ***procrastination***. In other words, do not delay or put off decisions or activities. Do not put off until tomorrow what you can do today. Do a little each day on long-term assignments. Suppose you are assigned a paper to be completed by the end of the term. Do not wait until the day before it is due to start. Start now and do a little each day.

- Reduce interruptions of your planned study time. If your friends call during your study time, spend a few minutes with them, but excuse yourself quickly. Let them know you have something to do. If they are true friends, they will understand. Remember, you cannot recapture lost time. Therefore, get in the habit of telling them you'll call back later. Return immediately to what you were doing before the interruption. Better yet, study in a place where common interruptions cannot occur. Do not let time thieves steal your time, 18-2.

- Focus on one task at a time. It is difficult to focus on your studies while watching television or talking to friends. You can study best when you devote your full attention to it.

> **IRS time (individual responsibility for saving time)**
> Taking whatever steps are needed to make the best use of time.
>
> **priorities**
> Everything that you consider highly important.
>
> **procrastination**
> The delaying or putting off of decisions or activities.

18-2

Watching TV, daydreaming, and talking on the phone can be "time thieves" that steal your time from more important activities.

Study Skills

Many students can improve their study habits. The most common cause of poor study habits is poor use of time. Study periods or study halls are often used as social periods. That is an unwise use of time unless you are working on a team project. The schoolwork that could be accomplished in a study period must then be done after school. One secret to becoming a better student and getting better grades is to use time wisely.

Begin your study period with a positive attitude. A good attitude will help you get right into your study assignment. Make up your mind to tackle the hardest part first. Set a time limit for study, perhaps two hours. Let others know that this is your time for study, not interruptions. Avoid trying to study in a noisy crowd. Instead, find a comfortable, quiet place at home, at school, or in the library. In this way, you can get the most accomplished in the least amount of time.

Make sure your desk or tabletop is clear of distractions. Don't leave anything on it that will keep you from your assignment. Put away magazines and books not needed for your assignment. Make sure you have everything you will need to complete the assignment. Gather the necessary books, papers, pens, pencils, and other supplies before you start. See 18-3. Don't waste valuable study time looking for these items while trying to get your assignment done.

18-3

Apple Computer

Good study habits include working in a quiet area with all your supplies at hand.

The hardest part of any job, even studying, is getting started. Once you sit down, make up your mind to begin. Then concentrate right away on your assignment. To *concentrate* means to focus your attention and effort. Stay involved in what you are doing. Don't waste valuable study time daydreaming or thinking about something else.

Plan to study when you are rested. Being rested is important because a tired person will find it difficult to concentrate. If you can't concentrate, you won't be able to remember what you have learned.

Another important study tip is to take a few moments after you study to think about what you have learned. Sometimes you can mentally review the material by just sitting back and thinking. Reflecting on your studies will improve your level of learning.

concentrate
To focus attention and effort on something.

Taking Notes

Taking notes is an important study skill to develop. Good notes come in handy when it's time to review what you have studied. They help you recall the important points of information.

Taking notes does not mean writing down every word that is said. In fact, people who are too busy writing generally do not hear everything being said. Try to listen carefully to your teacher or study partner and write down only the key points. Teachers often identify key points with phrases that focus attention, like "the cause was," " the result was," or "to sum up." See 18-4.

Helpful Tips

The following tips may help you learn to take good notes:

- Use one side of a sheet of paper.
- Number each page, especially for a loose-leaf notebook. It is easy for pages to shift out of order.
- Leave a margin at the top of the page. You can use this space to write down key information, such as the date an assignment is due. Also use this space to identify the class, topic, date, and teacher.
- Write down only important points.
- Use an outline format.

18-4

When taking notes, be sure to listen carefully and write down key points.

- Whenever possible, use symbols and abbreviations. Write = for *equals*, ≠ for *does not equal*, and + for *plus*. You may use other symbols, too, as long as you know what they mean.
- Write notes to yourself in the margins. They may be questions, suggestions, or reminders.

Good study skills will help you on the job, too. Your employer may ask you to attend a meeting and report to coworkers what was discussed. Being able to take good notes will help you prepare your report.

Taking Tests

Tests are given to find out how much you have learned. They provide feedback for both you and your teachers. Tests are not meant to scare you or to make you look bad. Their purpose is to measure how much you know and don't know. Your job is to do your best to show all that you know. To do that, you can't rely on magic or luck. You need to prepare yourself.

Before the Test

Cramming the night before is not the best way to prepare for a test. You need to keep up with what is being taught in your classes. Studying and doing your home-work regularly will help you understand information better and remember it longer. However, you may want to give extra effort to your studies the last few nights before a test. The following tips will help you as you give special attention to test material:

- Review the material in the textbook.
- Pay particular attention to your notes.
- Try to determine what questions will be asked.
- Recall what kinds of questions were asked on the last test in the class.
- Consider studying with a classmate, taking turns to ask each other questions.
- Get a good night's sleep.

See 18-5 for a summary of good study habits that are wise to develop. The chart also lists some poor study habits to avoid.

Good Study Habits	Poor Study Habits
■ Tackle the hardest parts first when you sit down to study.	■ Study the easiest parts first.
■ Study in a comfortable place where you will not be disturbed.	■ Study in a noisy crowd or another area where you will be easily distracted.
■ Clear the desk or tabletop of magazines, books, and other objects you are not going to use.	■ Study in a cluttered area.
■ Gather the books, papers, pens, pencils, and other supplies you need before you start to study.	■ Waste time looking for books, papers, pens, pencils, and other supplies you need.
■ When you sit down to study, begin concentrating right away.	■ Allow your mind to wander when you sit down to study.
■ Study when you are well rested.	■ Study when you are tired.
■ Take a few moments after you study to think about what you have learned.	■ As soon as you finish studying, go on to another activity.
■ Write down only the key points when taking notes.	■ Try to write down every word that is said when taking notes.
■ Get a good night's sleep before taking a test.	■ Stay up late studying the night before a test.
■ Begin projects and start studying for tests well in advance.	■ Try to cram all your studies into the last minute.
■ Give your studies your full attention.	■ Try to do something else while you study, such as watch television.

18-5

Using good study habits will help you benefit most from your study time.

Taking the Test

The way you take a test can affect how well you do on it. The following suggestions may help improve your test performance:

- Be relaxed and have a positive mental attitude.
- Look over the entire test before starting it.
- Read and follow directions carefully.
- Read each test question carefully.
- Think before you write your answer.
- If you get stuck on a question, skip it and return later after answering the other questions.
- Before handing in your test, review it and make corrections where necessary.

When You Get Your Test Back

Learning does not stop once you turn in your test. When you get the test back, you can use it to prepare for future tests. The following suggestions might help you get more from your tests:

- Congratulate yourself for everything you answered correctly.
- Learn from your mistakes.
- Read the teacher's comments and corrections.
- Ask for help on topics that gave you difficulty.
- Begin immediately to start preparing for the next test.

Summary

Time management is a key life skill. Although you can't change the amount of time in a day or week, you can change the way you use it. You can learn to make the best use of your time.

Good study habits help you make the most of your study time. They can also help you learn more and get better grades.

Taking notes is a study skill that improves with practice. The key is to listen carefully while writing down only the important points.

By taking tests, you find out how much you have learned. You can improve your performance on tests by following certain steps. The steps can help you prepare for tests, take the tests, and learn from the results of the tests.

Reviewing the Chapter

1. What is the purpose of a time log?
2. How can you get more time to do all the things you want to do?
3. List five suggestions for making the best use of your time.
4. Identify two phrases that teachers often use to highlight key points that should be written down in notes.
5. Give two examples of symbols or abbreviations you could use when taking notes.
6. What is the purpose of tests?
7. List five steps you can take to prepare for a test.
8. List five tips that can help you perform well when taking a test.
9. When you get a test back, list three steps to follow for improving your test-taking skills.
10. Rate each of the following study habits *good* or *poor.*
    A. Clear your desk or tabletop of distractions before beginning.
    B. Study when you are well rested and alert.
    C. Start with the easiest part of the task.
    D. Study while watching television.
    E. Take a few moments after you study to think about what you have learned.

Building Your Foundation Skills

1. Ask several people to tell you their best time management tips. Share your tips with the class.

2. Write a paper about successful habits for studying, note taking, or test taking. Submit it to the school paper.

3. Test your concentration. Go to the library and find two newspaper articles that are about equal in length. Study one article in a quiet place for a certain length of time, perhaps 15 minutes. Then write down as much of it as you can remember. Later, go to a noisy place or sit in front of a television. Study the second article for the same amount of time. Then write down as much of it as you can remember. Compare the results. Which setting allowed you to concentrate better? In class, discuss how study efforts are affected by a person's surroundings.

4. Practice taking notes during classes. Later, compare your notes with those of a classmate to make sure you wrote down all key points.

Building Your Workplace Competencies

Do a three-step study to compare how you think you spend your time with how you want to spend it and how you actually spend it. Using a computer, create a time sheet that lists all your activities and allows room for recording times. First, estimate how much time you think you spend with each activity. Then, imagine yourself leading an ideal life and estimate how much time you would like to spend on each activity. Finally, keep a daily log for two weeks to find out how you actually spend your time. Write a brief report about what you learned from this exercise. Include ideas on how you could improve your time management. *(This activity develops competence with resources, information, and technology.)*

Communication Skills

Objectives

After studying this chapter, you will be able to

- explain the importance of feedback in the communication process.

- list helpful tips for public speaking.

- demonstrate how to make and receive business telephone calls.

- write a business letter.

- identify several forms of nonverbal communication.

Words to Know

communicate

feedback

verbal communication

multitasking

nonverbal communication

body language

Methods of Communication

To *communicate* is to share ideas, feelings, or information. When people communicate, two things happen—a message is sent and a message is received. Communication can take place between just two people or among millions of people.

People communicate in many different ways. In this chapter, you will read about how to receive messages through listening. You will study how to send messages through speaking. You will also read about communicating through writing and body movements.

Although this chapter discusses many methods of communication, there are many others that are not discussed. Chart 19-1 lists some of the many ways people send and receive messages. This chart also lists some common channels through which people communicate.

Communication

Ways to Send Messages	Ways to Receive Messages	Channels of Communication	
speaking	listening	conversations	e-mail
writing	reading	meetings	art
drawing	seeing	speeches	music
touching	feeling	lectures	letters
singing		newspapers	books
using body language		magazines	
sending signals		telephones	
using sign language		photographs	

19-1

There are many ways to send and receive messages.

communicate
To share ideas, feelings, or information, both verbally and nonverbally.

Listening

Communication involves the sending and receiving of a message. Listening is the most common method of receiving messages. Listening is not the same as hearing. In order to listen, you must pay attention to the message being sent.

The world is full of so many sounds that people automatically block out many of them. They choose to listen only to certain sounds. As an example, think about an air conditioner. It makes noise when it is on. Most people can hear the noise, but they do not listen to it. They do not pay attention to it.

Have you ever missed part of the directions for a school project because you were not listening? You probably heard the teacher talking, but you didn't listen to what he or she was saying.

Often, communication fails because people are poor listeners. Instead of listening, they are daydreaming or thinking about something else. Some people fail to listen because they are not interested in what is being said. Others are too busy trying to guess what the speaker will say next. Several types of poor listeners are described in 19-2.

Poor Listeners	
Detail seekers	They try to memorize all the facts. As a result, they concentrate on small details while missing important information. They may even miss the main ideas of the speaker.
Daydreamers	They are easily distracted. Their minds drift. They do not concentrate on what the speaker is saying.
Emotional listeners	They let certain words or phrases upset them. They concentrate on the speaker's poor choice of words or phrases and not on the actual message.
Critics	They are more concerned with the speaker's visual impact than the message. These listeners spend too much time concentrating on such factors as the speaker's clothes and body motions.
Notetakers	They are too involved in writing everything down. They often miss the speaker's main ideas.
Arguers	They begin to disagree before the speaker is finished. They begin building their arguments before hearing the speaker's point of view.

19-2

Poor listeners have bad listening habits that prevent true communication from taking place.

You should try to be a full-attention listener. A *full-attention listener* concentrates on what is being said. Thoughts and ideas are absorbed. Main facts are understood. Questions are asked to clarify concepts. You can become a full-attention listener by practicing the following good listening skills:

- Pay close attention to what the speaker is saying.
- Don't let outside noises distract you.
- Keep an open mind. Don't jump to conclusions. Wait until the speaker's points have been made before you speak.
- Don't try to listen and talk at the same time.
- Don't try to memorize everything the speaker says. Concentrate on the speaker's main points.
- If you take notes, don't try to write everything down. List only the important facts and main ideas.
- Ask questions if you don't understand something or if you feel you have missed a point.

Feedback

Good, clear communication involves more than the sending and receiving of a message. It also requires that both the sender and the receiver understand the message in the same way. The link to this understanding is feedback. *Feedback* is the return of information to the sender by the receiver trying to understand the message. Good listeners provide feedback. They restate the message in their own words to respond to the speaker. This is a way to be sure both sides understand the message. See 19-3 for an illustration of the following example:

Employer: "Check these orders with our inventory. If there are problems, bring them to me."

Employee: "OK, I'll check to see if we have enough stock to fill all these orders. If there are any orders we can't fill, I'll bring them to you."

Employer: "Good, please start right away."

feedback
The return of information to a sender by a receiver trying to understand the message.

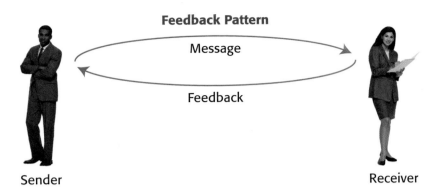

Feedback Pattern

Message

Feedback

Sender   Receiver

19-3
Feedback from the receiver allows the sender to be sure his or her message has been understood.

Recall a time when a teacher asked you to do a task. You did what you thought you were asked to do. Later you realized that your teacher was referring to something else. Who is at fault when a misunderstanding occurs? Many times, it is both the sender and the receiver. If no feedback is requested or given, both parties assume the message is clear. This is a major mistake many people make in the communication process.

You will receive many instructions on the job. Make sure you understand what the boss is telling you to do. Ask questions to clarify the assignment. Repeat in your own words what you understand the assignment to be. Feedback will improve your communication skills. It will help you become a better employee.

Speaking

Speaking is the most widely used form of **verbal communication**, which is communication involving the use of words. People speak to express ideas, give information, or ask questions.

Working in any career field requires the proper use of the spoken word, 19-4. Speaking clearly will help you express ideas to coworkers. Failure to communicate clearly can lead to hazardous situations. In some cases, you could lose your job if you do not communicate well.

A good speaker has a good chance for job success. For example, a salesperson who can tell customers about a product's good features is likely to make more sales. More sales mean more commission!

19-4
Good communication skills are required for most jobs. Your supervisors and coworkers need to understand what you say.

Improving Your Speech

Your speech is part of the image you project. It affects the impressions people form of you. If you speak clearly and use proper grammar, people are likely to form good impressions of you.

Keeping in mind some simple guidelines will help you improve your speech in day-to-day conversations. First, think about your message before you speak. Use just enough words to convey your idea clearly. Try not to talk too much. No one likes to listen to a person who talks on and on without expressing a clear message.

When you speak, use simple sentences. Use words that both you and your listener will understand. Use good grammar. Mispronouncing a word or using poor grammar is very distracting to the listener. Speak clearly and in a normal tone. The following tips will help you improve your speech:

- Always speak slowly and clearly. Rapid, mumbled speech is difficult to understand.
- Practice good grammar at all times. Poor grammar is often a sign of a poor education. People who use poor grammar are less likely to get good jobs.

verbal communication
Communication involving the use of words.

- Think about what you are going to say before you say it. Pause before answering a question or making a statement. This gives you a chance to think about what you will say. Then you can respond in the best possible way.

- Try to avoid using slang, such as "cool," "yeah," or " 'ya' know." Some employers think that using slang is unprofessional. They may be less likely to hire or promote an employee who frequently uses slang.

- Try not to drop the endings of words. Don't say "singin" instead of "singing." Always pronounce your words clearly and completely.

Public Speaking

Public speaking is the act of making speeches in public before audiences. It is much like talking to your friends. There are, however, more receivers of your message and the response is slower.

There are several reasons why you might give a speech. One common reason is to inform people. Another is to convince people to think your way.

While in school, you will be encouraged to make presentations to your classes. Perhaps you will speak before others at group meetings, too. These speaking opportunities can help prepare you for the career world. See 19-5.

19-5   *Cedar Bluff High School FCCLA, Cedar Bluff, Alabama*

Taking advantage of public speaking opportunities through student organizations will help prepare you to give business presentations in the future.

Being able to speak in front of a group is expected in the work world. Workers speak in front of audiences of coworkers and supervisors for many reasons. Members of production teams give progress reports at weekly group meetings. Researchers share their findings with people working to develop new products. Salespeople present product information to groups of customers.

When you prepare a speech, you should make an outline of the points you want to cover.

- Start with the *introduction*—a short statement telling the audience what the topic of your speech is.

- Move into the *discussion*—the main idea or message you want to get across.

- Finish with the *closing*—a short summary of what you have said.

Be sure you know your subject well. Be prepared to discuss the topic briefly and concisely. Don't memorize your speech, but practice it. You may want to tape your speech so you can listen to how you sound.

When you give the speech, speak clearly. Use a normal tone of voice, but be sure to speak loud enough to be heard. Keep eye contact with members of the audience. Show enthusiasm. Use gestures, like pointing, to emphasize important points. Do not overuse gestures.

Dress neatly and appropriately. Stand straight with good posture. Be friendly and firm in your presentation. Try to enjoy the experience. Remember, it is a chance for you to inform people or to convince them to think your way.

Multitasking

Employees who wear headsets while working are multitasking. **Multitasking** means doing more than one job at a time. Wearing headsets on the job is an increasingly common way to keep coworkers informed.

One example is a fast-food worker who takes your order. While talking with you, the order-taker's words are heard through the headset by the kitchen staff. A cook may reply, "It won't be ready for 10 minutes." After the order-taker warns you about the delay, you may decide to change your order. The headset allows coworkers who handle various parts of a job to work smoothly as a team.

Multitasking requires good speaking and listening skills. Headsets allow employees to do their job while hearing the status of related tasks at other locations.

multitasking
Doing more than one job at a time.

Using the Telephone

Many business operations are conducted on the telephone, 19-6. The telephone is a communication tool that requires good listening skills and good speaking skills. Learn to use your company's telephone wisely.

When using the phone, you must remember that the people with whom you talk cannot see you. They cannot see if you are shaking your head to convey a yes or no. Without facial expressions or gestures, your words and tone of voice are even more important. Use them carefully to convey the same friendliness, sincerity, and interest you would express in a face-to-face meeting.

19-6
Many businesses rely on telephone communication.

Receiving Calls

If you are responsible for receiving calls, answer the telephone promptly. Greet the caller and identify your company. Give the caller your full attention. What the caller has to say is important.

First impressions are lasting. How you sound on the telephone is important in creating a favorable impression. Make an effort to sound pleasant. Put a "smile" in your voice. Always be polite. Say, "thank you" and "you're welcome." Make the caller feel comfortable and let him or her know that you want to help.

Observe the following points when speaking on the telephone:

- Speak slowly and clearly. Don't mumble.
- Use a pleasant tone of voice.
- Never shout.
- Be courteous and polite.

- Speak directly into the telephone.
- Be patient.
- Be thorough. Be sure to give and get all information accurately.

If you direct a call to someone else, be sure the person is available. If the person is not available, take a message. When taking a message, get the following information:

- caller's name
- name of the caller's company
- caller's telephone number and extension
- reason for the call
- time and date of the call

Don't be afraid to repeat information to make sure you have it right. You cannot afford to make mistakes when taking messages. You must spell the caller's name correctly. You must get the company's name right. If the call is to be returned, you must write down the correct telephone number.

Types of Calls

Remember, you are representing your company when making calls on the job. To do your best, you need to be prepared and organized. You also need to speak clearly and use a pleasant tone of voice.

All business calls should be brief and to the point. Therefore, you should take time to plan your calls. Ask yourself, "Why am I making this call?" Is it to give information, get information, or place an order?

Before placing a call, have the necessary information in front of you. Outline your main points. Don't trust complex facts to memory.

Orders

If you are calling to place an order, have the facts in front of you. Read your notes slowly and clearly. Speak at a normal pace. Give the person a chance to ask questions and repeat information.

Tell the person who you are. State the name of your company and why you are calling. Give all part numbers or catalog numbers. Tell how many parts are needed. A typical business telephone order is illustrated in 19-7.

Placing a Business Order

"Good morning. Jeff's Auto Parts Company. May I help you?"

"This is John Anthony, parts manager of Ace Garage in Perth Amboy. We need a thrush muffler for a '94 Chevrolet, 250 engine, 6 cylinder, part number A984-7674B02."

"Ok, let me make sure I have the correct information. You need part A984-767 B02, a thrush muffler for a '94 Chevrolet, 250 engine, 6 cylinder."

"Right. Could I pick it up this afternoon?"

"Let me check on that and call you back. Could I have your name and telephone number?"

"John Anthony, Ace Garage, 555-4330."

"That's John Anthony, Ace Garage, 555-4330."

"Right."

"Thank you for calling. I'll check on this part and call you back as soon as possible."

"OK, good-bye."

"Good-bye."

19-7

Speaking clearly will help the person taking your telephone order to record the information correctly.

Emergency Calls

In the event of an emergency on the job, you must know what to do. Learn what the company expects of you. Many companies have guidelines to follow during emergencies. Check with your supervisor. Learn where emergency telephone numbers are posted. You may need to call the police, an ambulance, or the fire department. Most towns and cities call *911* to report an emergency. If you don't know what number to call in an emergency, just speak to the operator.

When reporting an emergency, remain calm. Clearly describe the injury or accident. Give your company's address. Stay on the line and do exactly as you are told until help arrives.

Writing Business Letters

Writing letters is a common way to communicate in business. Employees must be able to communicate with many individuals and outside groups. Knowing how to write business letters is an important job skill. A sample business letter is shown in 19-8. The essential parts of a business letter are described as follows:

- *Return address.* Use your personal address or the address of the company or organization for whom you are writing. (Usually this is included on the company's letterhead.)
- *Date.* Use the date you are writing the letter.
- *Inside address.* Use the complete name and address of the person to whom you are writing. Be sure to include the person's job title, too.
- *Salutation or greeting.* Begin your letter with a greeting. "Mr. Jones:" and "Dear Sir or Miss:" are examples.
- *Body of the letter.* This is the message you want the reader to receive.
- *Complimentary close.* Conclude your letter with "Sincerely," or "Yours truly."
- *Signature with typed name and title.* Always sign your letter.

The most difficult part of writing a letter is starting it. First, make an outline of the important facts or ideas you want to convey. If you are writing about events, list them in the order they occurred or are scheduled. If you are writing about ideas, cover the most important topic first and save the least important for last.

When writing a thank-you letter, state why you are thanking the person. Explain why you appreciate what was done. Send a thank-you letter as soon as possible after receiving the favor or gift.

When writing a letter requesting information, explain in detail what you need. Also indicate when you need the information. Close the letter with a short statement showing your appreciation for the person's help.

When you are providing information in response to a request, open the letter by thanking the person for requesting the information. Then give the information. Close the letter by assuring the person that you were happy to help. Be brief and to the point.

Sterling Enterprises, Inc.
123 East Avenue
Lansing, IL 60456

Date

Return Address

December 14, 2004

Inside
address

Ms. Jane Wright, Sales Manager
Greenbaugh Equipment Company
128 South Avenue
Freetown, PA 08956

Salutation

Dear Ms. Wright:

Body

Please send me your current catalog of commercial food equipment.
I would also like to receive information regarding ordering procedures,
shipping, warranties, and return policies.

I am planning to expand my operation this coming February. Therefore,
I would appreciate receiving these materials at your earliest convenience.

Thank you for your assistance.

Sincerely, ←——— Complimentary close

Alfred J. Sterling

Alfred J. Sterling
President

Signature and
typed name

19-8
Follow this format when writing business letters.

Nonverbal Communication

Not all messages involve words. ***Nonverbal communication*** is the sending and receiving of messages without the use of words. It is used by sailors aboard ships who send messages using flags or lights. It is used by mimes, who tell stories using only body movements and facial expressions. Musicians and artists also use it. The saying "a picture is worth a thousand words" refers to the power of this form of communication.

Nonverbal communication is as old as cave drawings, smoke signals, and drumbeats. It is part of modern society, too. Police officers use whistles and hand movements to direct traffic. Politicians smile, wave, and shake hands to express their goodwill. In the game of charades, players use nonverbal communication to help their partners guess the words.

A single body movement or gesture may have several meanings. This is especially true if the gesture is not accompanied by spoken words. Thinking about the situation in which a movement is used will help you determine its meaning.

Body Language

Your ***body language*** tells others a lot about you. In this form of nonverbal communication, you send a message with your use of body movements. You also speak with your facial expressions and hand gestures.

To learn more about body language, watch people without listening to them. Sit on a bench at a shopping mall and watch the crowd. Also, watch TV with the volume off. Pay attention to the movements, gestures, and expressions you see. What can you learn?

After watching body language, transfer what you have learned into action. Use body language to help you communicate more clearly. Make sure you are sending the signals and messages you want to send.

nonverbal communication
The sending and receiving of messages without the use of words.

body language
A form of nonverbal communication in which a person "speaks" with the use of body movements, facial expressions, and hand gestures.

Body Language on the Job

On the job, body language tells others about you. See 19-9. Slouching during an interview may suggest a lack of interest in the job. Even though you answer the questions thoughtfully, the interviewer may think you are lazy and sloppy. Staring into space while at a planning meeting may suggest that you are bored. Even if you contribute ideas, your boss may think you are uninterested.

You must stay aware of your body movements. Know what kind of an impression you are making. Then, go a step further. Use body language to make the kind of impression you want to make. Chart 19-10 lists various impressions your body movements might give.

Communication Tools

All forms of communication require some type of tool in order for communication to take place. With nonverbal communication, it may be a drum, smoke signal, or the human body. The telephone speeds spoken communications. Pens, paper, and

19-9

Body language can be used to emphasize important points during meetings.

typewriters once were the primary tools of written communication, but today it is the computer.

Computers process words quickly to create all types of business communications. These are hand-delivered, mailed, or transmitted as faxes, e-mails, and other forms of electronic communication. The same guidelines that apply to written communications also apply to electronic forms. Punctuation, spelling, and grammar should always be checked for accuracy. Messages sent from the workplace should always be related to business and never contain personal information.

Remember, the e-mail you send and receive while at work is not private. Your employer can check it at any time. Therefore, give it the same careful treatment you would give to any other form of communication.

Interpreting Body Language

Nonverbal Communication	Possible Meaning	Nonverbal Communication	Possible Meaning
Tears	joy sorrow love pain	Arms folded at chest	reservation displeasure disagreement defiance
A wink	a greeting a shared secret a signal teasing	Handshake	a greeting a farewell an agreement peace sportsmanship
A fist	power defiance a threat	Smile	friendliness humor happiness affection approval ridicule
Crossed fingers	a wish or hope good luck a lie		

19-10

Each body movement, gesture, and facial expression can convey a number of messages.

Summary

Communication is a major factor in all relationships—business and personal. Keys to success in communication include being a full-attention listener, using feedback, and speaking clearly.

When employees use headsets, telephones, and computers, they are communicating as representatives of their companies. They should be polite, thorough, accurate, and businesslike. In case of an emergency, they should know how to make emergency calls.

People are constantly sending messages about themselves without words. They do this through their body language. People should know what message their body language conveys so it is consistent with the one they want to send.

Reviewing the Chapter

1. Name three ways to send messages, three ways to receive messages, and three vehicles of communication.
2. Describe a full-attention listener.
3. Why is feedback important in the communication process?
4. List five tips for improved speech.
5. List and describe the three parts of a speech.
6. What five pieces of information should you record when taking a telephone message?
7. What are the seven essential parts of a business letter?
8. Which is a form of nonverbal communication?

    A. reading a book

    B. writing a letter

    C. painting a picture

    D. singing a song

9. How do you speak in body language?
10. Give an example of a message communicated on the job through body language.

Building Your Foundation Skills

1. Write a story, either factual or fictional, describing a problem created because feedback was not understood correctly.

2. Prepare and give a speech to the class on the importance of delivering speeches well.

3. Write a message on a piece of paper that you would send via e-mail.

4. Play a game of telephone. Begin with a message provided by the teacher. Have one classmate "telephone" the message to a second classmate in a place where they can't be overheard. Then have the second classmate "telephone" the message to a third classmate. Continue until all classmates have had a chance to receive the "call" and take the message. Then compare the final message to the original one. Did everyone give and receive the message accurately?

Building Your Workplace Competencies

Write a fictitious letter to a company requesting career information on specific types of jobs available. Work with two classmates on this project and use a computer. First, outline the points to include in the letter. Access the word processing program to view the business letter formats available. Decide on the best format to use, and compose a letter from your outline. Include everyone's signature on the letter. *(This activity develops competence with interpersonal skills, information, and technology.)*

Your Appearance

Objectives

After studying this chapter, you will be able to

- describe good grooming guidelines related to hair, skin, hands, breath, makeup, and fragrance.

- plan a wardrobe for work.

- judge the quality of clothes according to fabric, construction, and fit.

- summarize the proper care of clothing.

Words to Know

grooming

acne

dress code

wardrobe inventory

accessories

fads

Good Grooming

Your appearance is an important part of the first impression you make on people. They often form opinions about you based on your personal appearance. Therefore, it is always important to look your best. **Grooming** is the term used to describe how people take care of themselves. Good grooming means being clean, neat, and well dressed. See 20-1.

Hair

The appearance of your hair can add to or detract from your overall appearance. To look your best, keep your hair neatly trimmed and off your face. Whether you choose to keep your hair long or short, be sure to have it cut regularly. It should always look neat and fashionable.

People have different types of hair, so they need to follow different hair care routines to be well groomed. Some people need to wash their hair every day. Others need to wash their hair less often. You should be sure your hair is clean at all times. Ask you hairstylist or barber what type of shampoo and conditioner you should use to keep your hair clean and healthy.

If you choose to have a mustache or beard, keep it clean and neatly trimmed. Having a beard or mustache is acceptable at some jobs but not others. Some employers have rules about hair length and facial hair. Check to see if your employer has such rules.

Skin

To look fresh and healthy, your skin must be kept clean. That means your entire body. Bathe or shower daily. Be sure that you look clean and smell fresh when you go to work. Use deodorant or antiperspirant to help keep you fresh.

Many people, especially teens, have acne. *Acne* is a skin disorder caused by inflammation of the skin glands and hair follicles. It may result in blemishes on the face, neck, scalp, upper chest, or back. If you have acne, take extra care to keep your skin clean. If you are worried about your complexion, seek a doctor's advice.

grooming
The way in which people take care of themselves.

acne
A skin disorder caused by the inflammation of the skin glands and hair follicles.

20-1
A person who is well groomed is likely to make a good first impression.

Hands

In the workplace, shaking hands is a common practice. Since this gives people a chance to notice your hands, you should keep your hands clean and well manicured. You should be sure your nails are smooth and clean. Keep them at a reasonable length. Women may choose to polish their nails. Polished nails should always be kept fresh. Chips in the polish should be repaired daily.

Breath

Having fresh breath is important when you work with other people, 20-2. One factor that affects the freshness of your breath is whether your teeth and gums are clean and healthy. You need to brush and floss your teeth daily to keep them clean. You should visit your dentist regularly to keep your teeth and gums healthy. You may also want to use mouthwash to freshen your breath.

Makeup

Sometimes makeup is used to enhance facial appearance. If you choose to wear makeup, carefully select the proper type. If you like

Lab Volt

20-2

Working closely with others is more pleasant when everyone has fresh breath.

your appearance, you will be able to turn your attention away from yourself. You will be able to think of others and concentrate on your work.

Makeup is proper for women to wear on most jobs. The key to wearing makeup well is using flattering colors and keeping it light. If you are uncertain about what colors and products are right for you, go to a local department store. Ask the skin care consultants to help you choose the makeup that is best for you.

Fragrance

Sometimes individuals wear a fragrance to work. It might be from after-shave lotion, cologne, hair spray, or perfume. If you choose to wear a fragrance, be sure it is very light and pleasant. Fragrances that are too strong may annoy your coworkers or customers. See 20-3.

20-3
Most people do not want strong fragrances in the workplace. They prefer the fresh smell of good grooming.

Wardrobe

Different types of jobs require different types of clothes. People who work on farms or in construction can wear jeans and T-shirts to work. People in offices must wear more formal clothes to work, like jackets and dressy shirts. Whatever work you do, remember that your clothes say something important about you. The way you dress has an effect on how people think of you. Your clothes should always be neat and clean, no matter what work you do.

Dress Codes

Practically all workplaces have a dress code. A *dress code* is a set of clothing rules that employees must follow. Find out what your place of work requires. For instance, a company may require you to wear a uniform, special footwear, or a lab coat.

Some companies have dress codes because they have a certain image they want their employees to maintain. For instance, an accounting company may want its employees to convey a professional image by wearing suits and dressy clothing. See 20-4. Other companies have dress codes for safety reasons. A construction company, for instance, may require its employees to wear hard hats.

A trend in workplace is *relaxed dress codes*. This means wearing casual clothes, such as men wearing knitted shirts with collars and trousers, and women wearing informal blouses or sweaters with slacks. Other names for this trend are *corporate casual* and *workday casual*. Casual dress days were once reserved for Fridays, but more employers are allowing casual clothing on other days as well. However, business dress is usually required for meetings with clients or customers.

A relaxed dress code is not the same as no dress code. Ripped jeans, cut-offs, shorts, halter tops, and clothing you would wear to the beach are not suitable items for the work-place. With suitable casual clothes, workers can feel more comfortable on the job and still convey a professional image.

20-4

Many companies want their employees to wear clothes that will communicate a businesslike image.

Jewelry

Company dress codes may apply to jewelry as well as clothing. In some work settings, jewelry can get caught in machinery and become a safety hazard. Employees may not be allowed to wear long chains, earrings, rings, necklaces, bracelets, or watches. Where jewelry is allowed, it should be chosen with care and worn in moderation. Simple pieces that accent an outfit are a better choice than dramatic, overpowering items.

dress code
A set of clothing rules that workers must follow while at their places of employment.

Wardrobe Planning

Before you buy new clothes for work, take time to determine what you need. If you are unsure about what you should wear on the job, look at the clothes other people in the company wear. Then, review your wardrobe. Do your clothes seem compatible with that workplace? If not, you will need to do some planning to assemble an appropriate wardrobe.

The first step in wardrobe planning is to know what you already have. A good way to find out is to take a *wardrobe inventory*. This is a list of all the clothes and accessories you have in your closet and drawers. *Accessories* are items, such as shoes, handbags, belts, neckties, and jewelry, that are needed to complete outfits. As you make your wardrobe inventory, briefly describe the color and condition of each item. For instance, you may have a white shirt that is in good shape and a blue shirt that needs replacing.

Once you know what you have, you can decide what to add or replace. Make a list of exactly what you want or need to buy. Note the style and color of each item on the list. As you do this, think of what you will wear with each new piece of clothing or accessory. Plan complete outfits. Don't buy items that won't go with anything else in your closet.

If your job requires you to wear a dressy wardrobe, begin by buying a few basic pieces of clothing. You can add to them later when you can afford to do so. If your job does not require a special wardrobe, then you may be able to wear many of the clothes you have now. No matter what you wear to work, always be sure your clothes are clean and neat. See 20-5.

Nilfisk of America, Inc.

20-5

Even employees who do not have a dress code should make sure their work clothes are neat and clean.

Avoiding Fads

As you plan your wardrobe, remember that fashions constantly change, but many of the changes are fads. *Fads* are items that are popular for one or two seasons. Pants with flared legs and ankle socks with lace ruffles are examples of fads. Avoid spending a lot of money on fads. Instead, look for classic styles that will always be popular. Oxford shirts, straight-leg pants, and straight skirts are all classic styles.

Shopping for Quality

Always try to buy clothes of good quality. They may cost more, but they will look nicer and last longer than clothes of less quality. One well-made shirt for $30 may be a better buy than three shirts of less quality totaling $30.

The three signs of clothing quality are good fabric, construction, and fit. Check all three before you buy.

Fabric quality is judged by how the material looks and feels. In general, natural fibers, such as cotton, offer comfort. Synthetic fibers, such as polyester, help prevent wrinkles. The labels in your clothes list the fiber content and provide clothing care directions.

The construction of clothing refers to the way clothes are put together or sewn. In good quality clothes, the seams are straight and securely stitched. Zippers and pockets lie flat. Buttons are secure. Stripes, plaids, or other patterns in the fabric match at the seams.

Clothes must fit properly to look good. Use the following guidelines to judge fit:

- Movement should be comfortable when the garment is on.
- A garment should lie smoothly across the body without wrinkling, bunching, or sagging.
- Shirt or blouse sleeves should be a little longer than jacket sleeves.
- Men's ties should extend to the belt.
- Dress or skirt hems should not be too short.
- Pants should be long enough to extend to the tops of shoes but not the floor. See 20-6.

wardrobe inventory
A list of all the clothes and accessories found in a person's closet and drawers.

accessories
Items that complement a wardrobe, such as shoes, handbags, belts, neckties, and jewelry.

fads
Clothing items or styles that are popular for a very short period of time.

20-6

When shopping for clothes, look beyond first appearance and check construction and fit. Also read the care labels.

Laundry and Ironing

No matter how expensive your clothes are, they will look cheap if they are dirty or cleaned improperly. You need to make sure your clothes are cleaned appropriately. They will look better and last longer if you do.

The labels attached to clothes give their care instructions. See 20-7. Many clothing items can be washed in a washing machine. If not, you will need to wash them by hand or have them dry-cleaned.

Hand-washing means the clothes must be soaked in soapy water and washed by hand. After soaking them a few minutes in a clean sink or tub, gently rub them with your hands. Then rinse them thoroughly. Dry them on a hanger or flat on a rack, depending on the care instructions. Some hand-washed items can be dried in a dryer on a *gentle* setting with low or no heat.

Some clothes must be dry-cleaned if their labels say *dry clean only*. The cost of dry cleaning can be expensive. Shop around to find a cleaner that does a nice job at reasonable prices. If you must dry-clean clothing frequently, be sure to include this expense in your monthly budget.

In addition to having clean clothes, you should be sure your clothes are ironed. Ironed clothes have no wrinkles. They look smooth and neat. They give you a more professional appearance. Some fabrics need to be ironed more than others. Linen wrinkles easily, while polyester resists wrinkling.

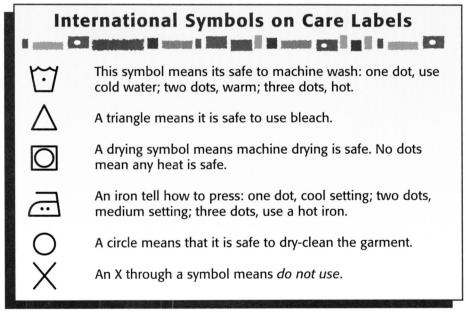

20-7

International symbols on care labels tell consumers how to care for their garments.

Summary

You should always try to look your best. Your appearance affects the way other people think of you. Looking your best also helps you feel good about yourself.

Good grooming includes keeping your hair, skin, and hands clean and attractive. It includes keeping your breath fresh and using makeup and fragrances wisely. It also includes wearing clothes that are clean, neat, and appropriate.

Different types of work require different wardrobes. When you start a job, find out what the other workers wear. Then make plans to put a similar wardrobe together.

As you shop for clothes, avoid spending a lot of money on fads. Look for signs of quality in clothing. After buying clothes, be sure to care for them properly.

Reviewing the Chapter

1. Give one good-grooming tip for each of the following:
   A. hair
   B. skin
   C. hands
   D. breath
   E. makeup
   F. fragrance

2. What are two reasons for a company dress code?
3. What is the first step in wardrobe planning?
4. List five examples of accessories.
5. As a person begins to build a wardrobe for work, should individual items or complete outfits be purchased?
6. Why avoid spending a lot of money on fads?
7. What are three signs of quality clothing?
8. Name three guidelines for judging the fit of clothes.
9. Why should clothes be properly maintained?
10. Where can you find washing and drying instructions for your clothes?

Building Your Foundation Skills

1. Develop a weekly grooming chart for yourself. List what you will do daily and weekly to stay well groomed.
2. Visit several stores that sell clothes of various styles, qualities, and prices. Look for both fads and classic styles. Compare the fabric, construction, and fit of different clothes. Give an oral report about what you learned.
3. Take an inventory of your wardrobe. Make a list of what you would need to add to your wardrobe to dress appropriately for an office.
4. Call three dry cleaners in your area. Make a comparison list of their prices for cleaning each of the following: a man's suit, dress, coat, sweater, and pair of slacks.

Building Your Workplace Competencies

Visit one place where you would like to work to observe how people are dressed. Make an appointment with someone in the personnel or human resources department to discuss the organization's dress code. Obtain a copy of the dress code, if one exists. Find out what type of clothing is forbidden and what the penalty is for wearing these to work. Present your findings to the class in an oral report. Create a poster to use during your report that shows the do's and don'ts of dressing for work. *(This activity develops competence with resources, interpersonal skills, information, and systems.)*

Good Health and Job Success

Objectives

After studying this chapter, you will be able to

- incorporate enough activity in each day to maintain fitness.

- list guidelines for choosing foods that will provide a balanced diet.

- determine ways to handle stress.

- explain why people should avoid smoking.

- describe the negative effects of abusing alcohol and drugs.

Words to Know

physical fitness
balanced diet
nutrients
stress
drug
drug abuse
addiction
drug screening

Staying Healthy

Maintaining your health is important to all areas of your life. If you are not in good health, you cannot do your best in school. You may not be able to fulfill your family responsibilities. Poor health can also affect your performance on the job.

Start caring about your eating and lifestyle habits while you are young. How you treat your body now will impact your health later. There are many ways to enjoy food and promote good health at the same time.

The *Dietary Guidelines for Americans* is the best guide to promoting good health. The U.S. Department of Agriculture and Department of Health and Human Services developed the 10-point plan. The *Guidelines* help children and adults make personal choices to achieve and maintain good health. See 21-1.

Aim for Fitness

Aim for fitness is the first challenge in achieving good health. Aiming for fitness involves two steps—maintaining a healthy weight and staying active. **Physical fitness** is the ability to perform daily tasks easily with enough reserve energy to respond to unexpected demands.

The best way to promote physical fitness is to incorporate activity into each day as much as possible. You don't need to set aside a special block of time to exercise. Simply accumulate at least 60 minutes of moderate activity throughout the day on most days of the week. Longer periods of activity or more vigorous activities are even better.

If possible, ride a bike to school instead of taking a bus. Use stairs instead of escalators or elevators. These are two easy activities you might be able to do. On the other hand, if you prefer to schedule a specific time of day for an exercise workout, then do that. The objective is to get the activity you need to maintain good health.

Before any vigorous activity, be sure to begin with warm-up exercises to help prevent strains and pulled muscles. A good warm-up prepares your muscles and joints for the strenuous motions to follow. Many coaches and trainers recommend at least 10 minutes of warm-up exercises.

physical fitness
The ability to easily perform daily tasks with enough reserve energy to respond to unexpected demands.

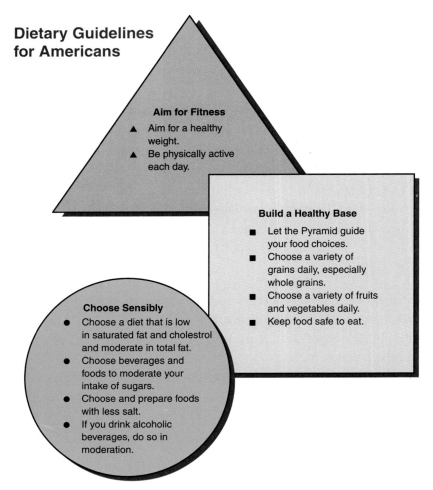

Dietary Guidelines for Americans

Aim for Fitness
▲ Aim for a healthy weight.
▲ Be physically active each day.

Build a Healthy Base
■ Let the Pyramid guide your food choices.
■ Choose a variety of grains daily, especially whole grains.
■ Choose a variety of fruits and vegetables daily.
■ Keep food safe to eat.

Choose Sensibly
● Choose a diet that is low in saturated fat and cholestrol and moderate in total fat.
● Choose beverages and foods to moderate your intake of sugars.
● Choose and prepare foods with less salt.
● If you drink alcoholic beverages, do so in moderation.

21-1
The Dietary Guidelines for Americans lists 10 basic steps to good health.

Brisk activity provides good conditioning for your heart and lungs. Walking, running, swimming, rowing, jumping rope, bicycling, playing tennis, and skiing are good forms of exercise. Team sports like basketball, soccer, and hockey are also good. You may want to try several activities.

Joining a health or tennis club, local park district programs, the YMCA, or the YWCA are good ways to get exercise. You should start any new exercise program slowly and build it gradually. As the activity becomes easier, you can do a little more. Don't try to do too much on your first or second try. You may overdo it and get sore muscles. Then you might lose your desire to continue. A word of caution: it is wise to consult a physician before beginning a strenuous exercise program.

Build a Healthy Base and Choose Sensibly

A good way to maintain a healthy body is to eat a balanced diet. A ***balanced diet*** is an intake of food that supplies all the nutrients in the needed amounts to maintain good health. ***Nutrients*** are chemical substances in foods that nourish the body. To create a balanced diet, you must choose the foods you eat with care. Eating foods that are good for you helps you feel good. That is why some people say, "You are what you eat."

No single food provides all the needed nutrients. Eating a wide variety of foods is the best way to obtain all the nutrients required for good health. The Food Guide Pyramid can help you recognize your food choices. See 21-2.

The Food Guide Pyramid is an eating plan that divides foods into groups according to the nutrients that they provide. It also recommends the number of daily servings from each group. Select the recommended servings from each food group every day.

Eat plenty of grain products, vegetables, and fruits. These foods are high in fiber and nutrients. They also tend to be low in fat and calories. You lose weight if you eat fewer calories than you use. You maintain your weight when the number of calories you eat equals the number of calories you use.

Choose a diet low in saturated fat and cholesterol, and moderate in total fat. No more than 30 percent of calories in your diet should come from fat. Fried or greasy food, butter, margarine, and oils are common fat sources. Too much fat in the diet has been linked to health problems. For that reason, the foods at the top of the pyramid should be eaten sparingly.

Sugars and other sweets also appear at the top of the pyramid. They contribute many calories and few nutrients. Use sugars, salt, and sodium in moderation. Too much sodium has been linked to high blood pressure in some people. Many processed foods contain large amounts of salt.

balanced diet
An intake of food that supplies the body all the necessary nutrients in the needed amounts to maintain good health.

nutrient
A chemical substance in food that nourishes the body.

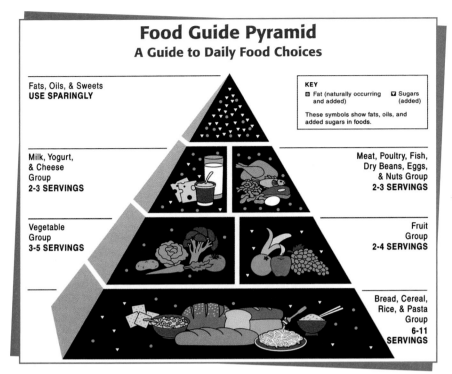

21-2

Eating the recommended number of servings from each group in the Food Guide Pyramid each day will help you get the nutrients you need.

Keep foods safe to eat by cleaning hands and work surfaces often. Always keep hot foods hot and cold foods colds. Keep raw, cooked, and ready-to-eat foods separate while shopping, preparing, and storing. When in doubt, throw it out instead of taking a chance on spoiled food.

A varied diet coupled with regular activity will help you maintain a healthy weight. Try to avoid eating too much of any one item. Bad habits are easy to form and hard to break.

Children and adolescents should not drink alcoholic beverages. Poor nutrition can result if alcohol replaces foods in the diet. Also, alcohol consumption is a major cause of accidents among teens.

Learn to Handle Stress

You face various types of stress every day. **_Stress_** is a feeling of tension, strain, or pressure. It is usually the result of some change. Stress can affect both the body and the mind. See 21-3.

Both good and bad changes create stress. Getting a new job causes stress; so does losing a job. Making the basketball team causes stress; so does an injury or illness. Dating someone new causes stress; so does ending a relationship.

Both big and little pressures create stress. Big worries, like money problems, drug abuse, divorce, and the death of a loved one, can cause extreme stress. Homework, tests, and deadlines can cause stress, too.

21-3

A person's body language can show signs of stress.

Some stress is good for you. It makes life interesting and exciting. It keeps you on your toes. It challenges you to react to new situations.

On the other hand, trying to handle too much stress repeatedly can be harmful. Severe stress can affect your behavior. You may not be able to concentrate on your work. You may feel frustrated. You may become rude to people. Too much stress can also harm your health. It can be a factor in the development of ulcers, heart problems, and strokes.

stress
A feeling of tension, strain, or pressure.

Since you cannot avoid stress in your life, you need to learn how to handle it. The following tips on managing stress often help:

- Practice good eating and sleeping habits. Avoid eating too many high-calorie snacks. Eat balanced meals. Get plenty of rest. Most students your age need eight or nine hours of sleep every night. Developing these habits will help keep you in good health. Healthy individuals are more able to handle stress.
- Use physical activity to relieve stress. Let off steam by working out, playing a sport, or pursuing other forms of exercise. See 21-4.
- Talk about your problems. Choose to talk to people you trust and respect. They may be able to help you see your problems from a different view. Sometimes professionals, such as psychologists, clergy, and counselors, can offer great help.
- Maintain a positive attitude. Keep away from complainers. Surround yourself with positive-thinking people who feel good about themselves. Develop a "can do" philosophy. Set realistic goals and objectives. Then go after them.
- Manage your time. Control your time by setting priorities. Develop a to-do list for each day and stick to it.
- Develop a positive work ethic and outlook on life. Associate with others who share your beliefs and value your personal priorities. Seek out those who find similar meaning for their lives and encourage their companionship.

Ways to Relax

A good way to reduce stress is to relax. When you are relaxed, you feel at peace with yourself and the rest of the world. You feel renewed and regain strength. It is important that you reserve some time for total relaxation.

Bergen County Vocational Technical School

21-4
Team sports are a fun way to exercise your body and relax your mind.

There are many ways to relax. Like exercise, you have to find the ways that suit you best. Consider the following possibilities:

- Read something inspiring, entertaining, or informative.
- Play a game of chess, checkers, or cards.
- Listen to music.
- Spend time alone to think about your goals and life plans.
- Talk with someone about a topic of mutual interest.
- See a movie, play, concert, lecture, or television program.
- Attend a social function.

The type of work you do may determine the relaxation that's best for you. If you read all day at school and work, you may want to rest your eyes while listening to music. No matter how you choose to relax, do so whenever you feel the need. Give your body and your mind some time to reduce the everyday stresses of life.

Avoid Tobacco Use

When it comes to tobacco use, there isn't much good to say about it. At best, it is a bad habit. At worst, it is a killer. The Surgeon General has warned that cigarette smoking is dangerous to your health. Smoking causes lung cancer, heart disease, and emphysema, and may complicate pregnancy. See 21-5. Smokeless tobacco—chewing tobacco and snuff—have also been linked to health problems, such as mouth and throat cancer. Besides the health issues, there are many reasons why tobacco users should quit.

> Surgeon General's Warning: Cigarette smoke contains carbon monoxide.

> Surgeon General's Warning: Quitting smoking now greatly reduces serious risks to your health.

> Surgeon General's Warning: Smoking causes lung cancer, heart disease, emphysema, and may complicate pregnancy.

> Surgeon General's Warning: Smoking by pregnant women may result in fetal injury, premature birth, and low birth weight.

> Warning: The Surgeon General has determined that cigarette smoking is dangerous to your health.

21-5

Recent warnings printed in cigarette ads and on cigarette packages underscore the health hazards associated with cigarette smoking.

- Smoking is an expensive habit. Heavy smokers spend hundreds of dollars every year on cigarettes.
- Smokers' clothes often carry a smoke odor.
- Tobacco use causes bad breath and discolored teeth.
- Tobacco use causes the senses of smell and taste to dull.
- Smokers are fire hazards. The National Fire Protection Association reports that smoking is a major cause of fatal residential fires.
- In most states, it is illegal for persons under a specified age to purchase and use tobacco products.

People who don't use tobacco should never start. Smokers are finding it more difficult to comply with the increasing strictness of nonsmoking policies in the workplace. Some employers allow smoking only in a designated smoking room for limited periods. In many workplaces, however, cigarette smoking is banned completely. See 21-6.

21-6
Workers are more productive in a tobacco-free environment.

How to Quit Smoking

There are many ways to quit smoking. People who smoke have to choose the methods that work best for them. The first step is to decide that they truly want to quit. Smokers must have the desire and the will to quit. The methods described in the following paragraphs have helped millions of Americans quit. Similar methods can help users of smokeless tobacco, too.

One way to quit smoking is known as *cold turkey*. With this method, smokers make the decision to stop smoking at a specific time. Then they do it. They never again smoke another cigarette. This method takes willpower and determination. It's tough, but it works.

Another way many people quit smoking is by gradually reducing the number of cigarettes they smoke. They may start with 20 cigarettes a day. They may cut down to 15, then 10, then five, then three, then two, then one, and finally none!

People who want to quit smoking may find that gum or candy can help. Whenever they have the urge to smoke, they can replace the cigarette with gum or candy. There also are commercial products available to help those who want to quit smoking.

Individual or group therapy is another option for those who want to quit smoking. Therapy can provide the professional support that people need. If you smoke, you may want to talk with your doctor about the best way for you to stop.

Avoid Drug Use

A *drug* is any chemical substance that brings about physical, emotional, or mental changes in people. *Drug abuse* is a term used to describe the reckless use of drugs. It means using a drug in a way that can damage a person's health or ability to function. No workplace permits drug use among employees.

Drugs such as marijuana, heroin, cocaine, crack, Ecstasy, PCP, and LSD are illegal. However, drugs do not have to be illegal to be abused. Drug abuse can easily occur with prescription medications and over-the-counter remedies.

drug
A chemical substance that brings about physical, emotional, or mental changes in a person.

drug abuse
The use of a drug in a way that can damage a person's health or ability to function.

Different drugs affect the body in different ways. Drugs may have harmful effects on the heart, lungs, brain, and reproductive system. Drugs can dull the senses, alter behavior, impede judgment, and impair driving skills. Drugs can cause dizziness, vomiting, convulsions, coma, and death.

Not only do drugs affect the user's body, they also affect the user's relationships. Drug abusers seldom live successful lives. Those who depend on drugs lose interest in school, family, and jobs. They spend most of their conscious time searching for drugs or stealing money to buy more. They usually develop an addiction. An *addiction* is the never-ending obsession to use a drug more often.

Typical drug abusers have few friends. Practically all begin their drug habit by simply experimenting, believing they can stay in control. In the end, drugs take over their lives. Eventually every drug abuser learns—the hard way—that drugs can't bring happiness or solutions to problems. Drugs only cause more problems.

Avoid Alcohol Use

Most people do not associate alcohol with drugs. They should. Alcohol is a drug. It can alter your behavior and damage your health. Alcohol abuse can ruin personal relationships. It can cause economic and legal problems. It can also lead to health problems such as brain damage, cirrhosis of the liver, and heart failure.

Are you aware that alcohol-related car accidents are the number one cause of death among teenagers? Here's why: alcohol moves quickly into the bloodstream and to the brain. When this happens, the person's vision, muscle coordination, and reaction time are impaired. Drinkers usually feel more powerful and in control. In reality, their body functions are slowed down. They have less control. See 21-7.

Just one drink can affect a driver's performance. The message is clear. Drinkers shouldn't drive, and anyone planning to drive shouldn't drink. If you plan on drinking at a party or event, you should also plan to have a designated driver. A designated driver is someone who agrees not to drink and will drive others home safely. Be responsible.

Alcohol and Other Drug Problems at Work

Practically all employers will require you to take a drug test before they hire you. This is called *drug screening*. Drug screening tests can reveal the presence of drugs in a person's body. During the workday, some employers periodically test their employees *randomly*. This means that a small percentage of workers are selected, without warning, to take an immediate drug test.

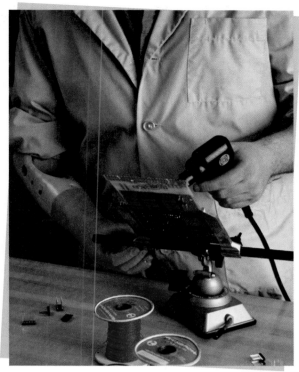

21-7
Workers who operate tools or machinery can't afford to have their motor skills impaired by alcohol.

Drug screening is one way for employers to reduce problems at work. Employee problems due to alcohol and drugs cost businesses billions of dollars each year. Many companies have policies that deal with alcohol and drug abuse on the job. Disciplinary action is taken against employees who are found intoxicated while on duty or who illegally use or possess drugs. In some cases, use of alcohol or drugs on the job is grounds for immediate dismissal.

addiction
The never-ending obsession to use a drug more often.
drug screening
Tests that can reveal the presence of drugs in a person's body.

Alcohol and drug abuse on the job contribute to the following problems:

- poor quality control
- more safety risks
- increased absenteeism and lateness
- more health risks
- poor relationships between coworkers
- increased risk of internal theft (to pay for drug or alcohol addiction)

Where to Get Help

Many organizations are available to help people who have alcohol or drug problems. These organizations can provide information, counseling, and treatment. If you or someone you know needs assistance, contact help immediately. Turn to the Yellow Pages of your phone book. Look under *Alcoholism Information* and *Treatment Centers*. Help may also be listed under *Drug Abuse and Addiction–Information and Treatment.*

People who need information or help can also turn to family members and friends. School nurses, counselors, teachers, coaches, and religious leaders may be able to suggest sources of help. Also, community agencies, religious organizations, and hospitals may offer programs for help. Remember this important point: when someone with a problem is ready to face it, immediate action should be taken. See 21-8.

Substance Abuse Treatment Programs

Assessment
Upon admission to a treatment facility, this process evaluates the patient's addiction and recommends an appropriate treatment program.

Detoxification
This process is designed to safely withdraw patients from addictive substances as an initial step in breaking their dependence on the substances.

Inpatient Care
In this program, patients become residents of the treatment facility to help them begin their recovery in a protected environment. Food, lodging, and 24-hour nursing care are provided in addition to the treatments included in outpatient programs. This program is often recommended for patients who are unable to abstain from substance use without constant supervision or whose health been weakened by their addiction.

Outpatient Care
In this program, patients visit the treatment facility for group therapy, individual counseling, and education exercises. Friends and family members may be encouraged to participate in some activities with patients. This program is often recommended for patients able to abstain from the use of substances without constant supervision. Patients who begin treatment on an inpatient bases may continue on an outpatient basis once their condition has stabilized.

Family Support Programs
These programs educate family members of addicted persons about addiction and its impact on the family. The programs allow family members to share experiences with other families in the same situation.

Aftercare
Aftercare programs provide continued support through group therapy and individual counseling sessions to help patients remain free of addiction. Programs also provide support for friends and family members.

21-8
Many types of treatment programs are available to help individuals and families affected by drug addiction.

Summary

Health is an important factor in all aspects of your life. Feeling well allows you to live your life to its fullest. When you are physically fit, you can perform well at school and work. You also have enough energy to enjoy your leisure time.

Regular activity and a balanced diet are two keys to good health. They give your body what it needs to function well.

Stress is a part of life. To maintain good health, you must learn to handle stress. Finding ways to relax will help.

Good health depends on what you do as well as what you don't do. It is important not to smoke and abuse alcohol and other drugs. If you have any problems in these areas, make an effort to solve them. Many sources of help are available.

Reviewing the Chapter

1. How much physical activity is recommended for good health?
2. Why should you warm up before vigorous exercise?
3. Why is it important to eat a variety of foods?
4. True or false. You lose weight if you eat more calories than you use.
5. Which of the following statements is true?

    A. Stress can affect both the body and the mind.

    B. Both good and bad changes create stress.

    C. Some stress is good for you.

    D. No stress is good for you.

6. List five ways to handle stress.
7. According to the Surgeon General, how is cigarette smoking dangerous to your health?
8. Describe the *cold turkey* method of quitting smoking.
9. Why should someone who has been drinking avoid driving?
10. List five problems caused by alcohol and drug abuse on the job.

Building Your Foundation Skills

1. Do further research and write a report on one of the following topics about stress: the causes, the effects, or ways to handle it.

2. Read current news stories about the problems businesses face because employees use alcohol and other drugs. Present your findings in an oral report to the class.

3. Ask a nutritionist or dietitian to talk to your class about choosing foods for a balanced diet. Be prepared to ask questions.

4. For one week, keep a time log that lists periods of moderate and vigorous activity. Determine if you are meeting the recommendations for physical fitness. If not, develop a plan of action to incorporate more activity in your daily routine.

Building Your Workplace Competencies

Working with your classmates, organize a reference file of community sources to help people who want to quit smoking or stop using alcohol or other drugs. Include the names, addresses, hours, and key contact people of the area organizations with a brief description of their services. Determine the most useful type of file (index cards, notebook, or computer) that would maintain a person's privacy. Before actually beginning work, report what you understand your part of the assignment to be. *(This activity develops competence with resources, interpersonal skills, information, systems, and technology.)*

22

Developing Leadership Skills

Objectives

After studying this chapter, you will be able to

- identify leadership traits.

- discuss how leadership traits and skills can be applied to work situations.

- name and describe the nationally recognized career/technical student organizations.

- explain the purpose of parliamentary procedure.

Words to Know

leadership

leader

career/technical student organization (CTSO)

agenda

parliamentary procedure

Robert's Rules of Order

326

Leadership

Leadership is the ability to direct others on a course or down a path. When thinking of people who have that quality, you tend to think of famous people. Many famous people are leaders, but many ordinary people are leaders, too.

A *leader* is a person who influences the actions of others. The captain of a sports team is a leader. However, the teammate who encourages the team to do its best is a leader, too. Many people are leaders because they inspire those around them to perform well, 22-1.

In the workplace, leadership is not reserved just for the head of the department or the company. A workplace that values teamwork

22-1
Leaders challenge other members of a group to do their best, no matter what the activity is.

encourages the development of many leaders. Sometimes a work team has *shared leadership* responsibilities. In this case, no single individual holds the position of leader. Instead, different members come to the forefront to lead a project when it involves their area of expertise. After the phase is complete, another team member leads the next phase.

Few people will become company presidents. However, all of us will need to be leaders on many occasions in our lives. The success of schools, businesses, cities, and nations depends on effective leaders.

Leadership Traits

Effective leaders have certain traits. These traits can be practiced and acquired. Having leadership traits is helpful in all aspects of everyday life.

leadership
The ability to lead or direct others on a course or in a direction.
leader
A person who influences the actions of others.

- *Leaders respect the rights and dignity of others.* They are willing to accept responsibility and work within the group. They are able to get along with people in a friendly and peaceful manner.
- *Leaders are straightforward.* They give praise where praise is due. They communicate their thoughts and feelings in a clear and understandable manner.
- *Leaders are well informed on matters that concern the group.* They are confident and honest. They trust their fellow group members.
- *Leaders are positive and excited about the group's work.* They are open-minded.
- *Leaders inspire accomplishments.* They can help a group set goals. They also know how to get a group started and keep it on track.

Effective Leadership at School and at Work

You may be surprised to learn that the traits and skills used by effective leaders in the workplace are the same as those used by effective students. Refer to the chart in 22-2. There you'll find common steps individuals can take to become leaders at school and at work.

Steps to Becoming a Leader

- Arrive a little early for meetings and apointments.
- Try to act and speak in a way that will leave a favorable impression.
- Develop good conversational skills. This includes being a good listener and an interesting speaker.
- Make a special effort to remember the names of everyone you meet.
- Stay out of arguments. No one ever wins an argument.
- Avoid complaining and being critical of others.
- Make an effort to find something good to say.
- Always appear interested, friendly, and pleasant.
- Say "please" and "thank you" often.
- Demonstrate your best effort at all times.
- Always try to make the best use of resources.

22-2
If you have accomplished some of these steps, you are well on your way to becoming a leader.

School Organizations Create Leaders

The best way to develop leadership skills and prepare for the world of work exists right in your own school. A variety of student organizations, clubs, and extracurricular activities are available to help you explore new interests and develop leadership skills.

Consider joining a *career/technical student organization (CTSO)*. These are school groups that help students learn more about certain occupational areas. You could join an existing organization, or you could ask a teacher to help you start a chapter of a student organization at your school. A teacher-advisor offers help when needed. In these organizations, students run the activities. They make the decisions. See 22-3.

22-3   *FCCLA*

This career/technical student organization wanted to focus on preventing violence in the community.

---

career/technical student organization (CTSO)
School groups that help students learn more about certain occupational areas.

As a member of a career/technical student organization, you share interests and career goals with other students. By working with them, you also share many benefits of an active club. You can learn about careers in your field of interest. You can enjoy social activities and participate in civic activities. You can develop leadership skills. You can participate in local, state, national, and even international conferences and competitions. Meanwhile, you will be building your self-confidence, self-esteem, and motivation.

The career/technical student organization to join should be the one that best matches your career goals. It should be related to your school program. The following career/technical student organizations are nationally recognized:

Business Professionals of America (BPA) is for students enrolled in business and office programs. The group's purpose is to help students learn job-related skills for business and office occupations. Members participate on local, state, and national levels. Activities focus on promoting job skills, leadership traits, and social awareness.

DECA–An Association of Marketing Students is for students who are interested in marketing. Programs focus on career development, economic understanding, leadership, and civic duties. Members learn about marketing, merchandising, management, and related careers, 22-4.

Family, Career, and Community Leaders of America (FCCLA) is open to students through grade 12 who have taken or will take courses in family and consumer sciences. This organization encourages personal growth, prepares students for careers, and fosters family and community involvement and leadership.

22-4
*Joining DECA will help prepare you for a
career in sales and customer relations.*

**Future Business Leaders of America–Phi Beta
Lambda (FBLA-PBL)** is for students interested in
business careers. The group helps students understand American business enterprise and set career
goals. It also helps them develop character and self-
confidence. Other goals of the group are to promote
sound financial management and competent business leadership. Activities focus on civic and
community service, career development, social
awareness, and economic education. Students can
compete in individual, team, and chapter events at
regional, state, and national levels.

Health Occupations Students of America (HOSA) is for students interested in health occupations. The group helps students develop leadership skills, civic responsibilities, and occupational skills. Students become aware of health care issues and concerns. They participate in group discussions, conferences, and educational projects.

National FFA Organization (FFA) is for students preparing to enter careers in agriculture, agribusiness, and agriscience. Competitive activities and award programs operate on local, state, and national levels. They give students practical experience in applying the agricultural knowledge and skills gained in the classroom. The group works to promote leadership, character development, cooperation, service, improved agriculture, and citizenship. See 22-5.

22-5
National FFA Organization projects and events give student members a chance to apply their knowledge of plants and soils.

Skills USA–VICA prepares students to enter trade, industrial, technical, and health careers. Its activities help students develop leadership and teamwork skills needed for job success. Programs provide students with training and employment opportunities and exposure to members of the workforce. Members compete in occupational skill olympics from the local to the international level.

Technology Student Association (TSA) is open to any student who is taking, or has taken, technology courses. Activities include individual and group projects, competitive events, and school and community services. Students gain insight into careers and learn job-related skills. They also develop the leadership, personal, and social skills needed for living in a modern, technical world.

How Student Groups Operate

Student groups have various names, such as clubs, organizations, and associations. They allow people with a common interest to meet and exchange information. When you join a school group, you will find its organizational pattern is similar to other groups.

All student groups have officers, who generally lead the group. The members elect the officers—usually president, vice president, secretary, and treasurer. Student groups also have one or more committees. Each committee focuses on one aspect of the group's work. Groups often use committees to handle events, publicity, and membership. See 22-6.

Meetings are usually held on a regular basis. They may be scheduled weekly, monthly, or quarterly. The highlight of most meetings is an informational program. A part of each meeting is devoted to conducting the business of the student group.

22-6

This project committee is preparing for a competition.

Good meetings require advance planning. Usually the officers or members of a program committee plan the meetings. The president of the group conducts the meetings.

An *agenda* is a list of activities that will occur during a meeting. An agenda is also known as an order of business. An agenda should be presented to the membership a few days before each meeting. That allows people to plan for the meeting. It helps them prepare to intelligently discuss the business of the group.

The success of a group depends primarily on the quality of its meetings. Good meetings are described in the following statements:

- The meeting agenda is carefully planned in advance.
- The meeting follows the agenda, and starts and ends on time.
- The meeting room has good lighting and comfortable seating.
- Officers use parliamentary procedure to run the meeting.

Parliamentary Procedure

Persons who attend meetings of various organizations find that the meetings usually follow the same pattern. Most groups conduct their gatherings according to *parliamentary procedure*. This is an orderly way of conducting a meeting and discussing group business. Its purpose is to help groups run their meetings fairly and efficiently.

Parliamentary procedure provides an orderly way to propose, discuss, and act on items of business. It provides a chance for fair discussion and action by the group. Both the majority and minority sides of an issue are handled fairly. Finally, parliamentary procedure provides rules for conducting group business quickly and according to the will of the majority.

Robert's Rules of Order is the most common reference used in parliamentary law. There are other references on parliamentary procedure that you may find easier to read. As an officer or member of a group, you should be familiar with parliamentary law. You should be knowledgeable so you can find the answers to problems that arise during club meetings.

agenda
An order of business that lists activities that will occur during a meeting.

parliamentary procedure
An orderly way of conducting a meeting and discussing group business.

Robert's Rules of Order
The most common reference book used to describe the parliamentary procedure used at business meetings.

Summary

Leadership traits can be practiced and acquired. They can help you be successful in many different settings. They are helpful in clubs, at work, and in everyday group situations.

Career/technical student organizations bring students with common career goals together. Eight career/technical student organizations are nationally recognized. Each focuses on a different career field.

As a member of such a group, you will learn how meetings are run. You will be able to practice parliamentary procedure. You may have the chance to serve as an officer or committee member. Participating in career/technical student organizations has other benefits, too. You can learn more about careers. You can take part in many activities and competitions. You can learn new skills and build self-confidence.

Reviewing the Chapter

1. List four leadership traits.
2. Name six steps for a student to take at school or work to become a leader.
3. What is the function of career/technical student organizations?
4. Name three benefits of being involved in a career/technical student organization.
5. Name two career/technical student organizations for students who are interested in business occupations.
6. A career/technical student organization for students who are interested in marketing is _____.
   A. TSA
   B. DECA
   C. BPA
   D. HOSA
7. True or false. FCCLA is for students who are preparing to enter careers in agriculture, agribusiness, and horticulture.
8. List four characteristics of a good meeting.
9. What is the purpose of parliamentary procedure?
10. What book is commonly used as a reference on parliamentary procedure?

Building Your Foundation Skills

1. Attend a meeting in your school or community. Take notes on the use of parliamentary procedure. Write a brief report on your findings.

2. Interview members of one of the career/technical student organizations in your school. Ask them about their participation in the group. What have they gained from belonging to the group? Also ask them how the organization has affected their career goals. Present your findings to the class in an oral report.

3. Contribute to a class discussion about the traits of effective leaders. Discuss how these same traits can be applied to situations at work and in everyday life.

4. Ask a member of a career/technical student organization in your school to talk to your class about the benefits of belonging to the group.

Building Your Workplace Competencies

Working with several classmates, research one aspect of parliamentary procedure. Possible topics include: order of business and programs, making a motion, committees and their reports, secretary's and treasurer's reports, nominating committee and elections, and officers and their duties. Have the group decide how to divide the tasks. Using a computer, create an informational handout to teach other members of the class about your topic. Make a brief presentation to the class using the brochure. After all groups have made their presentations, participate in a mock meeting to elect officers. *(This activity develops competence with resources, interpersonal skills, information, systems, and technology.)*

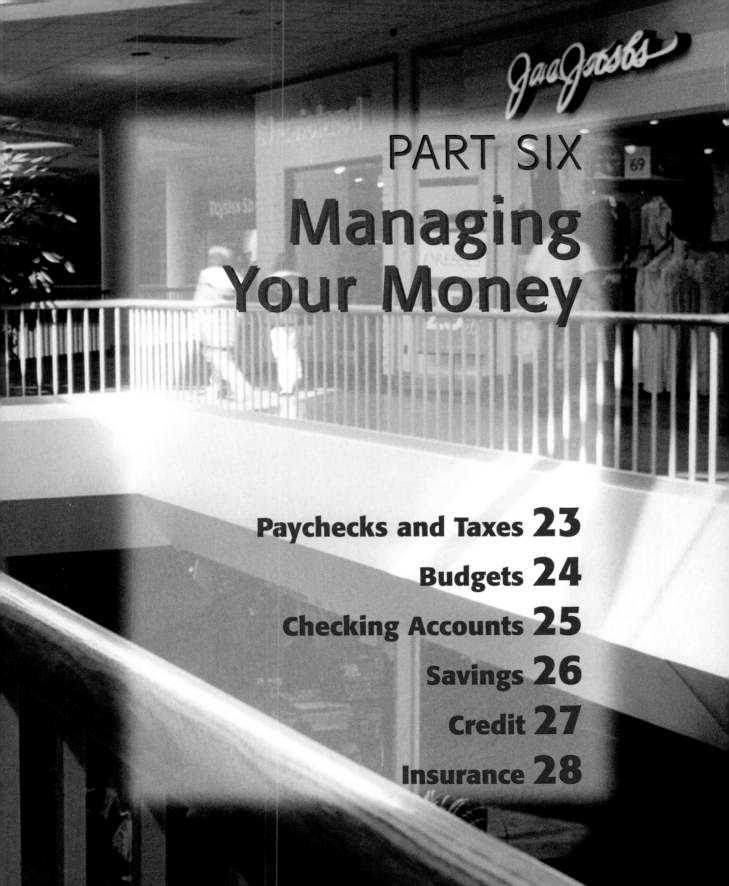

PART SIX
Managing
Your Money

Paychecks and Taxes

Objectives

After studying this chapter, you will be able to

- explain the difference between gross pay and net pay.

- discuss the use of W-4 and W-2 Forms.

- complete a Form 1040EZ federal income tax return.

Words to Know

pay period

gross pay

net pay

W-4 Form

dependent

W-2 Form

Internal Revenue Service (IRS)

income tax

Federal Insurance Contributions Act (FICA)

Form 1040EZ

Payday

Payday is usually a happy day. It is the day you are paid for the work you have done. Your paycheck, however, may be smaller than you expected. In this chapter, you will learn what goes into your paycheck—and what comes out of it.

Companies pay their employees for the work they did during a ***pay period***. Most companies have weekly, biweekly (every two weeks), semimonthly (twice a month), or monthly pay periods. In many companies, payday is not the last day of the pay period. Many companies delay pay for a week or a full pay period. For instance, suppose a company pays its employees every Friday. Each check covers the pay period that ends the previous Saturday. See 23-1. This delay allows the company to accurately pay employees for all the time they worked during the period.

23-1
Many companies delay payday for a week or more to do proper record keeping.

pay period
A length of time for which an employee's wages are calculated. Most businesses have weekly, biweekly, semimonthly, or monthly pay periods.

When you start working for a company that delays payment, wages earned during the delay time will be held back. Suppose you start a job on Monday with the company described earlier. You will not receive a paycheck on your first Friday on the job. The wages you earn during this period will be paid to you on the following scheduled payday.

Suppose you decide to quit your job, and your last day of work is Friday. The company will owe you a paycheck on the next payday. It will include the wages earned since the last pay period.

Paychecks and Paycheck Deductions

Most companies pay their employees by check. Using checks helps companies keep records of what was paid and when it was paid.

A typical paycheck has a stub attached to it. A *paycheck stub* provides detailed information. It states your ***gross pay***. This is the total amount of money you earned during the pay period. It is figured by multiplying the number of hours you worked by your hourly wage. Suppose you worked 17.5 hours at a wage of $6.75 per hour. Your gross pay would be $118.13 (17.5 x $6.75 = $118.13).

A paycheck stub lists all paycheck deductions. These are amounts of money subtracted from your gross pay. Examples of deductions include the following:

- federal and state income taxes
- social security taxes
- medicare tax
- health insurance contributions
- union dues
- saving plans
- pensions
- uniforms
- loans
- charity contributions

The amount of money left after all deductions are taken from your gross pay is called your net pay. Your ***net pay*** is your take-home pay. In this example, the total deductions are $24.22 ($13.56 + $2.34 + $6.54 + $1.78 = $24.22). Your net pay is $93.91 ($118.13 - $24.22 = $93.91). See 23-2 for how the following deductions are shown on a typical paystub.

- $13.56 for federal income tax
- $2.34 for state income tax
- $6.54 for social security tax (FICA)
- $1.78 for medicare tax

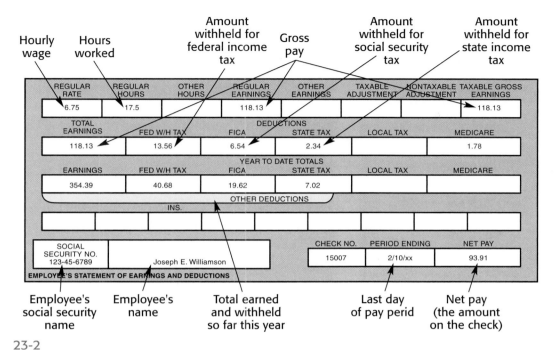

23-2

This important paperwork shows total earnings, deductions, and reasons for the deductions.

The W-4 Form

Each time you begin work with a new employer, you will fill out a *W-4 Form*. This form is also called an *Employee's Withholding Allowance Certificate*. It determines how much of your pay should be withheld for taxes.

The government allows taxpayers to claim certain allowances. Each allowance that you claim results in less tax taken from your pay. You may claim a personal allowance for yourself only if no one else can claim you as a dependent. Some taxpayers may claim additional allowances for age, blindness, and dependents. A *dependent* is a person who relies on the taxpayer for financial support, such as a child or nonworking adult.

gross pay
The total amount of money earned during a pay period.

net pay
The amount of money left after all deductions have been taken from the gross pay.

W-4 Form
Employee's withholding allowance certificate, a form filled out by an employee when beginning a new job. It determines how much of the employee's pay should be withheld for taxes.

dependent
A person, such as a child or nonworking adult, who relies on a taxpayer for financial support.

The W-4 Form is a two-part form. See 23-3. To fill it out, you generally follow these simple directions:

- Print or type your name in block 1 with your address directly below.
- Write your social security number in block 2.
- Check *single* in block 3.
- Enter a zero in block 5 to indicate that you are not claiming any allowances. (You cannot claim an allowance for yourself if a parent or guardian is claiming you as a dependent.)
- Sign your name and write the date on the appropriate line.

If you think you will owe taxes at the end of the year, you can enter an amount in block 6. Paying a little more each pay period is easier than paying a lot when your tax bill is due.

If you are married, have dependents, or have other sources of income, these directions may not apply to you. In these cases, complete a W-4 worksheet before filling out the form. (Brief worksheets also appear on other tax forms. Always be sure to fill them out to obtain the correct data.)

Your employer will compare your W-4 Form to withholding tables prepared by the government. Based on your income, your employer will determine how much money to withhold from each paycheck for income tax. The total amount withheld during the year should come close to your total tax bill for the year.

The W-2 Form

Every January, you should receive a *W-2 Form* from each employer that paid you wages in the previous year. The W-2 Form is also known as a *Wage and Tax Statement*. It states how much you were paid and how much of your income was withheld for taxes. An example is shown in 23-4.

When you receive your W-2 Forms, look at them carefully. You may want to compare them to your paycheck stubs. The information should be the same.

Keep your W-2 Forms in a safe place. You will need them to fill out your income tax return.

> **W-2 Form**
> Wage and tax statement, a form showing how much a worker was paid and how much income was withheld for taxes in a given year.

Form W-4 (2002)

Purpose. Complete Form W-4 so your employer can withhold the correct Federal income tax from your pay. Because your tax situation may change, you may want to refigure your withholding each year.

Exemption from withholding. If you are exempt, complete only lines 1, 2, 3, 4, and 7 and sign the form to validate it. Your exemption for 2002 expires February 16, 2003. See **Pub. 505,** Tax Withholding and Estimated Tax.

Note: You cannot claim exemption from withholding if **(a)** your income exceeds $750 and includes more than $250 of unearned income (e.g., interest and dividends) and **(b)** another person can claim you as a dependent on their tax return.

Basic instructions. If you are not exempt, complete the **Personal Allowances Worksheet** below. The worksheets on page 2 adjust your withholding allowances based on itemized deductions, certain credits, adjustments to

income, or two-earner/two-job situations. Complete all worksheets that apply. **However, you may claim fewer (or zero) allowances.**

Head of household. Generally, you may claim head of household filing status on your tax return only if you are unmarried and pay more than 50% of the costs of keeping up a home for yourself and your dependent(s) or other qualifying individuals. See line E below.

Tax credits. You can take projected tax credits into account in figuring your allowable number of withholding allowances. Credits for child or dependent care expenses and the child tax credit may be claimed using the **Personal Allowances Worksheet** below. See **Pub. 919,** How Do I Adjust My Tax Withholding? for information on converting your other credits into withholding allowances.

Nonwage income. If you have a large amount of nonwage income, such as interest or dividends, consider making estimated tax payments using **Form 1040-ES,** Estimated Tax for Individuals. Otherwise, you may owe additional tax.

Two earners/two jobs. If you have a working spouse or more than one job, figure the total number of allowances you are entitled to claim on all jobs using worksheets from only one Form W-4. Your withholding usually will be most accurate when all allowances are claimed on the Form W-4 for the highest paying job and zero allowances are claimed on the others.

Nonresident alien. If you are a nonresident alien, see the **Instructions for Form 8233** before completing this Form W-4.

Check your withholding. After your Form W-4 takes effect, use Pub. 919 to see how the dollar amount you are having withheld compares to your projected total tax for 2002. See Pub. 919, especially if you used the **Two-Earner/Two-Job Worksheet** on page 2 and your earnings exceed $125,000 (Single) or $175,000 (Married).

Recent name change? If your name on line 1 differs from that shown on your social security card, call 1-800-772-1213 for a new social security card.

Personal Allowances Worksheet (Keep for your records.)

A Enter "1" for **yourself** if no one else can claim you as a dependent . . . . **A** _____

B Enter "1" if: { • You are single and have only one job; or
• You are married, have only one job, and your spouse does not work; or
• Your wages from a second job or your spouse's wages (or the total of both) are $1,000 or less. } . **B** _____

C Enter "1" for your **spouse.** But, you may choose to enter "-0-" if you are married and have either a working spouse or more than one job. (Entering "-0-" may help you avoid having too little tax withheld.) . . . . **C** _____

D Enter number of **dependents** (other than your spouse or yourself) you will claim on your tax return . . . . **D** _____

E Enter "1" if you will file as **head of household** on your tax return (see conditions under **Head of household** above) . **E** _____

F Enter "1" if you have at least $1,500 of **child or dependent care expenses** for which you plan to claim a credit . **F** _____

(**Note:** Do **not** include child support payments. See **Pub. 503,** Child and Dependent Care Expenses, for details.)

G **Child Tax Credit** (including additional child tax credit):
• If your total income will be between $15,000 and $42,000 ($20,000 and $65,000 if married), enter "1" for each eligible child plus **1** additional if you have three to five eligible children or **2** additional if you have six or more eligible children.
• If your total income will be between $42,000 and $80,000 ($65,000 and $115,000 if married), enter "1" if you have one or two eligible children, "2" if you have three eligible children, "3" if you have four eligible children, or "4" if you have five or more eligible children. **G** _____

H Add lines A through G and enter total here. **Note:** This may be different from the number of exemptions you claim on your tax return. ▶ **H** _____

For accuracy, complete all worksheets that apply.
• If you plan to **itemize or claim adjustments to income** and want to reduce your withholding, see the **Deductions and Adjustments Worksheet** on page 2.
• If you have **more than one job** or are **married and you and your spouse both work** and the combined earnings from all jobs exceed $35,000, see the **Two-Earner/Two-Job Worksheet** on page 2 to avoid having too little tax withheld.
• If **neither** of the above situations applies, **stop here** and enter the number from line H on line 5 of Form W-4 below.

- - - - - - - - - - - - - - - - - - - **Cut here and give Form W-4 to your employer. Keep the top part for your records.** - - - - - - - - - - - - - - - - - - -

Form **W-4**
Department of the Treasury
Internal Revenue Service

Employee's Withholding Allowance Certificate
▶ For Privacy Act and Paperwork Reduction Act Notice, see page 2.

OMB No. 1545-0010

2002

1 Type or print your first name and middle initial Last name		2 Your social security number
Joseph E. Williamson		123 45 6789

Home address (number and street or rural route)	3 ☑ Single ☐ Married ☐ Married, but withhold at higher Single rate.
438 South Deerfield Drive	Note: If married, but legally separated, or spouse is a nonresident alien, check the "Single" box.
City or town, state, and ZIP code	4 If your last name differs from that on your social security card,
Pleasant View, IL 62935	check here. You must call 1-800-772-1213 for a new card. ▶ ☐

5	Total number of allowances you are claiming (from line **H** above **or** from the applicable worksheet on page 2)	**5**	0
6	Additional amount, if any, you want withheld from each paycheck	**6** $	
7	I claim exemption from withholding for 2002, and I certify that I meet **both** of the following conditions for exemption:		

• Last year I had a right to a refund of **all** Federal income tax withheld because I had **no** tax liability **and**
• This year I expect a refund of **all** Federal income tax withheld because I expect to have **no** tax liability.
If you meet both conditions, write "Exempt" here . . . . ▶ **7**

Under penalties of perjury, I certify that I am entitled to the number of withholding allowances claimed on this certificate, or I am entitled to claim exempt status.

Employee's signature
(Form is not valid unless you sign it.) ▶ *Joseph E. Williamson*   Date ▶ *January 4, 2002*

8 Employer's name and address (Employer: Complete lines 8 and 10 only if sending to the IRS.)	9 Office code (optional)	10 Employer identification number

Cat. No. 10220Q

23-3

A W-4 Form tells an employer the correct amount of federal income tax to withhold from an employee's pay.

a Control number	22222	Void ☐	For Official Use Only ▶ OMB No. 1545-0008		

b Employer identification number			1 Wages, tips, other compensation	2 Federal income tax withheld
98-7654321			$ 7231.13	$ 499.32

c Employer's name, address, and ZIP code		3 Social security wages	4 Social security tax withheld
Fill-It-Up Service Station 273 South Main Street Pleasant View, IL 62935		$ 7231.13	$ 528.00

5 Medicare wages and tips $ 7231.13   6 Medicare tax withheld $ 108.45

7 Social security tips $ 8 Allocated tips $

d Employee's social security number
123-45-6789

9 Advance EIC payment $ 10 Dependent care benefits $

e Employee's first name and initial   Last name

11 Nonqualified plans $ 12a See instructions for box 12 $

Joseph E. Williamson
438 South Deerfield Drive
Pleasant View, IL 62935

13 Statutory employee ☐ Retirement plan ☐ Third-party sick pay ☐   12b $

14 Other   12c $

12d $

f Employee's address and ZIP code

15 State	Employer's state ID number	16 State wages, tips, etc.	17 State income tax	18 Local wages, tips, etc.	19 Local income tax	20 Locality name
IL	987654321	$ 7231.13	$ 198.00	$	$	
		$	$	$	$	

Form **W-2** Wage and Tax Statement   **2001**   Department of the Treasury- Internal Revenue Service

Copy A For Social Security Administration- Send this entire page with Form W-3 to the Social Security Administration; photocopies are **not** acceptable.

Cat. No. 10134D

For Privacy Act and Paperwork Reduction Act Notice, see separate instructions.

Do Not Cut, Fold, or Staple Forms on This Page — Do Not Cut, Fold, or Staple Forms on This Page

23-4

A W-2 Form states an employee's earnings and tax withholdings for a year.

Taxes

One of the responsibilities you have as a wage earner is to pay taxes. The government gets money needed to run the country through taxes. Your tax money pays for government services. Tax money supports public education. It pays for government-assistance programs and certain health services. It pays for social security and veterans' benefits. Tax money also supports the nation's armed forces and police and fire departments.

The U.S. Congress passes federal tax laws. The *Internal Revenue Service* (*IRS*) is the agency that enforces the tax laws and collects taxes.

State and local governments work in similar ways. Legislatures pass tax laws. Revenue agencies enforce the laws and collect the taxes.

There are many different types of taxes. Two types of taxes that are deducted from your paycheck are income tax and social security tax.

Income Tax

As a wage earner, you have to pay income tax. *Income tax* is a tax on all forms of earnings. The federal government, most states, and many cities place a tax on income. It is figured as a percentage of the money you earn each year from wages, interest, and investments.

Your employer withholds tax from your paychecks. It is sent to the government. By April 15 of each year, you must file a tax return for the previous year. As you complete your income tax return, you may find that you have more tax to pay. On the other hand, you may find that too much was withheld during the year. In that case, you would receive a refund from the government.

Social Security Tax

Social security taxes are federal taxes based on income. Almost all workers in the United States pay them. People pay social security taxes while they work so they can collect monthly payments after they stop working.

Your employer deducts social security taxes from your paychecks. The deductions appear on your paycheck stubs under the heading *FICA*, which means *Federal Insurance Contributions Act.*

Social security taxes are figured as a percentage of your earnings. Whatever you pay, your employer makes a matching payment. For instance, suppose $5.26 is deducted from your paycheck for FICA. Your employer would also pay $5.26. Your employer would send a total of $10.52 to the IRS as your FICA contribution.

As you work and make contributions, you earn work credits. Later, if you become disabled or retire, you will receive benefits in the form of monthly payments. If you die, your survivors will receive monthly payments. *Medicare* is another kind of social security benefit. It is a form of hospital and medical insurance.

Internal Revenue Service (IRS)
The agency that enforces federal tax laws and collects taxes.

income tax
A tax on all forms of earnings.

Federal Insurance Contributions Act (FICA)
An act that allows the federal government to reserve a percentage of a paycheck for social security tax.

23-5
Filing taxes can be a hassle if a person waits until the last minute or misplaces important papers.

Filing a Federal Income Tax Return

Your federal tax return must be filed by April 15 each year. If you filed taxes last year, you should receive an income tax form in the mail by the end of December. This gives you enough time to prepare your return and file it by April 15. See 23-5.

When filing your first tax return, you will need to get a form from a local library, bank, post office, or IRS office. You should automatically receive a form in the mail each year thereafter. If you move, however, the form may not be forwarded to you. Failing to receive a form in the mail is no excuse for not filing a return. As a wage earner, it is your responsibility to prepare and file a tax return on time.

Form 1040EZ

Form 1040EZ is the simplest form to complete for filing an income tax return. As a new employee, you probably meet all of Form 1040EZ's conditions. If not, you must report your income to the IRS on another type of form. You will probably be able to use a Form 1040A or Form 1040. Each form includes instructions that explain which form to use.

With the example of a high school student, Joseph E. Williamson, you can see how to complete a Form 1040EZ. Joseph Williamson worked part-time as a gas station attendant. Income tax was withheld according to his W-4 Form. At the end of the year, Joe received copies of Form W-2 from his employer. It showed that $499.32 was withheld for income tax from Joe's total earnings of $7,231.13.

Joe can use Form 1040EZ to file his income tax return because he is single and has no dependents. In addition to his wages, Joe's savings account earned $55.44 in interest. See 23-6.

Form **1040EZ**

Department of the Treasury—Internal Revenue Service

Income Tax Return for Single and Joint Filers With No Dependents (99) **2001**

OMB No. 1545-0675

Label (See page 12.)
Use the IRS label. Otherwise, please print or type.

Your first name and initial   Joseph E.   Last name   Williamson

If a joint return, spouse's first name and initial   Last name

Home address (number and street). If you have a P.O. box, see page 12.   438 South Deerfield Drive   Apt. no.

City, town or post office, state, and ZIP code. If you have a foreign address, see page 12.   Pleasant View, IL 62935

Your social security number 123 45 6789

Spouse's social security number

▲ **Important!** ▲
You **must** enter your SSN(s) above.

Presidential Election Campaign (page 12)

Note. Checking "Yes" will not change your tax or reduce your refund.
Do you, or spouse if a joint return, want $3 to go to this fund? ▶

You ☐Yes ☑No   Spouse ☐Yes ☐No

Income
Attach Form(s) W-2 here.
Enclose, but do not attach, any payment.

1 Total wages, salaries, and tips. This should be shown in box 1 of your W-2 form(s). Attach your W-2 form(s).   1   7,231

2 Taxable interest. If the total is over $400, you cannot use Form 1040EZ.   2   55

3 Unemployment compensation, qualified state tuition program earnings, and Alaska Permanent Fund dividends (see page 14).   3

4 Add lines 1, 2, and 3. This is your **adjusted gross income.**   4   7,286

Note. You **must** check Yes or No.

5 Can your parents (or someone else) claim you on their return?
☐ **Yes.** Enter amount from worksheet on back.
☐ **No.** If **single,** enter 7,450.00. If **married,** enter 13,400.00. See back for explanation.   5   4,400

6 Subtract line 5 from line 4. If line 5 is larger than line 4, enter 0. This is your **taxable income.** ▶   6   2,886

Credits, payments, and tax

7 Rate reduction credit. See the worksheet on page 14.   7

8 Enter your Federal income tax withheld from box 2 of your W-2 form(s).   8   499

9a **Earned income credit (EIC).** See page 15.   9a

b Nontaxable earned income.   9b

10 Add lines 7, 8, and 9a. These are your **total credits and payments.** ▶   10   499

11 **Tax.** If you checked "Yes" on line 5, see page 20. Otherwise, use the amount on **line 6 above** to find your tax in the tax table on pages 24–28 of the booklet. Then, enter the tax from the table on this line.   11   448

Refund
Have it directly deposited! See page 20 and fill in 12b, 12c, and 12d.

12a If line 10 is larger than line 11, subtract line 11 from line 10. This is your **refund.** ▶   12a   51

b Routing number

c Type: ☐ Checking ☐ Savings

d Account number

Amount you owe

13 If line 11 is larger than line 10, subtract line 10 from line 11. This is the **amount you owe.** See page 21 for details on how to pay. ▶   13

Third party designee

Do you want to allow another person to discuss this return with the IRS (see page 22)? ☐ **Yes.** Complete the following. ☑**No**

Designee's name ▶   Phone no. ▶ (   )   Personal identification number (PIN)

Sign here
Joint return? See page 11.
Keep a copy for your records.

Under penalties of perjury, I declare that I have examined this return, and to the best of my knowledge and belief, it is true, correct, and accurately lists all amounts and sources of income I received during the tax year. Declaration of preparer (other than the taxpayer) is based on all information of which the preparer has any knowledge.

Your signature   Joseph E. Williamson   Date 3-16   Your occupation   Service attendant   Daytime phone number (708) 555-2121

Spouse's signature. If a joint return, **both** must sign.   Date   Spouse's occupation

Paid preparer's use only

Preparer's signature ▶   Date   Check if self-employed ☐   Preparer's SSN or PTIN

Firm's name (or yours if self-employed), address, and ZIP code ▶   EIN   Phone no. (   )

For Disclosure, Privacy Act, and Paperwork Reduction Act Notice, see page 23.   Cat. No. 11329W   Form **1040EZ** (2001)

23-6

Form 1040EZ takes a minimum of time and effort to complete.

Form 1040EZ
The simplest income tax return form to complete.

Completing Your Tax Return

You should read all instructions carefully before beginning your tax return. If you have questions about the instructions, you should seek help. You can ask parents or guardians for help. Teachers and counselors are also good sources of information. The IRS provides taxpayers with assistance, no matter which form they use. Simply contact the IRS at their Web site (irs.gov) or visit their local office.

Joe carefully read all the instructions on Form 1040 EZ. He felt confident that he could complete the form without additional help. (Refer back to Figure 23-6 frequently as you follow the steps described on this and the next two pages.)

Joe printed his full name, address, and social security number in this section. This is Joe's first year to file a tax return. Next year he will receive his 1040EZ from the IRS in the mail with a printed label containing this information. Joe will simply transfer that label to this section of the form and correct any errors.

Joe checked the *No* box for the Presidential Election Campaign Fund. This fund was established by Congress to help pay the campaign expenses of presidential candidates. If you pay income tax, you may contribute three tax dollars to this fund by checking the box.

Filing Status

Joe did not check either box under *Spouse* because he is single. If Joe were married and filing a joint return, he would checked *Yes*. Also, he would have filled in the line under his name.

Report Your Income

Line 1. Joe wrote in the total he received in wages, salaries, and tips. (Tips include cash, merchandise, or services you receive directly from customers or amounts an employer pays on behalf of charge customers.) The amount shown in Box 1 of his W-2 Form is $7,231.13. Joe wrote in $7,231 because taxpayers are allowed to round off figures to the nearest dollar. If Joe had more than one job, he would have included earnings from all of his employers.

Line 2. Joe wrote in the rounded amount of total interest he received. In this case, he earned $55.44 from his savings account. You should receive an interest statement from your bank and any other institution that pays you interest.

Line 3. Joe skipped Line 3. He would have completed this line if he had been laid off and received unemployment payments. Unemployment payments must be claimed as income.

Line 4. Joe added Lines 2 and 3—the $7,231.00 from wages plus the $55 from interest on his savings. Note that Joe wrote $7,286.00 on Line 4.

Line 5. Joe lives at home, so his parents claim him as a dependent. He checked the *Yes* box. Then he turned to the worksheet on the back of Form 1040EZ as directed. He completed the steps of the worksheet and calculated the figure of $4,400. This he wrote on Line 5

Line 6. Joe computed the amount of income he had to pay tax on by subtracting Line 5 from Line 4 ($7,286 − $4,400 = $2,886). Joe entered $2,886 on Line 6.

Payments and Taxes

Line 7. Joe checked the instructions for *Rate reduction credit.* He determined that it did not pertain to him.

Line 8. Joe looked at the W-2 Form he received from his employer. Box 2 of that form showed that his employer withheld $499.00 income tax. He wrote $499.00 on Line 7.

Line 9. Joe read the instructions for *Earned income credit (EIC).* Joe found that he was not eligible for the credit because he is single and his parents were claiming him as a dependent.

Line 10. Joe added the figures on Lines 7 and 9. He wrote $499.00.

Line 11. Joe is asked to look at Line 5 on his form. Joe found $2,886 on Line 5. This is Joe's taxable income. He then looked in the back of his 1040EZ booklet and found the tax table that applied to single taxpayers. The amount of tax due for $2,886 was $448. He wrote $448 on Line 11.

Refund or Amount You Owe

Line 12a. Joe compared Line 10 with Line 11. Because Line 10 is larger than Line 11, Joe subtracted the amount on Line 11 from the amount on Line 10 ($499 − $448 = $51).

Joe can receive a refund in two ways. He can get a check from the U.S. Department of the Treasury. The check will be mailed directly to Joe. Joe can choose to have a direct deposit made to his account. If Joe chooses the direct deposit, he must complete Lines 12b, 12c, and 12d.

Line 13. If Line 11 had been larger than Line 10, Joe would have owed tax. He would have subtracted Line 9 from Line 10. He would have entered that amount on Line 13. That would be the amount of additional tax Joe would have to pay. Then, he would have to attach a check for that amount to his tax form. However, since Joe was entitled to a refund, he did not write anything on this line.

Sign Your Return

Joe marked *No* in the block titled *Third party designee* because he had prepared his own return. If the IRS had questions, he was the best person to contact, not someone else. He simply left the rest of the block empty.

Joe read the statement, "Under penalties of perjury, I declare that I have examined this return, and to the best of my knowledge and belief, it is true, correct, and accurately lists all amounts and sources of income I received during the tax year." He followed the instructions carefully. He went back and rechecked his figures. To the best of his knowledge, Joe had correctly completed his return. He signed his name and wrote the date on the form. He also wrote in his occupation and phone number.

Finally, Joe attached his Copy B of Form W-2 to his Form 1040EZ. He mailed it to the Internal Revenue Service Center that serves his area.

As you've seen, filing a tax return using Form 1040EZ is not difficult if you carefully follow each step. A checklist appears in the instructions for Form 1040EZ to help taxpayers avoid making common mistakes. See 23-7.

State Income Tax

If your state collects income tax, that return is due at the same time as the federal income tax return. Since each state's form is different, you need to obtain one from your own state. Follow the directions provided.

Tax Penalties

The IRS has established certain penalties for filing late without permission, lying, and cheating. Take the time to do your taxes correctly and on time. If you need assistance, ask a family member or tax preparer to help you.

Don't panic if you are audited. An audit is simply the government's way of checking your return. The auditor may find that your return is correct. On the other hand, the auditor may find a mistake. Your may have made a math error, or perhaps you forgot to include interest earned on a savings account. Honest mistakes like these could be settled easily. You would have to pay any tax you owe and perhaps a penalty for late payment. For intentional errors and fraud, major penalties can be applied.

Checklist for 1040EZ Filers

1. Did you complete all the personal information on your form? If you received a label from the IRS, is the information correct?

2. Is your social security number correct? Did you write it in the blocks provided on the form?

3. Did you attach all your W-2 Forms and 1099 Forms to the left margin of your return?

4. Did you check your math? Errors in your math can delay your return.

5. Did you use the amount from Line 6 to find your tax in the tax tables?

6. Did you enter the tax you found in the tax tables on Line 11?

7. Did you check the correct box on Line 5? Can anyone else claim you as a dependent?

8. Did you enter the amount due as a refund on Line 12a? If you owe additional taxes, did you include a check or money order with your return?

9. Did you sign and date your return?

10. If you did not receive an envelope or label from the IRS, did you mail your return to the nearest IRS Center?

11. Do you want an electronic deposit of your refund? If so, did you provide both your routing number and your account number?

23-7

Asking these questions helps taxpayers avoid making common errors when completing Form 1040EZ.

Summary

When you accept a job and start working, you need to understand your paycheck. Some of the money you earn cannot be taken home. The stub attached to your paycheck will list deductions from your earnings for taxes and other expenses.

When you start a new job, you should fill out a W-4 Form. It will determine how much of your pay should be withheld for taxes. Each January, you should receive W-2 Forms from each of the places you worked during the previous year. The forms tell how much you were paid and how much of your income was withheld for taxes.

One of the responsibilities of wage earners is to file income tax returns. Form 1040EZ is the simplest to complete. Whatever form you use, you must file your return by April 15. If your state has an income tax, that return is due at the same time. There are penalties for failing to file, filing late without permission, and filing a false return.

Reviewing the Chapter

1. In many companies, why is payday not the last day of the pay period?
2. Explain the difference between gross pay and net pay.
3. List five types of paycheck deductions.
4. What is another name for the W-4 Form? What is its purpose?
5. What is another name for the W-2 Form? In general, what information does it give?
6. Name five ways tax money is used.
7. Who passes federal tax laws? Who enforces them?
8. Which of the following statements is true?

   A. Social security taxes are federal taxes based on income.

   B. On paycheck stubs, deductions for social security taxes appear under the heading FICA.

   C. Whatever employees pay in social security taxes, their employers pay matching amounts.

   D. All of the above.

9. What is the deadline for filing a federal income tax return?
10. If you are a wage earner and do *not* receive a tax return form in the mail, what should you do?

Building Your Foundation Skills

1. Poll several businesses to find out when their paydays occur. (Inform them that you are requesting the information for a class project.) Share your findings in class.

2. Ask parents and friends about the different types of deductions made from their paychecks. Discuss their answers in class.

3. Research how tax money is collected and spent by your state or local government. Design posters to illustrate your findings. Display the posters throughout your school in April.

4. Prepare a presentation on how to file Form 1040EZ. Your presentation might include the use of skits and/or visual aids.

5. Ask an IRS auditor to talk to your class. Be prepared to ask questions about tax forms and audits.

Building Your Workplace Competencies

Research the social security system using the Internet to find out as much information as possible. Work with two or three of your classmates. Together decide who will do which tasks. Find out when social security began and why. Who is eligible for social security payments today? Why do a growing number of people believe that the system should have an overhaul? Present your key findings to the class in charts and/or posters. *(This activity develops competence with interpersonal skills, information, systems, and technology.)*

Budgets

Objectives

After studying this chapter, you will be able to

- identify sources of income.

- list fixed and flexible expenses that may be included in a budget.

- develop and evaluate a spending calendar.

- prepare a want list with both short-range and long-range goals.

- plan a budget.

Words to Know

budget
fixed expense
flexible expense

The Need for Money Management

You need money to buy the things you need and want. The amount of money you earn affects what you are able to buy. However, how you spend your money can have just as much effect as how much you earn.

No matter how much money they earn, some people find it difficult to live on what they make. The more they earn, the more they spend. On the other hand, others seem to have few money problems. They usually have enough money for what they need. They are even able to save money.

You must learn to manage your money wisely in order to live on what you earn. If you do not, you will probably have money problems. Wise planning will help you live within your income. Planning will help you buy what you really need and still have money left to get the things you want. See 24-1.

A plan for the use or management of money is called a ***budget***. Now is a good time to start following a budget. Learn to manage the money you earn now. As your income grows, you will be able to adjust your money management decisions.

24-1
People need money to buy food and other basic daily needs.

| **budget** |
| A plan for the use or management of money. |

Sources of Income

The first step in making a budget is to identify your sources of income. You need to know how much money you can expect to receive within an average week, month, and year. Knowing your expected income will help you plan how to manage your money.

Start identifying your sources of income by listing the money you are sure to receive. If you work, you should list your average monthly take-home pay. Include tips you receive on a regular basis in your budget plan. Since no two days or weeks are exactly alike, you cannot always accurately estimate an exact figure on tips. Use a conservative average and plan on a minimum amount.

Some additional sources of income are bonuses, commissions, and overtime pay, which are offered by some jobs. Interest on savings and dividends from investments are also sources of income. Cash gifts for birthdays and special occasions count as income, too. Such sources of income generally vary from month to month. Including them in a budget may be risky. It is safer to base a budget on sure and steady sources of income.

Types of Expenses

The next step in making a budget is to list your expenses. Expenses are usually described in terms relating to how often they are paid. If you pay bus fare every day, it is a daily expense. Many expenses are paid weekly or monthly. See 24-2. Quarterly expenses are paid four times a year. *Semiannual* expenses are paid twice a year. *Annual* expenses are paid once a year.

24-2

Paying back the loan for a new or used car usually involves several years of monthly payments.

Fixed and flexible are other terms used to describe expenses. A *fixed expense* is a set amount of money due on a set date. Examples of fixed expenses include the following:

- rent or mortgage payments
- insurance premiums
- tuition
- membership dues
- property taxes
- installment payments (for a car loan, major purchase, or credit card balance)

As a rule, fixed expenses must be paid when due. They cannot be changed, delayed, or reduced. Therefore, they are considered first when making a budget. *Flexible expenses* are expenses that vary in amount. The most common flexible expenses include the following:

- food
- clothing
- home furnishings
- utilities
- transportation
- medical needs
- savings
- recreation and entertainment

You have more control over flexible expenses than fixed expenses. Some flexible expenses vary with your wants. You can often adjust how much money you spend for these expenses. For instance, suppose you want to eat in nice restaurants. This will make your food expense higher than eating at home. However, if you adjust this expense by eating more meals at home, you can save money. This money might be used for another flexible expense, such as clothing or recreation.

As you manage your money, try to keep your fixed expenses to a minimum. Plan ahead and save for major purchases instead of making installment payments. This will keep

fixed expense
Something for which a set amount of money must be paid regularly, such as rent, insurance, or tuition.

flexible expense
An expense that varies in amount and does not occur on a regular basis, such as food, transportation, or entertainment.

your money available for flexible expenses. As a result, you will have more control over the use of your money.

How Do You Spend Your Money?

Do you know where your money goes? How much of your income goes toward fixed expenses? How much goes toward flexible expenses? In order to use your money wisely, you must know how you spend it.

A Spending Calendar

Use a spending calendar like the one shown in 24-3 to find out how you spend your money. Start the calendar when you receive your next paycheck. Record all your expenses for each day on your calendar. Total your expenses for each week. Use the column at the far right to record your weekly totals.

How you spend your money will vary from week to week. No two weeks of spending are exactly alike. Using a spending calendar for a full month will help you get a pattern of your spending habits. At the end of the month, you will have a good idea of where your money was spent. You will have taken a big step toward controlling your money. This is how to make your money work for you.

Spending Calendar

Sunday	Monday	Tuesday	Wednesday	Thursday	Friday	Saturday	Weekly Total
3 Church $2.00	**4** Lunch $1.00	**5** Lunch $1.65 stamps $5.00	**6** Lunch $1.25	**7** Lunch $1.00	**8** Lunch $1.00 Football Ticket $3.00 Pizza $5.20	**9** Hamburger, fries, drink $2.14	**$23.24**
10 Church $2.00	**11** Lunch $1.25	**12** Lunch $1.25	**13** Lunch $1.00 Birthday gift $14.43	**14** Lunch $1.25	**15** Lunch $1.00	**16** New shirt $17.11	**$39.29**
17 Church $2.00 Movie $3.00	**18** Lunch $1.00	**19** Lunch $1.00	**20** Lunch $1.25	**21** Lunch $0.90	**22** Lunch $1.25	**23** CD $12.44	**$22.84**
24 Church $2.00 Ice cream $1.07	**25**	**26** Lunch $1.25 Greeting Cards $3.48	**27** Lunch $1.25	**28** Lunch $1.00 Haircut $18.00	**29** Lunch $1.00	**30** Pizza $7.43 Movie $5.50	**$41.98**

24-3

A spending calendar can help you keep track of what you do with your money.

How Do You Want to Spend Your Money?

A good money management system helps you use your money to get what you want. Do you know what you want? Are you putting your money to work for you? Are you using it to reach your goals?

A "Want" List

As you prepare to plan a budget, develop a list of things you want. Make two columns on your "want" list. Label one *now* and the other *later*. Estimate the cost of each item you list to help you plan your savings goals.

Your *now* column is for those things you want quickly. You should be able to obtain these items in a year or less. Such items might include new clothing, membership at a sports club, and a CD player.

Your *later* column is for your long-range goals. This column is for items you want that may take more than a year to get. This list might include continuing your education, buying a car or a home, and taking a trip to Europe. See 24-4.

Look at your completed "want" list. Remember that you can't afford to buy everything at once. You will need to set priorities for your spending. What is most important to you now and in the future? What can you afford to buy with the money you have now or will earn? What can you do without? What don't you need? How can you trim expenses to get what you want? Could you delay some purchases? Are you beginning to think about opening a savings account?

By asking yourself these questions, you are developing money management skills. You are learning how to make your money work for you.

"Want" List			
Now	**Cost**	**Later**	**Cost**
Golf clubs	$225	video camera	$ 500
35 mm camera	280	computer	2,000
answering machine	75	car	11,000

24-4

Deciding what things are important to you now and in the future will help you set goals for budget planning.

Planning a Budget

A budget helps you make wise money decisions. It is your personal guide to spending and saving. You develop it and make it work.

A review of your spending calendar can help you plan a budget. It shows how you are spending your money. It helps you see your options for flexible expenses. Your spending calendar helps you identify areas where you can make changes in your use of money.

A review of your "want" list can also help you plan a budget. It gives you direction. It helps you focus on your goals.

You don't need to account for every penny in your budget. Instead, work with estimates and follow this guide:

1. Estimate your income.

2. List your fixed expenses.

3. Review your short-range and long-range goals.

4. Estimate your flexible expenses.

5. Set aside a portion of each paycheck for savings and miscellaneous expenses.

Different people plan for different time periods in their budgets. Some plan weekly budgets. Some who are paid every two weeks set up two-week budgets. Others prefer monthly budgets because most of their fixed expenses are paid monthly.

How you set up your budget is up to you. Just be sure to be consistent. If you set up a monthly budget, convert all income and expenses to monthly figures. The following formulas may help you:

- Weekly income ÷ 52 weeks = yearly income.
- Yearly income ÷ 12 = monthly income.
- Quarterly expense ÷ 3 = monthly expense.
- Semiannual expense ÷ 6 = monthly expense.
- Annual expense ÷ 12 = monthly expense.

Once you set up a budget, make a sincere effort to follow it. Review your budget often. Make adjustments for changes in income or expenses.

Follow the budget-planning guide in 24-5 to design your budget. Remember, this is your money-management plan. Your budget should help you reach your goals. It should not force you to live by strict rules that do not work for you. Be patient. Learning to use a budget takes time, but it is worth the effort. A workable budget will help you manage your money.

Monthly Budgeting Guide

Estimated Income

Net income (wages)	$1180
Tips	
Other_____	
Total	$1180

Estimated Fixed Expenses

Housing

Rent or mortgage payments	$350
Maintenance fees	
Other *GARAGE RENTAL*	20

Insurance Premiums

Life	
Health/medical	
Automobile	9
Home	
Other_____	

Debts and Obligations

Automobile loan payments	120
Other installment loan payments	45
Contributions	30
Tuition	
Membership dues	8
Other_____	

Taxes and Licenses

Property Taxes	
Automobile license plates	4
Other *VEHICLE STICKER*	2
Total	$648

Estimated Flexible Expenses

Food

At home	$80
Away from home	$40

Clothing and Accessories

New clothes	$50
Cleaning and laundry	15
Accessories	10
Grooming aids	20

Household

Home furnishings	5
Maintenance and repair	
Gas	10
Electricity	35
Water	
Telephone	30

Transportation

Gasoline	40
Automobile maintenance	20
Public transportation	

Medical Needs

Doctor	3
Dentist	4
Other_____	

Savings

Savings account	
Bonds	
Other_____	

Recreation and Entertainment

Movies	12
Vacation	50
Sport events	
Books and magazines	
Other_____	
Total	$479

Summary

Total estimated income	$1180
Total estimated expenses ($648 fixed + $479 flexible)	-1127
Balance (income minus expenses)	$53

24-5
To have a workable budget, the total estimated income must be equal to, or greater than, the total estimated expenses.

Summary

Learning to manage money is an important skill. No matter how much money you earn, it may not be enough if you don't use it wisely.

A plan for the use of money is called a budget. Its purpose is to help you manage your money so you can reach your goals. To design a budget, you must know your total income and total expenses. To have a workable budget, your income must be equal to or greater than your expenses.

A spending calendar and a want list will help you design a budget that will work for you. They will help you see your options and focus on your goals.

Reviewing the Chapter

1. Name five sources of income.
2. List five fixed expenses.
3. List five flexible expenses.
4. True or false. You have more control over fixed expenses than flexible expenses.
5. Why should you try to keep fixed expenses to a minimum?
6. What is the benefit of developing and using a spending calendar?
7. How can a "want" list help you plan a budget?
8. List five steps to use as a guide for setting up a budget.
9. Convert each of the following amounts to monthly figures:
   A. weekly income of $150
   B. quarterly expense of $120
   C. semiannual expense of $60
   D. annual expense of $72
10. What is the purpose of planning and using a budget?

Building Your Foundation Skills

1. Write a fictional story about money management skills. If the character has money problems, explain why and suggest solutions. If the character has no money problems, describe the management techniques he or she uses to achieve money-management success.

2. Ask a financial counselor to talk to your class about money management and budgets. Be prepared to ask questions.

3. Collect several printed budget forms. Discuss their usefulness in class.

4. Discuss options that are generally available for handling the flexible expenses of a budget.

Building Your Workplace Competencies

Following the examples in this chapter, develop a spending calendar, "want" list, and monthly budgeting guide. Begin by creating a spending calendar that describes and itemizes everything you buy for one month. Include short-term and long-term goals in your "want" list. With that information, prepare a monthly budgeting guide that addresses your income, expenses, and selected "wants" for which you plan to begin saving. Use a calculator to total and check your figures. Also estimate when you believe you will achieve each of the short-term and long-term goals in your "want" list. Describe in a one-page report what you learned from this exercise. *(This activity develops competence with resources, information, systems, and technology.)*

Checking Accounts

Objectives

After studying this chapter, you will be able to

- list factors to consider when selecting a financial institution.

- explain how to open a checking account and make a deposit.

- demonstrate how to write a check and endorse it.

- explain how to balance a checkbook.

- describe four special types of checks.

Words to Know

check
overdraw
deposit slip
endorse
bank statement
certified check
cashier's check
money order
traveler's check

The Convenience of Checking

A ***check*** is a written order to pay someone. It instructs a bank to take money from the checking account of the person writing the check. The amount specified on the check is paid to the party named on the check. See 25-1.

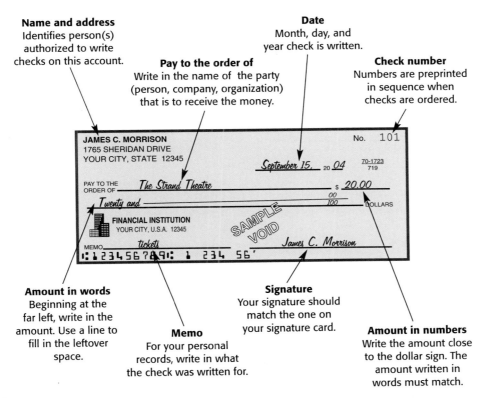

Name and address
Identifies person(s) authorized to write checks on this account.

Date
Month, day, and year check is written.

Pay to the order of
Write in the name of the party (person, company, organization) that is to receive the money.

Check number
Numbers are preprinted in sequence when checks are ordered.

Amount in words
Beginning at the far left, write in the amount. Use a line to fill in the leftover space.

Memo
For your personal records, write in what the check was written for.

Signature
Your signature should match the one on your signature card.

Amount in numbers
Write the amount close to the dollar sign. The amount written in words must match.

25-1
Checks allow people to transfer money without handling cash.

A checking account is a money management tool that helps you keep a record of your expenses. A checking account is also a safe place to keep your money. If a check is lost or stolen, you can stop payment on it. To stop payment on a check, you should contact your bank and fill out a form. You will need to pay a fee, which may be $25 or more.

check
A written order instructing a bank to take a specified amount of money out of the account on which the check is drawn and give it to the person whose name appears on the check.

You can pay your bills through the mail by check, and your canceled checks serve as proof of payment. Never send cash through the mail. If cash is lost or stolen, the money is gone.

Where to Open an Account

The first step in opening a checking account is to select a financial institution. *Commercial banks* offer a full range of services to both individuals and corporations. *Savings and loan associations* also offer a variety of services to individuals. *Credit unions* offer services to certain groups of people, such as employee groups.

When choosing a financial institution, consider the following factors:

- convenience
- services
- types of accounts
- fees

Shopping for a financial institution is much like shopping for a CD player or car. You would want to compare the features of several before making a choice.

Convenience

A convenient financial institution is one that is near your home or workplace. This would allow you to bank on your lunch hour or on your way to or from work. If the institution has branch offices, it provides even more convenience. You can deposit or withdraw money at any branch office. Therefore, you might find it convenient to have a branch where you shop or spend leisure time.

Another aspect of convenience is its hours. It should be open at times when you can get there. It may have early, late, or Saturday hours.

Services

Financial institutions offer a variety of checking and savings accounts as well as other services. See 25-2. If certain services are important to you, find out which institutions offer them. Compare services before making your choice. Service might include the following:

- automated teller machines (ATMs)
- drive-up banking
- credit card services

- cash cards
- debit cards
- loans

25-2

An automated teller machine is one of the many services offered by most financial institutions.

- safe-deposit boxes
- cashier's checks
- traveler's checks
- certified checks
- money orders
- overdraft protection

Many new services have been added to bank offerings. Several of these services involve the use of cards, similar to credit cards. In some cases, these cards can be used at cash terminals to obtain money from your account. At other times they can be used like cash. Other types of cards, called *debit cards*, take money directly from your bank account when you make a purchase.

These cards offer a great deal of convenience. However, these cards also make it easy for some people to overspend. You must have enough in your account to cover debit card purchases. If you **overdraw** your account, you spend more than is in your account. When you overdraw, you can be charged high interest rates as well as fees.

overdraw
To write a check for more money than what is in the account.

Types of Accounts

As a single person, you will probably open an *individual account*. Only your signature can be used to authorize a check. When you are married, you may want to open a *joint account*. This type of account permits either of the owners to sign a check.

Some checking accounts pay interest. An *interest-paying account* works much like a savings account. Interest is paid according to how much money is in the account.

Fees

A checking account usually costs money, but fees differ among financial institutions. Some charge a fee for each check you write. Others offer free checking if you keep a savings account there. Others provide free checking if you maintain a minimum balance in either your checking or savings account.

You must usually pay a fee for your checks. That fee varies depending on the design you choose. Consider all the various fees when choosing a bank. Fees vary among banks. Check out large and small banks to determine the right one for your needs.

Opening a Checking Account

Once you select a financial institution, you are ready to open your checking account. The process is an easy one. Ask to see the person in charge of new accounts. That person will have you fill out an application form. This form includes spaces for your name, address, telephone number, and if you work, your business address.

You will be asked to sign a *signature card*, which will be used to check the signatures on your checks. See 25-3. This helps prevent the crime of forgery. Falsely imitating someone else's signature on a check is forgery. You will also be asked to show some form of identification, such as a driver's license. Remember to bring your social security number. Banks must have your social security number on file for tax purposes.

Checking Account Application

OUR TOWN BANK
ANY ONE AUTHORIZED SIGNATURE WILL BE SUFFICIENT
FOR EACH WITHDRAWAL, CHECK OR OTHER ORDER.

ACCOUNT NUMBER

TITLE

THIS ACCOUNT WILL BE SUBJECT TO THE RULES AND REGULATIONS OF THE BANK, ALL LAWS, REGULATIONS AND RULES OF THE UNITED STATES, AND OF THE STATE OF NEW JERSEY, AND ALL CHANGES IN THOSE RULES, REGULATIONS, AND LAWS THAT MAY IN THE FUTURE BECOME EFFECTIVE. I FURTHER AGREE BY MY SIGNATURE BELOW THAT I HAVE RECEIVED A COPY OF--

☐ BASIC CHECKING AGREEMENT
☐ SAVINGS AGREEMENT
☐ TIME DEPOSIT OPEN ACCOUNT AGREEMENT
☐ JOINT ACCOUNT SUPPLEMENTAL AGREEMENT

☐ NOW ACCOUNT AGREEMENT
☐ STATEMENT SAVINGS AGREEMENT
☐ TRUST ACCOUNT SUPPLEMENTAL
  AGREEMENT

_____   _____
DEPOSITOR'S SIGNATURE   DEPOSITOR'S SIGNATURE

TYPE

☐ NOW   ☐ CHECKING   ☐ SAVINGS

SPECIFY TYPE OF ACCOUNT

- - - - - - - - - - - - - - - - - FOLD - - - - - - - - - - - - - - - - -

ADDRESS
WRITE
ZIP CODE
AFTER
STATE

SOCIAL SECURITY NO.		BIRTH DATE	SOCIAL SECURITY NO.		BIRTH DATE
HOME PHONE NO.	BUSINESS PHONE NO.		HOME PHONE NO.		BUSINESS PHONE NO.
EMPLOYER			EMPLOYER		
JOB TITLE			JOB TITLE		

DATE OPENED	DATE CLOSED	RELATED ACCOUNT NUMBERS	
IDENTIFICATION SOURCE	BRANCH NO.	OFFICER NO.	OPENED BY:

SIGNATURE CARD

25-3

This is a combined application form and signature card for opening a checking account. Some institutions use two separate forms.

Making a Deposit

You must put money into your checking account before you can write checks. The teller will ask you to complete a deposit slip. Use the *deposit slip* to record how much money you are going to put into your checking account. Space is provided for you to list cash and/or checks.

Give the completed deposit slip and your money to a teller. The teller will record your deposit and give you a receipt. You will be given temporary checks and deposit slips to use. Later, you will receive your own personalized checks and deposit slips in the mail. See 25-4.

You can deposit money electronically. You can transfer money from your other existing accounts or between accounts. If you transfer money electronically, you will not have a deposit slip. It is important that you keep accurate records if you wish to use this method.

Writing a Deposit Slip

Write the date you deposit the money.

List all coins.

List all currency (bills).

List all checks separately.

JAMES C. MORRISON
1765 SHERIDAN DRIVE
YOUR CITY, STATE 12345

DEPOSIT

CURRENCY
COIN
LIST CHECKS SINGLY
123 56
20 00
TOTAL FROM OTHER SIDE
SUB-TOTAL 146 56
LESS CASH RECEIVED 50 00
TOTAL DEPOSIT 93 56

DATE _____ August 10

_____ James C. Morrison
SIGN HERE ONLY IF CASH RECEIVED FROM DEPOSIT

FINANCIAL INSTITUTION
YOUR CITY, U.S.A. 12345

⑆123456789⑆ 1 234⁄567⑈

DEPOSIT TICKET
PLEASE ITEMIZE ADDITIONAL CHECKS ON REVERSE SIDE

Sign the slip if you are receiving cash back.

Total your bills, coins, and checks.

Write amount of cash you wish to keep out of the deposit.

Subtract amount of cash received and write in net deposit.

25-4

Personalized deposit slips come with checks to make it easy to add money to a checking account.

Endorsing a Check

When depositing a check made out to you into your account, you must first endorse it. To *endorse* a check, you sign your name on the back of its left edge. Your signature must be within one and one-half inches of the edge. Sign your name exactly as it is written on the front of the check. See 25-5.

Endorsed checks can be cashed as well as deposited. Do not endorse a check until just before you cash or deposit it. Once your check is endorsed, anyone can cash it. If an endorsed check is lost or stolen, the money is gone.

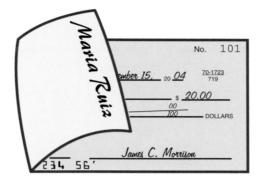

25-5

A check endorsement must be written on the back of the left edge of the check. It must not fall more than one and one-half inches from the edge.

Writing a Check

Checks should be written in ink. This will prevent others from changing the amount or the name on the check. The bank will return checks unpaid when information has been erased, crossed out, or changed in any way.

Using Check Registers

Most checks come with check registers. A *register* is simply a place to record all the deposits and credits that affect your account. Keeping your register up to date will help you keep track of how much money you have in your checking account.

You should complete the register before you write a check. Record each check and each deposit on the register. Deposits and interest are added to your balance. Checks and service fees are subtracted from your balance. See 25-6.

Instead of a register, some checks come with stubs or duplicates. Both serve as written records of the check numbers, dates, amounts, and parties to whom checks are written. If you have check stubs, you must

deposit slip
A form filled out before depositing money into a bank account.

endorse
To sign the back of a check in order to deposit or cash the amount specified.

NUMBER	DATE	DESCRIPTION OF TRANSACTION	PAYMENT/DEBIT (-)	√ T	FEE (IF ANY) (-)	DEPOSIT/CREDIT (+)	BALANCE $ 169 23
		RECORD ALL CHARGES OR CREDITS THAT AFFECT YOUR ACCOUNT					
164	5-6	FIRST UNITED METHODIST	$ 25 00		$	$	25 00
							144 23
165	5-12	TURNING HEADS SALON	23 00				23 00
							121 23
166	5-16	ILLINOIS BELL	33 17				33 17
							88 06
	5-18	DEPOSIT				173 32	173 32
							261 38
167	5-21	COMMONWEALTH ELECTRIC	23 65				23 65
							237 73
168	5-24	B & B TIRE & AUTO	20 28				20 28
							217 45
	6-1	DEPOSIT				192 82	192 82
							410 27
169	6-1	DORCHESTER REALITY	210 00				210 00
							200 27
170	6-2	AMERICAN CANCER SOCIETY	10 00				10 00
							190 27

25-6

Recording each deposit and withdrawal in a check register helps checking account holders keep track of their account balances.

write this information on the stub for each check. If you have duplicates, the information is automatically recorded as the check is written.

Whether you use a register, stubs, or duplicates, you should always know how much money is in your account. That way you can avoid overdrawing your account.

Your check will *bounce* if you do not have enough money in your account. The bank will charge a fee for any checks written against insufficient funds and will return those checks unpaid.

Using Electronic Checking

You can also use electronic checking. Electronic checking allows you to pay bills using your computer. To use your computer to pay bills, you must have a program that allows you to write checks. You can also transfer funds from another account to your checking account.

Bills can automatically be paid at the end of a billing cycle with an automatic debit to your account. This is just like writing a check. Automatic payment is usually applied to a bill that occurs every month for the same amount. For example, it can be used to pay your automobile insurance monthly or quarterly. If you use an automatic payment method, be sure your account balance will cover the payment. Also, deduct the amount from your account when the payment comes due.

Using this form of payment requires careful bookkeeping on your part. If you don't make proper deductions on time, your account won't balance. You may cause an overdraft.

Balancing Your Checkbook

You should receive a monthly or quarterly statement from the bank. The **bank statement** lists all your deposits, cash withdrawals, check withdrawals, service charges, and interest payments. It also lists your beginning and ending balances. See 25-7.

When you receive your bank statement, check off your canceled checks in your checkbook. Some banks return cancelled checks with each statement, but some do not. It is up to you to make sure your checkbook balance agrees with the bank statement. Instructions for balancing your checkbook are given on the back of most bank statements.

Also check off all the deposits listed on your statement. Add any interest shown on your statement to the balance in your checkbook. Subtract any service charges from your checkbook balance.

As you go over your statement, you may notice that several of your checks have not cleared your bank. Checks clear the bank at different times. People and companies often hold checks for a while before cashing them. Checks that have not cleared are called *outstanding checks*. When balancing your checkbook, list outstanding checks and subtract them from the bank's statement. See 25-8.

bank statement
A balance sheet listing deposits, withdrawals, service charges, and interest payments on an account with a financial institution.

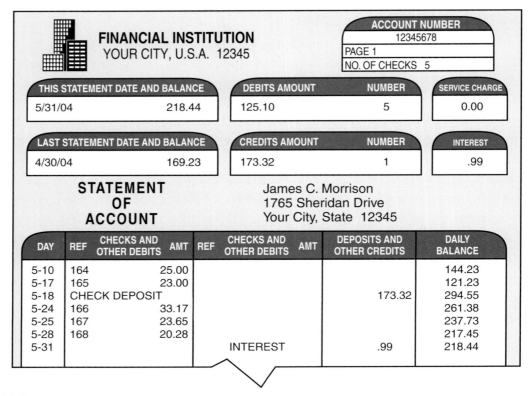

25-7
A bank statement provides a periodic summary of checking account activity.

When you have completed balancing your checkbook, the bank's statement should match your records. If you find the bank has made an error (such as incorrectly recording a deposit), call the bank and explain the problem. Before you call, however, make sure the error is the bank's, not yours.

Special Types of Checks

In addition to personal checks, there are several other types of checks:

- certified checks
- cashier's checks
- money orders
- traveler's checks

The use of these checks is explained in the following sections.

Balancing a Checking Account

OUTSTANDING CHECKS	
Check No.	Amount
169	210 : 00
170	10 : 00
TOTAL	220 : 00

Enter statement balance	218 : 44
List deposits not credited on this statement and add to statement balance.	192 : 82
Subtotal	411 : 26
Subtract checks outstanding	220 : 00
Total should agree with checkbook	191 : 26

Enter current checkbook balance	190 : 27
Add any interest shown on statement	: 99
Subtract any charges shown on statement	—0—
New checkbook balance	191 : 26

25-8
Most bank statements have a form similar to this on the back to help customers balance their checkbooks.

Certified Checks

Sellers of very expensive items often require payment by certified check. A ***certified check*** is one for which the bank guarantees payment. The bank withdraws the requested amount from your checking account. The bank teller stamps your check "certified." A bank official signs the check, guaranteeing the bank has set aside your money for payment. A small fee is charged for this service. See 25-9.

certified check
A check for which a bank guarantees payment.

25-9
Certified checks are often used when purchasing expensive items, such as jewelry.

Cashier's Checks

A *cashier's check* is drawn by a bank on its own funds. A bank officer, usually the cashier, signs it. People who don't know you may feel safer accepting a cashier's check than a personal check.

You don't need a checking account to get a cashier's check. You can go to any bank and buy a cashier's check. You pay the amount of the check plus a small service fee. The teller fills in the check amount and gives it to you. You then fill in the name of the company or person to be paid.

Money Orders

A *money order* is an order to pay a certain amount of money to a certain party. Money orders can be used to pay bills safely by mail. In those ways, money orders are like personal checks. You don't need a checking account to get money orders.

You can purchase money orders from several places:

- financial institutions
- U.S. post offices
- American Express agencies
- Railway Express agencies
- Western Union offices

To buy a money order, you pay the amount of the money order plus a small service fee. The agent prepares the money order and fills in the amount. You fill in the name of the person or company to be paid. If you have a checking account, you would not normally need this service.

Traveler's Checks

You may have seen television commercials showing people who lose cash while on vacation. If you lose your traveler's checks, they can be replaced. *Traveler's checks* are checks purchased in common denominations that are replaceable if lost or stolen. There is a service fee for buying traveler's checks. See 25-10.

When buying traveler's checks, you sign your name in front of the teller on each check you purchase. Later, when you go to cash the checks, you again have to sign them. The person receiving a check compares the second signature with the first one. If the signatures match, the person knows the check is really yours.

You can buy traveler's checks from banks and credit card companies. You do not need an account at the institution to buy traveler's checks.

25-10

Vacationers often carry traveler's checks instead of cash to guard against loss or theft.

cashier's check
A check drawn on a bank's own funds and signed by an officer of the bank.

money order
Used like a check, this is an order purchased for a specific amount to be paid to a certain party.

traveler's checks
Checks purchased in common denominations that are replaceable if lost or stolen.

Summary

A checking account provides both convenience and safety. Before you open a checking account, shop for the best financial institution for you. Compare the features of several before you make your choice.

Once you have a checking account, use it responsibly. Learn the correct way to fill out deposit slips, endorse checks, and write checks. Know how to use check stubs or a check register. Understand how to balance a checkbook. Then be sure you put your knowledge to good use. A checking account can be a helpful money management tool. However, if you misuse and overdraw it often, you will have problems.

At times, you may want to use cash or debit cards. Other types of checks available to you are certified checks, cashier's checks, money orders, and traveler's checks. All these services are for your convenience. Become familiar with them now so you will know how to use them when you choose to do so.

Reviewing the Chapter

1. Name two advantages of having a checking account.
2. What four factors should be considered when choosing a financial institution?
3. When you open a checking account, why are you asked to sign a signature card?
4. What form do you fill out when you want to put money into an existing checking account?
5. Why should a check be written in ink?
6. What is the purpose of using check stubs or a check register?
7. What checking account information is given on a bank statement?
8. You need a checking account to write a _____.
   A. certified check
   B. cashier's check
   C. money order
   D. traveler's check
9. Which of the following can be purchased at a post office?
   A. certified check
   B. cashier's check
   C. money order
   D. debit card
10. What is the primary reason for buying traveler's checks?

Building Your Foundation Skills

1. Your bank statement last month showed you had a balance of $1,723.34. You had three checks outstanding, totaling $67.89. This month you deposited $487.53. You wrote checks totaling $134.80. Your bank charges were $4.50. What is the total in your bank account?

2. Write a short paper on the advantages and disadvantages of using a debit card.

3. Invite a representative of a financial institution to visit your class. Ask questions about various services, fees, and types of accounts.

4. Investigate the consequences of having a check bounce. Talk to store managers and bank officials to get both sides of the story. Discuss your findings in class.

5. Design posters to illustrate the topics discussed in this chapter. Display them throughout your school.

Building Your Workplace Competencies

Visit three financial institutions in your area and compare them for convenience, services, fees, and types of accounts available. Work as a team with two or three of your classmates and assume you are opening a joint account. When you visit each institution, speak to a bank representative and explain the purpose of your visit. Be sure to obtain relevant brochures. What are the costs and requirements of a joint checking account at each institution? Using a computer, create a report that compares the facts you gathered. Decide which institution you would choose to open the new account. Make a brief presentation to the class explaining your team's decision. *(This activity develops competence with resources, interpersonal skills, information, systems, and technology.)*

Objectives

After studying this chapter, you will be able to

- determine reasons for saving.

- list three types of financial institutions that offer savings accounts and the agencies that insure them.

- explain the various ways to save.

- list reasons for buying U.S. savings bonds.

Words to Know

interest

principal

compound interest

direct deposit

savings club

certificate of deposit (CD)

money market account

U.S. savings bond

mutual fund

annuity

Reasons for Saving

Saving money is sound personal money management. You should save a portion of each paycheck based on your take-home pay and personal needs. The more you make, the more you should save.

There are many reasons for saving for the future. These reasons are as varied as everyone's wants and needs. See 26-1. The following events are common reasons for saving:

- emergencies
- future income reduction
- travel and recreation
- advanced education
- major purchases such as a car or home
- retirement
- financial security

Where to Save

You have several options for saving your money. Become familiar with the types of financial institutions that offer savings accounts. Find out how much interest each pays on the accounts. Then decide where you want to deposit your money.

- **Commercial banks** are known as the department stores of finance. They offer a full variety of banking services. They make loans and transfer funds. They also provide financial advice and offer savings accounts.

26-1
Saving money allows people to meet future financial goals, such as paying for a trip abroad.

- **Savings and loan associations** are primarily known for lending money to homebuyers. They usually pay slightly higher interest rates on savings accounts than commercial banks do.
- **Credit unions** are nonprofit financial institutions. They are owned by and operated for their members. Most credit unions serve people in a particular community, group, company, or organization. Credit unions make loans to their members at low interest rates. Also, they usually pay higher interest rates than banks do on savings accounts.

Will Your Savings Be Safe?

Financial institutions that are insured are safe places to keep your money. You get more protection from them than you would if you kept your money at home. Each account is insured up to $100,000. Should the institution go bankrupt, your money would be covered up to that amount. Before you open a savings account, check to see that it would be insured.

Two agencies are responsible for insuring most of the money in savings accounts. The *Federal Deposit Insurance Corporation (FDIC)* protects deposits in most commercial banks and savings and loan associations. The *National Credit Union Association (NCUA)* protects deposits in most credit unions. See 26-2.

Ways to Save

There are many ways to save. You should discuss your options with customer service representatives in local financial institutions. They will be happy to describe the various savings plans offered. Savings accounts, savings clubs, certificates of deposit, and U.S. savings bonds are some of the most common ways to save.

26-2
The FDIC sign assures bank customers their deposits will be safe.

Savings Accounts

A common way to save is to open a *regular savings account*. In this type of account, you can make deposits and withdrawals at any time. You receive a monthly or quarterly statement in the mail. All deposits and withdrawals are recorded in the statements. Be sure to double-check your account activity when you receive your statement. See 26-3.

Your savings account will earn interest. **Interest** is money paid to you for allowing a financial institution to have and use your money. The longer you leave your money in a savings account, the more interest you will earn. Interest will be paid in one of the following ways:

- daily
- quarterly (four times a year)
- semiannually (twice a year)
- annually (once a year)

ACCOUNT NO. 29-3689865	Security Convenience Personal Service				FINANCIAL INSTITUTION YOUR CITY, U.S.A. 12345		
DATE	MEMO	INTEREST	WITHDRAWALS	DEPOSITS	BALANCE	TELLER
06-15	--			200.00	200.00	04
06-22	--			50.00	250.00	07
06-26	CW		15.00		235.00	02
06-29	--			50.00	285.00	04
06-30		.51			285.51	05
07-06	--			52.00	337.51	01
07-13	--			50.00	387.51	04
07-21	CW		150.00		237.51	04

26-3
Savings account deposits and withdrawals are recorded in a statement.

interest
The money paid to customers for allowing a financial institution to have and use their money.

A savings account earns interest only on money that is on deposit for the full interest period. This is usually three months (quarterly). Suppose you withdrew money before the end of the interest-bearing period. Then you would receive interest only on whatever money you left in the account.

Many savings accounts pay interest from the day of deposit to the day of withdrawal. Interest is paid for every day the money is in the account. Suppose you withdrew money in the middle of a month. Then you would still earn interest for the number of days the money was in the account.

As interest is added to a savings account, it too begins to earn interest. Both the deposit, known as *principal*, and the earned interest continue to earn interest. This is known as *compound interest*.

Opening a Savings Account

Convenience is important when deciding where to open a savings account. Focus on financial institutions close to your home or workplace with hours that meet your needs. Next, find out which financial institution pays the highest interest rates for the type of savings account that interests you. Different institutions pay different rates of interest.

Finally, keep in mind that you do not need to choose the same institution for all your financial needs. For convenience, you may wish to have your checking account and your savings account in the same place. However, you can have your checking account in one place and your savings account in another. Shop around for the service that best meets your needs.

Comparing Fees

Some banks require you to maintain a minimum balance in your account. If you do not maintain that balance, you may be charged a service fee. Some banks have student accounts that may not require a minimum balance. It is important that you know what fees you will be charged when you open an account.

Often banks will have special programs for minors. Usually these are offered to minors of parents or guardians who already have an account at the bank. The programs allow you to keep an account with a small balance without a bank charge.

Making a Deposit

To deposit money in your savings account, you need to fill out a savings deposit form, 26-4. It is important to fill out the form correctly by following the steps on the next page:

26-4

Savings account customers must complete deposit slips to add money to their accounts.

- Write your name, the date, and your account number. (Personalized forms that are printed with your checks already contain your account number.)
- On the *currency* line, list the total amount of paper money you are depositing.
- On the *coin* line, list the total amount of pennies, nickels, dimes, and other coins you are depositing. (Currency and coin may be combined on a single cash line.)
- List each check separately on the lines provided.
- Add all the money you have listed and write the total on the line provided.
- Indicate the amount of cash, if any, you would like to receive.
- Subtract the amount of cash to be received from the total of the coins, currency, and checks. Write the amount of the net deposit.
- Present your money and the completed deposit form to the teller. The teller will record your deposit in your account. Any interest earned on your savings will be figured into your account at the end of each interest period.

principal
A savings account deposit.
compound interest
Interest figured on the principal plus the earned interest of a financial account.

Using Direct Deposit

Some employers have a direct deposit plan. A **direct deposit** program allows your employer to deposit your paycheck into your account. In a direct deposit program, you can split your deposit into one or more existing accounts. To take advantage of a direct deposit plan, you must complete a form provided by your employer. Then, your pay goes directly to your account on paydays.

Withdrawing Money

As with depositing, you need a form for withdrawing money from your savings account. See 26-5. Follow these steps to fill out a withdrawal form:

- Write your name, the date, and your account number.
- Write the amount of money you wish to withdraw.
- Sign your name on the withdrawal form.
- Present your completed withdrawal form to the teller. The teller will deduct your withdrawal from your account, update your balance, and give you your money.

Savings Clubs

A **savings club** encourages you to form a habit of saving money. When you open a savings club account, you set up a savings plan. You decide to deposit a set amount of money every week or every month. You are given a savings club book with an account number on it.

Every time you make a deposit, you use a deposit slip from your savings club book. At the end of your savings period, you receive a check for the amount you saved plus

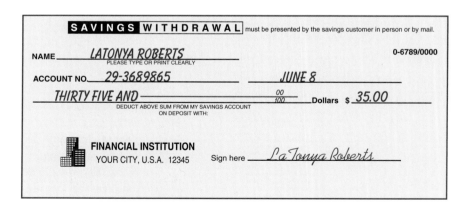

26-5
Completing withdrawal slips allows bank customers to take money from their savings accounts.

the interest you earned. You can then use the money you saved to reach a goal you set for yourself. Many people use savings clubs to save money for Christmas presents or vacations. See 26-6.

Certificates of Deposit

As your earnings and savings increase, you should consider expanding your savings. You may wish to invest in a *certificate of deposit*, known as a *CD*. You can buy them at a bank, savings and loan, or credit union.

At the time of purchase, you must decide how much you want to deposit and for how long. CDs are usually sold in amounts of $500 or more. The money is held for a set period of time. The time period may be as short as 31 days or as long as several years.

Interest rates for CDs vary. Overall, CDs earn higher rates of interest than savings accounts or clubs. Also, larger CDs usually earn higher rates of interest. However, there are penalties for early withdrawal. If you withdraw money from a CD before the end of the set time period, you will lose some interest.

Before you buy a CD, contact several financial institutions. Compare interest rates, minimum amounts of deposit, and penalties for early withdrawal. Choose the CD that best meets your needs.

26-6
Opening a savings club account helps some people save money to buy gifts and special purchases.

direct deposit
Program that allows an employer to deposit a paycheck directly into an employee's account.

savings club
A savings plan into which a set amount of money is deposited regularly until a savings goal is reached.

certificate of deposit (CD)
A savings certificate earning a fixed rate of interest that is purchased for a specific amount of money and held for a set period of time.

Money Market Accounts

Your banking institution also offers money market accounts. A ***money market account*** is similar to a CD, but has no time period restrictions. Money can be withdrawn or added at any time with this type of savings account.

Money market savings accounts usually have a rate of interest that is higher than a regular savings account, but lower than a CD. The rate may vary monthly. This type of account also permits check-writing privileges.

U.S. Savings Bonds

Many people choose to save money by buying a ***U.S. savings bond***. This is a certificate of debt issued by the federal government. People choose this savings option for several reasons.

- *Safety*—If the bonds are lost, stolen, or destroyed, they can be replaced. The U.S. government issues them.
- *Convenience*—They are available at most financial institutions for as little as $25. Also, many companies offer payroll savings plans. In such plans, an amount determined by the employee is deducted from paychecks for the purchase of the bonds.
- *Higher interest rate*—U.S. savings bonds earn a higher rate than regular savings accounts and savings clubs. Also, the interest earned on Series EE bonds is not taxed until the bonds are cashed.
- *Patriotism*—Buying U.S. savings bonds is a way to support the government. The money used to buy them goes to the government treasury. See 26-7.

Once you buy a U.S. savings bond, you must keep it for at least six months. You can cash it any time after that. The longer you keep it, the more interest it earns.

Mutual Funds

A ***mutual fund*** is a long-term investment that provides a way to invest in stocks and bonds. It generally provides a greater return than other forms of savings accounts.

When you purchase a mutual fund, your money is pooled with many other investors. The money is then invested by a fund manager in various stocks, bonds, or other money instruments. Investing in a mutual fund gives you professional assistance with your investment. You own a share of many different stocks and bonds.

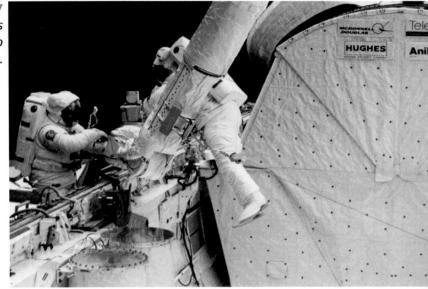

26-7
The government treasury, which includes money from U.S. savings bonds, is used to fund projects such as space exploration.

Mutual funds are listed in the business section of the newspaper that reports the performance of stocks and bonds. You can start some mutual funds with as little as $25.00. Others may require an initial investment of $1,000.00 or more. It is important to do a little research on mutual funds before you invest.

Many banks offer mutual funds as a service to their depositors, but extra fees may be involved. The value of a mutual fund rises and falls with the value of the stocks and bonds they contain. Unlike a checking account or savings account, the government does not insure a mutual fund.

Annuities

Another form of savings is an ***annuity***. An annuity provides both insurance and savings. Annuities are usually invested for 10 or 15 years. They may be issued longer or the term can be extended. In the event of the owner's death, benefits of an annuity are often paid like life insurance. An annuity is a useful investment for retirement or future security.

money market account
A type of savings account that is similar to a CD, but has no time restrictions.

U.S. savings bond
A certificate of debt issued by the federal government that serves as a safe way to save money.

mutual fund
A long-term investment that provides a way to invest in stocks and bonds.

annuity
A form of investment that lasts 10 or 15 years and provides insurance as well as savings.

Summary

Saving money is an important part of a personal money management plan. However, the reasons people save vary widely. The ways people save also vary.

Before you choose a financial institution, make sure its deposits are insured. Also check its interest rates and services. A savings account is a common way to save. It allows you to make deposits and withdraw money. A savings club can also help you form the habit of saving money.

You need to plan carefully before buying a certificate of deposit. It will earn a fixed rate of interest and your money will be tied up for a set period of time. A money market account is an alternative to a certificate of deposit. The rate of interest may go up or down. Money market accounts can have deposits or withdrawals at any time.

Buying U.S. savings bonds is a safe and easy way to save. The bonds earn good rates of interest and help support the government. Other forms of savings for the long-term are mutual funds and annuities. Long-term savings should be part of your planned saving strategy.

Reviewing the Chapter

1. List five reasons for saving.
2. Which financial institutions are known as the department stores of finance?
3. Which financial institutions are primarily known for lending money to homebuyers?
4. Which financial institutions are owned by and operated for their members?
5. Which types of financial institutions are protected by FDIC? Which are protected by NCUA?
6. When both the principal and the earned interest continue to earn interest, that interest is known as _____.
7. True or false. Different financial institutions pay different rates of interest on savings accounts.
8. When you have a savings club account, what happens at the end of your savings period?
9. Why are U.S. savings bonds a safe way to save?
10. Which form of savings is linked to insurance?

Building Your Foundation Skills

1. Design posters to illustrate reasons for saving. Display them throughout your school.

2. If you deposit $135.00 in your bank account and receive 5 percent interest per year, how much interest will you receive in three months if interest is accumulated quarterly? What will your investment be worth in one year?

3. Ask a representative of a financial institution to talk to your class about ways to save.

4. Research U.S. savings bonds to find out how they originated. Share your findings with the class in a brief oral report.

5. Visit or call two financial institutions in your area. Request information on their current interest rates for a one-year, $1,000 CD. Also ask about the penalties for early withdrawal. If you were to buy the CD, where would you deposit your money? Explain your findings in a brief written report.

Building Your Workplace Competencies

Visit two financial institutions in your area, checking the types of accounts that are available for students your age. Work with two or three students on this activity. Check the requirements, penalties, fees, and other obligations for each account. Also check the convenience, location, and banking hours of each institution. In which account would your money grow fastest? After finding answers to all the questions, determine where your team would prefer to bank. Explain why in a brief report to the class. *(This activity develops competence with resources, interpersonal skills, information, and systems.)*

Credit

Objectives

After studying this chapter, you will be able to

- discuss the advantages and disadvantages of using credit.

- describe four major types of credit.

- list ways to begin building a credit history.

- describe a person whom creditors would view as a good credit risk.

- explain the importance of a good credit rating.

Words to Know

credit line
collateral
assets
cosigner
credit bureau
credit rating
credit agreement

Common Uses of Credit

Billboards and store windows are covered with signs that say, "Buy now, pay later!" Newspaper ads read, "Easy credit terms with no down payment!" Radio and TV commercials advertise offers for "one-day credit approval." These are familiar slogans. They encourage people to buy on credit. They make buying easy—sometimes too easy. They don't mention the fact that credit ends up making items cost more.

Credit can be good. It can help people buy homes, cars, and furniture. It can help people live more comfortably.

Credit, however, can be dangerous. It becomes dangerous when it is overused or abused. It can cause financial problems when people can't make the payments they owe. In some cases, financial problems may lead to other problems. They may cause family arguments. They may also cause stress, which can affect health.

Credit used wisely can enrich your lifestyle. Credit used poorly can create major problems. You need to know when and how to use credit.

Advantages of Credit

When used properly, credit has the following advantages:

- Credit is a convenience. You can shop and travel without the worry of carrying large amounts of cash, 27-1.
- Credit allows you to use goods and services while paying for them. Saving enough money to buy expensive items can be difficult. Credit helps you buy such items and pay for them over a period of time.

27-1
People often use credit cards while traveling to avoid the need to carry a lot of cash.

■ Credit helps you meet financial emergencies. Unexpected costs due to sicknesses, accidents, and repairs can be handled through credit.

Disadvantages of Credit

Credit has some drawbacks, especially if it is overused. The following disadvantages of credit can become problems if credit is used unwisely:

■ Credit encourages impulse buying. You might buy more than you need. You may overspend and have trouble repaying.

■ Credit can get you into serious debt. Many people lose items purchased with credit if they can't make the payments. The items are repossessed or taken back by the sellers.

■ Credit makes the cost of goods and services higher. It is usually cheaper to pay cash than to use credit.

■ Credit ties up your future income. Any raises you get may need to be used to pay off past credit charges.

When to Use Credit

You should always think carefully before using credit to make a purchase. Ask yourself the following questions: Can you do without the item now? Will you have problems paying back the debt? Are you already spending more than 20 percent of your take-home pay on installment debt? If you answer "yes" to these questions, try to avoid more credit at this time. It is likely that you cannot handle any more payments. Credit should work for you, not against you.

Types of Credit

As a consumer, you should be aware of the following types of credit available to you:

■ charge accounts

■ credit cards

■ installment credit

■ loans

Charge Accounts

A charge account is the oldest type of credit offered by business to consumers. Usually no down payment is required nor is any interest charged. The consumer agrees to pay at a later date. If the consumer does not pay by the assigned date, a fee is usually added to the amount owed. An example of a business offering this type of credit is a utility company that provides natural gas or electricity.

Credit Cards

Banks, stores, and many other types of companies issue credit cards. See 27-2. When you apply for one, the issuer sets a maximum amount you can charge, called a *credit line*. This amount is based on how much you earn and your ability to repay. For example, your maximum credit line may be $1,000. You can make any number of purchases as long as the total does not exceed $1,000.

27-2
Department stores issue credit cards for consumers to use when buying clothing and household purchases.

Once a month, you receive a bill. You can pay the entire bill by the due date, which involves no added interest. The other option is to make monthly installment payments. You then have to pay interest on the unpaid balance.

> **credit line**
> The maximum amount that can be charged on a credit card.

Installment Credit

Many expensive household items, like computers and refrigerators, are purchased with installment credit plans. In such a plan, you agree to make set payments over a given period of time. For this convenience, you pay the going interest rate plus any service charges. If you fail to make payments, the company can repossess the goods.

Loans

Banks and other lending institutions offer credit in the form of loans. People take out loans to borrow money to pay for the following types of expenses:

- cars and homes
- further education
- outstanding bills
- home improvements
- start-up expenses for a business
- vacations

The important point to remember about loans is that you have to pay back what you borrow plus interest. You can get a signature loan, which is a loan backed by your signature or promise to repay. Many loans, however, require you to put up collateral before you get the money. *Collateral* is something of value held by a lending institution in case you fail to repay. For instance, a bank may hold the title for your car until you have repaid your car loan. See 27-3.

When you need a loan, find out more about the different types of loans available to you. The interest charged and the repayment terms can vary considerably.

27-3
Any car you purchase does not legally belong to you until you have paid for it completely. The creditor keeps the title as collateral.

How to Obtain Credit

If you have never used credit, you have no credit history. If this is the case, you need to begin building a credit history. The following suggestions may help you:

- Open a savings account and a checking account, and use them. This shows creditors that you can handle money.
- If your place of employment has a credit union, join it. Credit unions make loans available to their members at low interest rates.
- If you drive, apply for a gasoline credit card. Make occasional gas purchases on the card. Make sure you pay the total due on time.
- Purchase an item in a local department store using a lay-away plan. Make payments on time to develop a good credit record.
- Apply for a local department store's credit card. Use the card for items you need. Stay within your budget plan.
- Always pay your bills promptly.

Creditors Look for Good Credit Risks

Creditors want to issue credit to people whom they feel are good credit risks. These are people who repay their debt. Therefore, creditors look for certain traits in people, 27-4. From a creditor's point of view, a good credit risk is a person who has the following traits:

- is honest
- has a job with a steady income
- made regular payments on past loan or credit purchases
- lived in the same community for a few years
- has assets

Assets are valuable possessions you own, such as a house or a car. Assets also include money you have in bank accounts and the value of stocks and bonds you own

collateral
Something of value held by a lending institution in case a loan is not repaid.
assets
The valuable possessions a person owns, such as a house or a car.

27-4

Most creditors consider steady employment a requirement for someone who wants to obtain credit.

Getting a First Loan

As a minor, it is difficult to borrow money. Generally, a person must be at least 18 years old. Even then, it may be difficult to borrow without a cosigner. A *cosigner* signs the loan agreement with the person who is borrowing the money. The cosigner must have a good credit history and guarantee repayment of the loan. In the event the borrower does not make the payments, the cosigner must make them.

You might need to ask a relative or friend to cosign your first loan. Be sure you make your payments. Before you sign for a loan, figure out whether you can afford to pay it back. It would be unfair to the cosigner if you failed to live up to your responsibility. It could also damage your ability to obtain credit in the future.

Credit Applications

Before credit is granted to anyone, the person's job history, credit history, and ability to repay are checked. When you apply for a credit card or loan, you must fill out a credit application, 27-5. You will be asked to give the following information:

- name, address, and previous addresses
- current and former employers, including their addresses
- current job title (or military rank), salary, and number of years employed
- sources of additional income
- name of a close relative who is not living at your address
- existing sources of credit, including credit card accounts and loans
- all financial accounts, their account numbers, and the names and addresses of the financial institutions

Credit Bureaus and Credit Ratings

Complete all credit applications honestly. The information on your applications will be checked by *credit bureaus*. Businesses depend on credit bureaus to gather financial information on individuals. Businesses make their decisions to grant or deny credit based on information in reports from credit bureaus.

Don't lie or try to hide information. If you give false information, you run the risk of being denied credit. Credit bureaus keep track of all your loans and lines of credit. They not only know how much credit you already have, they also know if you repay your debts on time.

A credit bureau reports your credit rating. Your *credit rating* is an estimate of how likely you are to pay your bills on time. The rating is based on past records of your credit behavior.

If you handle credit well and pay your bills on time, you will have a good credit rating. However, if you abuse credit and fail to repay your debts, you will have a bad credit rating. If you have a bad credit rating, you may have trouble getting credit in the future. Creditors do not lend money to people who have a history of not paying their bills. Work hard to protect your credit rating. Use credit wisely. Don't abuse it.

There may be times when you may not be able to make loan payments. If that happens, call your creditors and tell them the facts. Be honest. You may have lost your job. You may be very ill. Special arrangements could be made until your situation improves. When it does improve, make every effort to meet your obligations.

Examine All Credit Agreements

Always read a credit agreement before you sign it. A *credit agreement* is a contract. It legally binds the lender and the borrower to the credit terms defined. It is important for you to read and understand what you are signing. See 27-6.

cosigner
A person who signs a loan with a borrower and is held responsible if the borrower does not pay back the loan.

credit bureau
An organization that gathers financial information on individuals for businesses to use as a credit reference.

credit rating
An estimate of how likely a person is to pay bills on time based on past records.

credit agreement
A written contract that legally binds a lender and a borrower to specific credit terms.

SEARS, ROEBUCK AND CO. INDIVIDUAL CREDIT ACCOUNT APPLICATION

APPLICATION TO BE COMPLETED IN NAME OF PERSON IN WHICH THE ACCOUNT IS TO BE CARRIED.

COURTESY TITLES ARE OPTIONAL   **PLEASE PRINT**

☐ MR. ☐ MRS. ☐ MISS ☐ MS. _____

First Name _____ Initial _____ Last Name

Street Address _____ Apt. # _____ City _____ State _____ Zip Code

Phone No: Home _____ Phone No: Business _____ Soc. Sec. No. _____ Age _____ Number of Dependents _____ (Excluding Applicant)

Are you a United States citizen? ☐ Yes ☐ No   If NO, explain immigration status: _____

How Long at Present Address _____ Own ☐ Rent-Furnished ☐ Rent-Unfurnished ☐ Board ☐ Monthly Rent or Mortgage Payments $ _____

Name of Landlord or Mortgage Holder _____ Street Address _____ City and State

Former Address (If less than 2 years at present address) _____ How long _____

Employer _____ Street Address _____ City and State

How long _____ Occupation _____ Net Income $ _____ (Take Home Pay) Monthly ☐ Weekly ☐

Former Employer (If less than 1 year with present employer) _____ How long _____

> ALIMONY, CHILD SUPPORT, OR SEPARATE MAINTENANCE INCOME NEED NOT BE REVEALED IF YOU DO NOT WISH TO HAVE IT CONSIDERED AS A BASIS FOR PAYING THIS OBLIGATION.

Alimony, child support, separate maintenance received under:
☐ Court order   ☐ Written agreement   ☐ Oral understanding   Amount $ _____   Monthly ☐ Weekly ☐

Other Income, if any: Amount $ _____ Monthly ☐ Weekly ☐ Source _____

Name and Address of Bank _____ Savings ☐ Checking ☐ Acc't No. _____

Name and Address of Bank _____ Savings ☐ Checking ☐ Acc't No. _____

Previous Sears Account? ☐ Yes ☐ No   At What Sears Store do you usually shop? _____ Account No. _____   Is Account Paid in Full ☐ Yes ☐ No   Date Final Payment Made _____

Relative or Personal Reference not living at above address _____
(Name) _____ (Street Address) _____ (City and State) _____ (Relationship)

CREDIT REFERENCES (Attach additional sheet if necessary.)   List all references   (Open or closed within past two years)

Charge Accounts Loan References Bank/Store/Company Address	Date Opened	Name Account Carried In	Account Number	Balance	Monthly Payments

Authorized buyer _____ First Name _____ Initial _____ Last Name _____ Relationship to applicant

Authorized buyer _____ First Name _____ Initial _____ Last Name _____ Relationship to applicant

THE INFORMATION BELOW IS REQUIRED IF: (1) YOUR SPOUSE IS AN AUTHORIZED BUYER OR (2) YOU RESIDE IN A COMMUNITY PROPERTY STATE (ARIZONA, CALIFORNIA, IDAHO, LOUISIANA, NEVADA, NEW MEXICO, TEXAS, WASHINGTON) OR (3) YOU ARE RELYING ON THE INCOME OR ASSETS OF ANOTHER PERSON, INCLUDING A SPOUSE OR FORMER SPOUSE, AS A BASIS FOR PAYMENT.

Name of spouse ☐ Name of former spouse ☐ Name of other person ☐ _____ Address _____ Age

Employer _____ Street Address _____ City and State

How long _____ Occupation _____ Soc. Sec. No. _____ Net Income $ _____ (Take Home Pay) Monthly ☐ Weekly ☐

Name and Address of Bank _____ Savings ☐ Checking ☐ Acc't No. _____

Name and Address of Bank _____ Savings ☐ Checking ☐ Acc't No. _____

THE PERSON ON WHOSE INCOME OR ASSETS YOU ARE RELYING AS A BASIS FOR PAYMENT MUST SIGN BELOW, HOWEVER, YOUR SPOUSE NEED NOT SIGN IF YOU RESIDE IN A COMMUNITY PROPERTY STATE OR IF YOUR SPOUSE IS AN AUTHORIZED BUYER.

SEARS IS AUTHORIZED TO INVESTIGATE MY CREDIT RECORD AND TO VERIFY MY CREDIT, EMPLOYMENT AND INCOME REFERENCES.

X _____
(Signature of person on whose income or assets applicant is relying.)   Date _____

27-5

The information on a credit application helps creditors evaluate an applicant's ability to make credit payments.

SEARS, ROEBUCK AND CO.
SEARSCHARGE SECURITY AGREEMENT

On all charges to my SearsCharge account, I agree to the following:

1. **OPTION TO PAY IN FULL EACH MONTH TO AVOID FINANCE CHARGES.** I have the right each month to pay the total balance on my account. If I do so within 30 days (28 days for February statements) of my billing date, no **Finance Charge** will be added to my account for that month. The billing date will be shown on a statement sent to me each month. The total balance on my billing date will be called the New Balance on my monthly statement.

2. **OPTION TO PAY INSTALLMENTS PLUS A FINANCE CHARGE.** If I do not pay the total balance in full each month, I agree to make at least a minimum payment within 30 days (28 days for February statements) of the billing date shown on my monthly statement. The minimum payment required each month is shown in the Schedule of Minimum Monthly Payments below.

3. **SCHEDULE OF MINIMUM MONTHLY PAYMENTS.** The required minimum monthly payment is based on the highest New Balance on the account.

When the Highest New Balance Reaches:	The Minimum Monthly Payment will be:	
$ .01 to $ 10.00	Balance	You may always pay more than the required minimum monthly payment. The minimum payment will change only if charges to the account increase the balance to a new high. The minimum payment will not decrease until the New Balance is paid in full.
10.01 to 200.00	$10.00	
200.01 to 240.00	11.00	
240.01 to 280.00	12.00	
280.01 to 320.00	13.00	
320.01 to 360.00	14.00	
360.01 to 400.00	15.00	
400.01 to 440.00	16.00	
440.01 to 470.00	17.00	
470.01 to 500.00	18.00	

over $500.00 - 1/28th of Highest Account Balance rounded to next higher whole dollar amount.

4. **FINANCE CHARGE.** If I do not pay the entire New Balance within 30 days (28 days for February statements) of the monthly billing date, a **Finance Charge** will be added to the account for the current monthly billing period. The **FINANCE CHARGE** will be either a minimum of 50¢ if the Average Daily Balance is $28.50 or less, or a periodic rate of 1.75% per month **(ANNUAL PERCENTAGE RATE** of 21%) on the Average Daily Balance.

5. **HOW TO DETERMINE THE AVERAGE DAILY BALANCE.** Sears will determine each day's outstanding balance in the monthly billing period and divide the total of these daily balances by the number of days in the monthly billing period. The result is the Average Daily Balance. Sears will include the current month's charges but will not include unpaid Finance or Insurance Charge(s), if any, when determining a daily balance. All payments and other credits will be subtracted from the previous day's balance.

6. **FAILURE TO MAKE MINIMUM PAYMENT.** If I do not make at least the minimum required monthly payment when due, Sears may declare my entire balance immediately due and payable.

7. **SECURITY INTEREST IN GOODS.** Sears has a security interest under the Uniform Commercial Code in all merchandise charged to the account. If I do not make payments as agreed, the security interest allows Sears to repossess only the merchandise which has not been paid in full. Upon my default, Sears may charge me reasonable attorneys' fees. I am responsible for any loss or damage to the merchandise until the price is fully paid. Any payments I make will first be used to pay any unpaid Insurance or Finance Charge(s), and then to pay for the earliest charges on the account. If more than one item is charged on the same date, my payment will apply first to the lowest priced item.

10897-051   Rev. 9/83
Illinois, Kentucky, South Dakota

8. **CHANGE OF TERMS — CANCELLATION.** Sears has the right to change any terms or part of this agreement by sending me a written notice. Sears also has the right to cancel this agreement as it relates to future purchases. I agree to return all credit cards to Sears upon notice of such cancellation.

9. **STATE OF RESIDENCE CONTROLS TERMS.** All terms of this agreement are controlled by the laws of my state of residence.

10. **CHANGE OF RESIDENCE.** If I change my residence, I will inform Sears. Sears has the right to transfer the account to a unit servicing my new residence. If I move to another state, the account, including any unpaid balance, will be controlled by the credit terms which apply to Sears credit customers in my new state of residence. Sears will provide me with a written disclosure of any new terms, including the amount and method of calculating the **Finance Charge.**

11. **AUTHORIZED BUYERS.** This agreement controls all charges made on the account by me or any person I authorize to use the account.

12. **CREDIT INVESTIGATION AND DISCLOSURE.** Sears has the right to investigate my credit, employment and income records, and has the right to verify my credit references and to report the way I pay this account to credit bureaus and other interested parties.

13. **WAIVER OF LIEN ON DWELLING.** Sears gives up any right to retain or acquire any lien which Sears might be automatically entitled to by law on my principal dwelling. This does not apply to a lien created by a court judgment or acquired by a filing as provided by statute.

14. **ACCOUNT SUBJECT TO APPROVAL OF SEARS CREDIT SALES DEPARTMENT.** This agreement and all charges on the account are subject to the approval of Sears Credit Sales Department. The agreement will be considered approved when Sears delivers a Sears credit card or other notice of approval to me.

15. **ASSIGNMENT OF ACCOUNT — PROTECTION OF BUYER'S RIGHTS.** I understand this account may be sold or assigned by Sears to another creditor without further notice to me. If so, the notice below, which is required by Federal law, is intended to protect any claim or right I have against Sears.

NOTICE: ANY HOLDER OF THIS CONSUMER CREDIT CONTRACT IS SUBJECT TO ALL CLAIMS AND DEFENSES WHICH THE DEBTOR COULD ASSERT AGAINST THE SELLER OF THE GOODS OR SERVICES OBTAINED PURSUANT HERETO OR WITH THE PROCEEDS HEREOF. RECOVERY HEREUNDER BY THE DEBTOR SHALL NOT EXCEED AMOUNTS PAID BY THE DEBTOR HEREUNDER. Errors or Inquiries on Monthly Statements.

NOTICE: SEE STATEMENT ACCOMPANYING CREDIT CARDS FOR IMPORTANT INFORMATION REGARDING YOUR RIGHTS TO DISPUTE BILLING ERRORS.

NOTICE TO BUYER: DO NOT SIGN THIS AGREEMENT BEFORE YOU READ IT OR IF IT CONTAINS ANY BLANK SPACES. YOU ARE ENTITLED TO AN EXACT COPY OF THE PAPER YOU SIGN. YOU HAVE THE RIGHT TO PAY IN ADVANCE THE FULL AMOUNT DUE.

RECEIPT OF A COPY OF THIS AGREEMENT IS ACKNOWLEDGED.

SEARS, ROEBUCK AND CO.

(Customer's Signature)   (Date)

(Please Print Name)

(Address)   (City)   (State)   (Zip Code)

(Account Number)

27-6

Signing a credit agreement indicates a consumer's willingness to meet the conditions set up by a creditor.

Don't be rushed into signing a credit agreement. Study the agreement before you sign it. Never sign a credit agreement that has blanks. Make sure that all numbers are correct. Don't overlook the finance charges.

Ask questions if you are not sure of something in the agreement. You could also seek advice from someone knowledgeable in money matters. If you are in doubt, you should write *no*. When you are satisfied with the contract, sign it. Then be sure to live up to the agreement.

Summary

Credit is easily available in today's society. Used wisely, it can be helpful. If abused, it can be dangerous. Always think carefully before using credit. Be sure you will be able to pay for it later.

Four major types of credit are charge accounts, credit cards, installment credit, and loans. Before using them, you should understand how they work. Know what costs and responsibilities are involved.

Although you may not need credit now, you should start thinking about building a credit history. Learn about credit applications, ratings, and agreements. Become familiar with the different types of credit and credit terms.

Reviewing the Chapter

1. List three advantages of credit.
2. List four disadvantages of credit.
3. True or false. A charge account usually involves a large down payment and a high interest rate.
4. When you receive a monthly credit card bill, what are your two options?
5. True or false. To buy something using an installment credit plan, a person agrees to make set payments over a given period of time.
6. Why might a lending institution ask for collateral before making a loan?
7. Name three ways to begin building a credit history.
8. Describe five traits of a person who is a good credit risk.
9. What risk does the cosigner of a loan take?
10. Why is it important to have a good credit rating?

Building Your Foundation Skills

1. Investigate the costs and interest rates of three different credit cards. Use the information to prepare a comparison chart.
2. Agree or disagree with this statement: credit companies should not issue credit cards to students. Prepare a five-minute oral report that explains your position and present it to the class.

3. Research what is involved in using an installment credit plan to buy a computer. What steps do you need to take? How much interest would you pay? What is the final cost of the computer with the added cost of the interest? Prepare a written report on your findings.

4. Collect credit agreements from several sources. Become familiar with the terms used. Then, display the credit agreements on a poster with a message about credit.

Building Your Workplace Competencies

Working with three or four of your classmates, find the least expensive way to buy a new car, financing it for four years. (As a class, choose one category to explore, such as a two-door compact or a sports utility vehicle.) Check the cost of the car through local dealers versus sources available on the Internet. Check at least five different credit sources. Together, decide who will handle which tasks. Prepare a written report indicating where your team would buy the car, at what cost, and with what type of financing. What are the monthly payments? What is the cost of financing? Are there any special costs involved? What is the total cost of the new car with all the related costs added? Present your conclusions to the class. *(This activity develops competence with resources, interpersonal skills, information, and technology.)*

28 Insurance

Objectives

After studying this chapter, you will be able to

- describe types of automobile insurance coverage.

- explain the importance of health insurance as a fringe benefit of a job.

- compare and contrast the three forms of life insurance.

- list reasons for buying property insurance.

Words to Know

policy

premium

deductible

health maintenance organization (HMO)

preferred provider organization (PPO)

whole life insurance

dividend

term life insurance

Financial Protection

Determining your insurance needs should be part of your money management plan. Insurance provides you with financial protection. It is important to shop for insurance just as you would shop for a car. Compare the policies of many insurance companies. Then choose one that is right for you.

Insurance is purchased in the form of a policy. A *policy* is a legal contract. It describes your rights and responsibilities as well as those of the insurance company. As you read an insurance policy, you will see the terms *insured* and *insurer*. When you purchase insurance, you are the insured. The insurance company is the insurer. The amount of money you pay for insurance is called a *premium*.

To purchase insurance, you must complete a written application. Read the application carefully. Be sure you understand the questions before you complete and sign the form. If there is something you do not understand, ask questions. Get help by talking to an insurance agent, a person familiar with insurance, or a lawyer. Understand the policy's benefits. Don't wait until you need to file a claim. *Filing a claim* means requesting payment from the insurance company for damages or losses.

Automobile Insurance

Several types of coverage should be considered when purchasing automobile insurance. One type is liability insurance. *Liability insurance* protects you against the claims of other people. It also protects you if you give someone else permission to drive your car and that person has an accident. Liability insurance is not required in all states, but it is very important to have.

Liability insurance is divided into two categories: bodily injury and property damage. *Bodily injury insurance* protects you against court actions or claims for injuries to other people. It protects you against lawsuits for accidents for which you are responsible.

Property damage insurance protects other people's property against damage that you cause. It covers the cost of repairs to the other driver's car if you are at fault in an accident. It also covers the cost of repairing telephone poles, traffic lights, and guardrails if you damage them in an accident. Property damage does not cover the costs of repairing your own car. See 28-1.

policy
A legal contract describing the rights and responsibilities of a person purchasing insurance and those of the company offering it.

premium
The amount of money paid for insurance.

28-1
An insurance agent can help people decide what type of insurance coverage they need.

Collision insurance pays for repairs to your car even if you are at fault, 28-2. Usually, you must pay a certain amount of money for the repairs. The insurance company pays the rest. The amount you pay is called the **deductible**. It is usually $200, $500, $1,000, or a percentage of the total cost. If your car is several years old, you may not need to purchase collision insurance. The car may not be worth the cost of the premiums and the deductible.

Car insurance premiums vary a great deal. They are determined by a rating system used by insurance companies. The rating system includes the following factors:

- driving record of the owner(s)
- ages of the driver(s)
- home address
- type of car driven
- whether the car is used for business or personal use

28-2
In many states, it is unlawful to drive without having insurance coverage.

- number of miles traveled each year
- whether the car is kept in a garage or outdoors
- satisfactory completion of a driver education course (for new drivers)

The amount of deductible a driver is willing to pay also affects the cost of car insurance. The most important factor is probably your driving record. People with good driving records pay lower insurance premiums.

Health Insurance

Health insurance helps people pay the costs of medical care. Some health insurance plans pay for all the costs. Most plans only provide for partial payments.

Health insurance usually covers hospital stays and examinations by physicians. Some also pay for prescription drugs, eyeglasses, and dental work.

Most employers usually provide a group insurance plan for full-time employees and pay a portion of it. Getting group insurance through a company usually costs less than buying health insurance on your own. Company-sponsored health insurance is a valuable fringe benefit. When you begin a job, study the health care plan your employer offers. Find out what it covers. See 28-3.

Even if you have health insurance, some doctors require payment when you receive treatment. Other doctors will wait until the insurance company pays them. Then they will send you a bill for the balance due.

deductible
The amount a policyholder must pay before an insurance company will pay a claim.

Many employers offer their employees membership in a *health maintenance organization (HMO).* These organizations cover most health care services. Set fees are paid in advance. Then when you need medical attention, you go to a doctor or hospital associated with the HMO. Depending on your policy, you receive care at no additional charge or a low fee.

Another form of health insurance is offered by a *preferred provider organization (PPO).* A PPO is an organization of doctors or hospitals. They contract with an insurance company to provide health services. Like an HMO, if you use doctors in the PPO, the fees are minimal. You can choose other doctors and hospitals, but the fees are higher and you will be responsible for paying the difference.

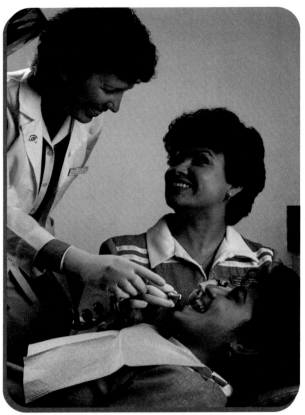

28-3

Members of a health insurance plan often have the option to buy dental and eye-care coverage for an extra fee.

Life Insurance

Life insurance is designed to provide financial security to the family of the insured, should that person die. Like health insurance, life insurance is often provided to full-time employees as a fringe benefit.

After the death of the insured, the face value of the policy is paid to the beneficiary. The policy owner names the beneficiary when he or she buys the policy. In most cases, the beneficiary is a spouse or family member.

Whole life insurance provides the insured with permanent coverage. The policy is in effect until the insured dies or the policy is cashed in. Premiums for most of these policies do not increase over the life of the policy.

Whole life insurance gains cash value over a period of years. This is because a portion of what you pay in premiums earns interest like the money in your savings account. Some whole life policies pay dividends. A *dividend* is a payout on money earned. They are usually paid on an annual basis. The dividends can be left in the policy and accumulate interest, or they can be applied toward the purchase of additional insurance. As long as you keep the policy, the cash value grows. After a period of time, you can turn in your policy for its cash value. However, once you cash in your policy, you are no longer insured under that policy.

Term life insurance is purchased for a limited period of time, such as five or ten years. At the end of this time, the policy may be renewed. The premiums for term life insurance are less than the premiums for whole life insurance. However, the premiums increase with each renewal. Term life policies do not gain cash value.

Variable-rate life insurance is another form. In many respects, a variable-rate insurance contract is similar to whole life insurance. The policy provides a guaranteed life benefit. This form of insurance is also an investment tool. You contribute a part of your premiums to investment options. The cash surrender value of this type of policy can greatly increase if your investments are successful. It can also decrease if your choices are unsuccessful. This form of policy is not for everyone. However, they do offer both the single and married person an option. The policy offers a guaranteed life benefit. It also builds cash that can later be withdrawn, similar to an annuity (discussed in Chapter 26).

Deciding how much life insurance to buy is not easy. Each person has different financial needs. Generally, a single person has few financial responsibilities. Thus, he or she needs less life insurance than a married person with children.

---

health maintenance organization (HMO)
A health insurance for which members pay a set fee and receive medical care, as needed, from a participating doctor or hospital.

preferred provider organization (PPO)
An organization of doctors or hospitals that contract with an insurance company to provide health services.

whole life insurance
An insurance plan that offers the insured permanent coverage.

dividend
A payout, usually annual, on money earned on whole life insurance.

term life insurance
An insurance plan that offers coverage for a limited period of time.

Disability Insurance

For many young workers, disability insurance is even more important than life insurance. Disability insurance provides for people who become unable to work due to serious illness or injury. It allows disabled employees to receive a percentage of their incomes for an extended period of time.

Employers often provide this type of coverage as part of their fringe benefit packages. However, policies vary greatly. If you have disability coverage through your employer, read the policy carefully. Evaluate the specific benefits and terms of the policy. Then decide whether you need to purchase additional coverage.

Property Insurance

Whether you rent or own a home, you should insure your property. Property insurance protects your possessions against fire, theft, or other types of loss. Property insurance also provides liability coverage in the event that someone is injured in your home.

A home fire occurs at least once a minute. Home fires account for billions of dollars in property damage each year. Much more than that is lost each year in thefts and burglaries. Property insurance is a way to protect yourself against such losses.

Be certain the policy you purchase has the type of coverage you need. A renter's insurance policy should cover personal belongings, furniture, appliances, and jewelry. A homeowner's insurance policy should cover all that and the building itself.

Standard property insurance covers your belongings for what they are worth at the time you file a claim. For instance, suppose your four-year-old television is stolen. Your insurance company may only give you about 60 percent of what you paid for it four years ago.

An option in property insurance that pays the full cost of new items is called *replacement value coverage*. This type of coverage costs more. However, you may find the extra cost worthwhile if you ever need to make a claim.

An inventory, or list, of all of your possessions can help you decide how much property insurance to buy. An inventory also provides a record of your valuables. Such a record would help you file a claim if your valuables were stolen or destroyed in a fire. See 28-4.

Filing a Claim

Filing a claim means requesting payment from your insurance company. For instance, you would file a claim on your car insurance after an accident. You would file a claim on your property insurance after a fire.

Each insurance company may want you to file your claim a bit differently. You will need to provide a list of the valuables that were damaged or destroyed. Other types of information may be required. You may need to describe the details of the accident. Talk with your agent to find out what action you should take.

Inventory of _LIVING ROOM_ Item Description (Include model #, serial #, or brand name when possible)	Date of Purchase	Purchase Price and Tax	Place of Purchase
1. SOFA THOMASVILLE, SINWP	5-2-02	$699.00	HOMEMAKERS
2. COFFEE TABLE BRASS/GLASS, 141F	11-26-02	$167.47	SERVICE MERCHANDISE
3. CEILING FAN W/LIGHT FIXTURE OAK/BRASS, C781153	1-7-03	$160.18	SPIEGEL
4. BOOKCASE O'SULLIVAN, 121LLY	2-1-03	$139.00	SERVICE MERCHANDISE
5. FLOOR RUG HANDMADE, INDIAN, 5'7" X 8'4"	6-11-03	$413.93	PIER 1 IMPORTS
6. TELEVISION RCA COLOR TRAK 2000, #F27160WN	10-2-03	$698.67	HIGHLAND SUPER STORE

28-4

A personal property inventory can help determine the amount of coverage needed.

Summary

You should shop for insurance to be sure you get the kind of financial protection you need. Read the policies. Know what they cover. Understand the benefits they offer.

Liability insurance is an important part of automobile insurance. It includes both bodily injury insurance and property damage insurance. You may also want to buy collision insurance to pay for repairs to your own car.

Health insurance helps pay the costs of medical care. Employers usually provide some form of health insurance to full-time employees. It is a valuable fringe benefit.

Life insurance provides financial security to survivors after the death of the insured. Whole life insurance stays in effect until the insured dies or until the policy is turned in for its cash value. Term life insurance is for a limited period of time. When the time period is over, the insured is no longer protected. Variable-rate insurance provides you with an opportunity to determine your own rate of dividend return.

Property insurance protects personal possessions. It also protects the policyholder against liability. A renter's policy covers the contents of a home. A homeowner's policy protects the building as well as its contents.

When you need to file an insurance claim, contact your agent. Follow the steps necessary to receive benefits from your insurance policy.

Reviewing the Chapter

1. What is the name of the money a person pays for insurance?
2. What legal contract describes the rights and responsibilities of a person buying insurance and the insurance company?
3. What type of insurance would protect you if you caused a car accident that dented someone else's car and a guardrail?
4. What type of insurance would protect you if you caused a car accident in which people were hurt?
5. What type of insurance pays for repairs to a car you own?
6. What term identifies the amount paid to cover loss or damage before the insurance company pays the remainder?
7. What is paid to the beneficiary of a life insurance policy when the insured dies?
8. What is paid to the insured when a whole life policy is turned in before death?

9. What is permanent life insurance called?
10. What is the term for life insurance that covers a certain number of years?

Building Your Foundation Skills

1. Investigate the difference between buying a health insurance policy and becoming a member of an HMO. Which would you prefer? Why? Explain your answers in a written report.
2. Study several life insurance policies. Make a comparison chart of their costs and benefits.
3. Make an inventory of your possessions. Decide how much property insurance you would need to cover them in case of loss. Call an insurance company to find out how much the premium would cost.
4. Design a poster illustrating the need for insurance. Display it in a visible location at school.
5. Find out what you should do to file a claim when you are in a car accident.

Building Your Workplace Competencies

Talk to an automobile insurance agent about the cost of automobile coverage and the factors that affect premiums. Find out specific premium costs for the car of your choice for a person with a new driver's license and no driving experience. What can be done to reduce the premiums? Obtain information about premium costs from two other car insurers either via phone or the Internet. Use the same make and model of car throughout this exercise. Using a computer, create a chart comparing premiums. Where would you buy insurance for your imaginary car? Make a brief presentation to the class. (*This activity develops competence with resources, interpersonal skills, information, systems, and technology.*)

PART SEVEN
Growing Toward Independence

A Place to Live

Objectives

After studying this chapter, you will be able to

- weigh the advantages and disadvantages of living at home, with a roommate, and on your own.

- list ways to look for a place to live.

- evaluate housing options according to a person's needs and budget.

- describe ideas for furnishing an apartment on a limited budget.

- explain the legal responsibilities involved in signing a lease.

Words to Know

real estate agency
rental agency
verbal agreement
lease
security deposit

Where Will You Live?

As you mature and grow toward independence, you will face many decisions. One may be where to live. You may be able to choose whether to live at home, with a roommate, or on your own. Before deciding where to live, consider the advantages and disadvantages of each option you have. See 29-1.

Living at Home

Many people look forward to leaving home once they enter the workplace. They want the change of pace and new challenges that living away from home offers. On the other hand, some people feel comfortable with their home lives. They are in no hurry to move out.

Living at home has many advantages for young workers. One big advantage is cost. Even if you pay room and board, living at home usually costs less than renting an apartment.

Another advantage is having the company of your family. Not only do family members provide companionship, they also provide assistance. Household chores, such as cooking, cleaning, and laundry, can be shared with others.

However, living at home can have some disadvantages. For instance, you may not be able to be as independent as you want. Your family's social activities may be different from yours. Your family's routines may be different from yours, too.

29-1
When young people begin earning full-time incomes, they often consider new living arrangements.

29-2
Friends who share common interests usually make compatible roommates.

Living with a Roommate

Choosing to live away from home is a big decision. If you want to live with a roommate, try to find someone with a lifestyle similar to yours. A roommate can become a lifelong friend or a terrible enemy. See 29-2.

Living with a roommate has some of the same advantages of living with family members. You can share expenses with a roommate. You have companionship and may meet new friends. You also have someone with whom to share household work.

Living with a roommate may also have some disadvantages. You may not get along with each other or with each other's friends. You may have different tastes in food and decorating. Your roommate may be sloppier or neater than you are. Your roommate may not understand your way of life.

Living on Your Own

Only you can decide if you are ready to live alone. This new experience may be a big change from the environment you know best.

The chief advantage of living alone is that you are totally independent. You decide when, where, and how you are going to do things. You can choose your own furnishings, food, TV programs, and music.

As a disadvantage, living alone can be lonely sometimes. Also, you are responsible for all the household expenses. In addition, you must do all the cleaning, cooking, and laundry.

Looking for a Place to Live

You can start to look for a place to live by asking your family and friends if they know of anything available. You can also look in the newspaper for apartments, rooms, or houses to rent. Check the classified ads in the real estate section of the newspaper. See 29-3. Look under the heading *Rental Properties* or *Apartments for Rent*.

Other sources of information are **real estate agencies**. They deal primarily with the buying and selling of houses. However, some real estate agents can help you find places to rent. Look in the Yellow Pages of the phone book to find real estate agencies that handle rental apartments and houses.

29-3
The classified ads in the newspaper are a good place to start a search for an apartment.

A **rental agency** can also help you find an apartment. It is a business that assists customers in the renting of apartments for a fee.

A rental agency is different from a real estate agency. The apartment owner pays the real estate agency a commission after the property is rented. You pay a fee to a rental agency before you find an apartment. After you pay the fee, the rental agency will refer you to apartments or houses available to rent. However, paying the fee is no guarantee that you will find a place to live.

> **real estate agency**
> A business that assists customers with buying and selling houses.
>
> **rental agency**
> A business that, for a fee, assists customers with renting apartments.

Housing Needs and Costs

As you look at places to live, think about your housing needs. Also think about the costs related to housing. The following questions may help you:

- Do you need a single room, apartment, or house?
- How much rent can you afford to pay? Some guidelines say to allow one-fourth of your salary for housing costs. Others suggest that you limit rent and utilities to one-third of your take-home pay. You must decide what you can afford based on your income and other expenses.
- How much should you expect to pay for utilities? Check to see which utilities are included in your rental payments, if any. Utilities may include electricity, gas, water, telephone, and waste disposal. Most utility bills must be paid monthly. Many companies require deposits from new utility users until they have proved they pay their bills on time.
- What furnishings and utensils do you need to buy? A bed, sofa, table, and chairs come to mind right away. Have you thought about sheets, towels, dishes, pots, and pans? Cleansers, buckets, and brooms cost money, too. Setting up a household can be expensive. See 29-4.
- If you need to use public transportation, is it available nearby?
- If you have a car, is safe parking available nearby?
- Is the place reasonably close to your work?
- Is the neighborhood safe and clean?

29-4
Checking the placement of electrical outlets and measuring closets are part of a thorough evaluation of an apartment.

When you look for a place to live, don't think only about the rent. Running a household costs more than just paying the rent. Having a home means more than having a roof over your head. Look for a place where you can feel safe and comfortable.

Furnishing Your New Home

Most apartments include a refrigerator and stove. If you rent an *unfurnished* apartment, you will need to supply your own furniture. If you rent a *furnished* apartment, the rent will be considerably higher because it will have furniture.

If you shop for furniture, you will see that it costs much more than you expect. You may not be able to afford many new items. Used furniture may be more in keeping with your budget. Look for affordable furniture and household items in newspaper classified ads. Also check garage and yard sales, auctions, and store clearances. See 29-5.

Your Legal Responsibilities

When you rent housing, both you and the owner have legal responsibilities. State and city laws regulate what the owner must provide for the tenant, known as the *renter*. The owner is responsible for caring for the building, hallways, and grounds. In return, you, the *tenant*, must remember the building is not your property. You are simply paying to use it for a period of time. Therefore, you must take good care of it.

When you rent a place to live, you and the owner agree to certain terms. The simplest form of agreement is a ***verbal agreement***. This is an agreement in which certain terms are specified but not written down. As a general practice, you should avoid verbal agreements.

A written rental agreement is called a *lease*. It is a legal contract. A lease explains the rights and responsibilities of the tenant and the owner.

verbal agreement
The simplest form of an agreement in which certain terms are specified but not written down.

lease
A written rental agreement, which defines the rights and responsibilities of the tenant and the owner of a rental property.

29-5

Clearance sales are a good source of bargains for someone furnishing an apartment on a budget.

Before signing a lease, be sure you understand all its conditions. A lease contains the following information:

- the length of the lease, usually six months or one year
- what the rent is
- when the rent is due
- responsibilities of the renter regarding the condition of the apartment
- what must be done before moving out of the apartment

The lease will also describe the terms concerning the security deposit. See the example in 29-6. A *security deposit* is usually equal to a month's rent. Most owners require a security deposit from a new tenant. If you damage the apartment, the owner will use the money to make the necessary repairs. If no damage is done, your deposit will be returned to you when you move away.

> **security deposit**
> An amount of money, usually equal to a month's rent, paid to the owner of rental property by new tenants when the lease is signed.

English Manor Apartments

I N C O R P O R A T E D

203 WINDSOR ROAD • LAKE SHORE, N.C. 28001

THIS AGREEMENT OF LEASE, MADE THIS __1st__ DAY OF __May_____ BETWEEN ENGLISH

MANOR APARTMENTS, INC., HEREINAFTER CALLED LESSOR: AND _____

_____ HEREINAFTER CALLED TENANT, WHETHER ONE OR MORE.

WITNESSETH, That the Lessor leases and lets unto the Tenant, premises known as _____ Lake Shore, N.C. 28401, for a term of not less than thirty (30) days from this date at the rental of $__400.00___ per month, to be paid in advance at the office of English Manor Apartments on the first day of each month without formal demand. This lease shall be renewed automatically for successive terms of one month each so long as the terms hereof are complied with at the same rental as hereinabove set forth payable in advance on the first day of each said renewed term, which renewed term shall expire of its own limitation at midnight on the last day of said term.

This will acknowledge the receipt of $__400.00___ as a deposit to cover any indebtedness to the Lessor for charges made for breakage or damage to the property. Any or all of deposit to be returned to the Tenant upon proper termination of the lease providing (1) THE TENANT HAS REMAINED IN POSSESSION AND PAID RENT ON ABOVE PROPERTY FOR AT LEAST SIX (6) MONTHS: (2) KEYS TO THE ABOVE PROPERTY HAVE BEEN RETURNED (3) THE PREMISES ARE LEFT IN A CLEAN CONDITION, AND ALL OTHER CONDITIONS OF THIS AGREEMENT HAVE BEEN MET TO THE SATISFACTION OF THE LESSOR. IT IS FURTHER UNDERSTOOD AND AGREED THAT THE TENANT SHALL GIVE A FIFTEEN (15) DAYS WRITTEN NOTICE BEFORE VACATING PREMISES. IF SAID NOTICE IS NOT GIVEN, TENANT WILL BE CHARGED FOR SAME.

TENANT will pay for any damage other than normal deterioration, wear and tear to the premises of Lessors property and will be responsible for the stoppage of sewer and drainage facilities chargeable to his use of the premises. Tenant will pay all utility bills as they come due. TENANT AGREES TO PAY A $5.00 GAS SERVICE CHARGE UPON VACATING.

LESSOR and its agents reserve the right to cancel this lease for any reason at any time by mailing a written notice to Tenant specifying a day of termination of the lease, which date shall be seven (7) days from the date of mailing the notice of cancellation. The mailing of such written notice by first class mail will constitute the giving of this notice. Any unearned portion of the rent will be refunded to the Tenant.

Should Tenant fail to make payment of the rental herein specified in advance by the first day of the month, this lease shall terminate at midnight of the last day of the preceding month without the necessity of any written notice; and Tenant agrees upon such termination to immediately vacate the premises. Should Tenant fail to vacate the premises, Lessor shall have the absolute right to lock the premises and forbid the use thereof by the Tenant.

The Lessor and its agents shall have the right to enter upon the premises at any reasonable time to assure that this agreement is being complied with and not being violated.

Time shall be of the essence of this agreement. It is agreed that no failure of the Lessor to insist on the strict terms hereof shall constitute a waiver of its rights to insist on such terms on any later occasion. Tenant will comply with the general rules and regulations promulgated by the Lessor for the operation of the apartment of which the subject premises are a part.

I/We accept the foregoing conditions.   ENGLISH MANOR APTS.

_____   _____

Tenant   Agent

_____

Tenant

29-6

Tenants are usually required to sign a written lease when they rent an apartment.

Summary

As you grow toward independence, you may need to decide where to live. Before making a decision, be sure to think about the advantages and disadvantages of each option. Ask your family and friends for leads. Read the classified ads in the newspaper. You may want to contact a real estate or rental agency.

Think about both housing needs and costs as you look for a place to live. The home you choose should be one that you can afford. It should also be one where you can feel safe and comfortable.

Furnishing a new home can be expensive. Look for ways to buy what you need while staying within your budget.

If you choose to rent a place to live, you will probably be offered a lease. Read it carefully. Understand the legal responsibilities it involves. Once you sign it, you are bound to fulfill your responsibilities.

Reviewing the Chapter

1. Name two advantages and two disadvantages of living at home.
2. Name two advantages and two disadvantages of living with a roommate.
3. Name two advantages and two disadvantages of living alone.
4. What is the difference between a real estate agency and a rental agency?
5. List five questions related to housing needs and costs you should consider when choosing a place to live.
6. Name three places where you might find affordable furnishings for a home.
7. True or false. In a verbal agreement, no contract details are in writing.
8. A lease _____.
    A. is a written rental agreement
    B. is a legal contract
    C. explains the rights and responsibilities of the tenant and the owner
    D. All of the above.
9. List five pieces of information included in a lease.
10. A security deposit _____.
    A. is usually equal to a month's rent
    B. is used by the owner to repair damages to the property caused by the tenant
    C. is returned to the tenant when he or she moves away if the property has not been damaged
    D. All of the above.

Building Your Foundation Skills

1. In a local newspaper, find ads for five places to rent. Find out the location and the rent for each place. Also find out how much space and what facilities each apartment has to offer. In a written report, explain why some cost more than others.

2. Obtain a lease from an apartment complex. Discuss the aspects of the lease in class. What parts of the lease seem to favor the tenant? Which parts seem to favor the owner?

3. In a local newspaper, find an ad for a furnished apartment. Call the apartment manager or visit the site to learn what furnishings are included.

4. Decide which living option seems best for a young person holding his or her first full-time job: living at home, with a roommate, or alone. List four or five reasons for your opinion and share them with the class.

Building Your Workplace Competencies

Find an unfurnished apartment for rent in your area and investigate sources of affordable furnishings for it. Working with two or three classmates, decide who will do which tasks. Obtain a floor plan of the rental unit or create one. The floor plan should show the room dimensions and locations of doors and windows. Find items to furnish the apartment to suit the needs and tastes of an 18-year-old on a tight budget. Record each item's cost, size, color, and condition (if used). Make an inventory list of the furnishings and their total cost using a computer. List the items in the order of importance, since all items cannot be purchased right away. Present your ideas to the class using fabric swatches, illustrations, product brochures, or photographs wherever possible. *(This activity develops competence with resources, interpersonal skills, information, and technology.)*

Transportation

Objectives

After studying this chapter, you will be able to

- identify two forms of self-powered transportation.

- determine the pros and cons of driving to work.

- describe three types of mass transportation.

- rephrase the information in a mass transportation schedule.

Words to Know

car pool

mass transportation

schedule

carrier

transfer

Self-Powered Transportation

Choosing where you work is sometimes as important as choosing what you do. When you are looking for a job, you must consider transportation. You must think about how you will get to and from work.

Two forms of self-powered transportation are walking and riding a bicycle. If you live close to your workplace, you can walk. In that case, changes in your work schedule won't create any transportation problems for you. You are completely independent and can come and go as you please without waiting for a ride. Walking is good exercise, and it is free. As long as the area is safe and the weather is suitable, walking is a good form of transportation. See 30-1.

Riding a bicycle is another option. It is best in areas with good weather, light traffic, and short distances to work. In areas with heavy traffic, it may be too dangerous.

Automobile Transportation

Many people choose to drive to work in their own cars. This option provides great flexibility. Drivers who have their own vehicles can travel whenever and wherever they want.

Driving has some drawbacks, too. If you choose to drive to work, you must have a driver's license. You must also have a car. Many new workers cannot afford to buy a new car. Even used cars are very expensive.

30-1
Walking to work is a good way to get exercise and save transportation costs.

Buying a car is not the only expense involved. You must also consider insurance. Car insurance premiums vary. In general, premiums are usually higher for younger drivers, new cars, and urban areas. The cost of gasoline should also be considered. How much you spend will depend on the type of car you drive and how far you travel.

Be careful not to overlook maintenance and repair costs. Even new cars require some maintenance such as oil changes. The maintenance and repair bills for older cars can be expensive and unpredictable.

If you own a car, you must also think about where you will park it. A garage is the best place to keep a car to protect it from accidents, theft, and bad weather. However, some apartments do not have garages or parking lots. If parking is not available where you live, you may have to park on the street. Renting garage space may be another option, but this would add to the cost of owning a car.

Driving a car gives you flexibility and independence, but it is expensive. Before you accept a job that would require you to drive, think carefully. Decide if you can afford to drive a car. Decide if you want to pay the costs related to driving. Also decide if you want the responsibility of driving. See 30-2.

Annual Car Costs

Total Ownership Cost	$ __5,204__
Total Operating Cost	__1,278__
Total Driving Cost	$ __6,482__

Ownership Costs		**Operating Costs**	
Depreciation (cost of car minus trade-in value, divided by number of years car is owned)	$ __3,444__	Gas (total miles driven divided by miles per gallon, multiplied by cost per gallon)	$ __575__
Insurance premiums	__1,612__	Maintenance (tune-ups, oil changes, tire balancing, etc.)	__168__
license and registration	__148__	Repairs (tires, battery, muffler, brakes, etc.)	__135__
		Miscellaneous (parking, car washes, accessories, etc.)	__400__

30-2

All the costs of owning and operating a car must be counted when considering the option of driving to work.

Car Pools

One way to cut driving costs is to join a car pool. A ***car pool*** is a group of people who take turns driving, usually to work. In this arrangement, you drive your car less. You still have the costs involved in owning a car. However, you can save money on fuel, maintenance, and repairs.

Car pools are as reliable as the people who form them. Members of a car pool must cooperate with each other. Each member must do his or her fair share to get everyone safely to work on time.

If you join a car pool, remember that members of a car pool can get sick. They can have appointments, meetings, and other responsibilities. Be sure to have a backup transportation plan ready in case your car pool arrangements change suddenly.

As a new employee, find out if your coworkers have car pools. You can usually get information about car pools from the company's personnel office.

When you join a car pool, you give up some of the flexibility and independence you have when you drive your own car. On the other hand, you gain companionship and reduce transportation costs.

Mass Transportation

Mass transportation is transportation used routinely by the general public. Buses, trains, and airplanes are used for mass transportation. One or more of these types of transportation are available in almost all large towns and cities.

Some mass transportation systems are privately owned and operated. Others are publicly owned. The government supports public mass transportation systems from tax money.

car pool
A group of people who take turns driving, usually to work.

mass transportation
Transportation used routinely by the general public.

Schedules

When using public transportation, plan your travel carefully. Check mass transportation schedules. A *schedule* lists the expected arrival and departure times for buses, trains, and airplanes. By reading a schedule, you can decide which ride will allow you to arrive at work on time. Schedules also list where stops are located. This allows you to find the stops that are closest to your home and your job. See 30-3.

When you use a schedule, remember that posted times are approximate. Drivers try to stay on schedule, but they can't always control delays. Choose a ride that will get you to work early. This will allow for any delays that may arise along the way.

Printed schedules are available from all carriers. A *carrier* is an organization that operates a transportation system. Carriers also provide more detailed information about schedules by phone.

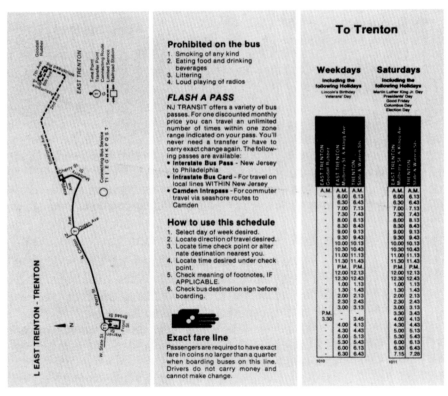

30-3
Bus and train schedules give passengers the information they need to use the system.

Buses

When you take a bus, remember that drivers can't control traffic and road conditions. If traffic is heavy or the weather is bad, your bus may be late. You, in turn, may arrive late for work. Listening to traffic and weather reports will help you foresee problems. If you hear warnings of storms or traffic delays, adjust your schedule accordingly.

Buses follow specific routes. In other words, they do not go down every street and stop at every corner. You are unlikely to find a bus that will drop you off right at your home or job. You may need to walk a few blocks to get to and from the bus stop. See 30-4.

30-4
Bus stops are located every few blocks along most city routes.

If you work in a large city, you may need to take several routes and transfer between them. To *transfer* is to change from one bus or train route to another. Usually a transfer costs nothing extra or a small fee. You should find out if you must transfer when scheduling your transportation.

Most bus lines require a ticket purchase in advance. Many bus companies offer reduced fares if you purchase a monthly pass or a quantity of rides. A monthly pass may also save you money by allowing you to make unlimited transfers at no extra cost. In some cities, monthly passes can save you as much as 25 percent. A 25 percent savings means that you get one free ride after three rides. Usually a ticket expires on a certain date.

schedule
A list of the expected arrival and departure times and locations for buses, trains, and airplanes.

carrier
An organization that operates a transportation system.

transfer
To change from one bus or train route to another.

You can call the bus company for information about using the bus system. You can get information about schedules, routes, and transfer locations. You can also find out about fares and possible discounts.

Trains and Subways

Large cities often have high-speed transportation systems. Subways and trains are not subject to traffic jams and other delays that slow buses. As a worker in a large city, you may be able to choose among different types of transportation. Plan your route just as you would if you took a bus. See 30-5.

30-5
Many large cities run trains as well as buses for mass transportation.

Airplanes

People on business trips often travel by airplane. Airplane schedules are like other mass transportation schedules. They give approximate arrival and departure times. However, airplanes are subject to many delays. It is a good idea to call and check on your flight before going to the airport.

Plan to arrive at the airport at least two hours before your flight is scheduled to depart. See 30-6. This will allow you time to check in, go through security, and get to your departure gate.

Airline passengers must also plan how they will get to and from the airport. Perhaps they drive to the airport or a friend drops them off. In addition to these options, various forms of ground transportation exist. These include buses, trains, limousines, taxis, and rental cars.

30-6
Airplanes provide fast transportation for people traveling long distances for work.

Summary

As an employee, you must be able to get to work on time. You should plan your transportation when you plan your job search. You must find a reliable form of transportation to and from your workplace.

You may be able to walk or ride a bicycle. You may choose to drive your own car or to join a car pool. Depending on where you live, mass transportation may be an option for you. In that case, you would need to read the schedules and plan your routes.

Reviewing the Chapter

1. Name two advantages of walking to work.
2. When would riding a bicycle be a good option for getting to work?
3. List three expenses related to driving a car to work.
4. How can joining a car pool reduce transportation costs?
5. True or false. The government uses tax money to support public mass transportation systems.
6. What can a traveler learn by reading a mass transportation schedule?
7. Changing from one bus, train, or subway to another to take a different route is a _____.
8. If you ride a bus every day, what is the benefit of buying a ticket for the month or a quantity of rides?
9. Why are subways and trains often much faster than buses?
10. Why should a traveler plan to arrive at the airport at least two hours before scheduled departure time?

Building Your Foundation Skills

1. Identify a place where you would like to work. Prepare a written comparison of three different ways of getting there and back. Consider the following factors: time, cost, convenience, and reliability. State which method of transportation you think would be best for you.
2. Talk to someone who is in a car pool. What are the pros and cons of this method of transportation? Share your findings with the class.

3. Using your home as the starting point, plan a bus (and/or train) route to the nearest shopping mall. Assume that you are scheduled to begin working as a salesclerk at 9 a.m. Where and when would you catch the bus? What time would the bus arrive at the stop nearest the shopping mall?

4. Plan how you would travel to an interview at your dream job. In an oral report, describe the trip from your home to the job site. List all forms of transportation you would use. Estimate how long the trip would take and how much it would cost.

Building Your Workplace Competencies

Prepare a budget that lists the complete costs of owning a car. Work with the same team and the same car example you researched for Chapter 27. In addition to the car expenses you learned from that activity, find out all other costs of owning the car. These may include the sales and/or state tax, license cost, registration fees, and city sticker fee. Also figure the operating costs by interviewing parents and others about gas and maintenance costs and service fees. Present your findings to the class. *(This activity develops competence with resources, interpersonal skills, and information.)*

Being a Responsible Citizen

Objectives

After studying this chapter, you will be able to

- recognize the importance of voting in elections.

- explain how laws are made.

- name the two categories of laws in the United States.

- determine situations that might require the services of a lawyer.

- state the rights and responsibilities of consumers.

Words to Know

citizen
register
bill
proposition
civil laws
public laws
monopoly
competition
recourse

The Right to Vote

A *citizen* is a person who owes allegiance to a government. As a citizen of the United States, you have many rights and responsibilities. Your rights are protected by the laws of the government. You are responsible for obeying those laws.

One of the most important rights of U.S. citizens is the right to vote. The law does not force citizens to vote. It simply gives them the opportunity to do so. See 31-1.

In general, any citizen of the United States who is at least 18 years old has the right to vote. It is the responsibility of each citizen to exercise that right. Voting is one way to express yourself on public issues. If you are eligible, you should vote in national, state, and local elections.

31-1
Exercising the right to vote gives citizens a chance to participate in their government.

The people who are elected to office make and enforce the laws. As a responsible citizen, you should vote to elect people who will support the kinds of laws you support. When you vote for someone, you are saying, "I want this person to represent me in government." You are also saying, "I think this person will do the best job for the town (or state or nation)."

Registering to Vote

In order to vote, you must register. When you *register*, you add your name to the official list of citizens eligible to vote in elections. To be eligible, you must be at least 18 years old. You must be a citizen of the United States. You must have lived in the state and county where you are

citizen
A person who owes allegiance to a government.
register
To submit one's name to the official list of citizens eligible to vote in elections.

registering for at least 30 days prior to the election. When you go to vote, election officials check to see if your name is on the list of registered voters. If it is, you can vote.

You can register to vote at the office of the county commissioner, the election supervisor, or the municipal clerk. Just before a major election, mobile units for voter registration may visit your neighborhood. They are run by representatives of political parties. They want all eligible citizens to be registered so they can vote in the upcoming election.

The Laws of the Land

Laws are rules by which people live. A society could not function if people did whatever they desired. Living in a society without laws results in total confusion and turmoil.

As a citizen, you have many rights that are protected by laws. If your rights are violated, the laws outline what course of action you may take to correct the situation. As a citizen, you also have a responsibility to obey laws. If you fail to do so, the laws define what penalties you will face.

How Laws Are Made

Laws are made by the legislative branches of the various levels of government. Lawmakers at every level are elected to public office. Federal laws are made by the United States Congress, 31-2. State laws are made by state legislatures. Local laws are made by town or city councils.

To make a new state law, a state legislator introduces a bill to the members of the legislature. A *bill* is a proposed law. The members of the legislature discuss the proposed law. They discuss the reasons for having the law and the reasons for not having the law. This discussion is called a *debate*. The members of the legislature vote on the bill. If it passes, it is sent to the governor. Once the governor signs it, it becomes a law.

Federal laws are made in a similar way. A bill is introduced. If it is passed by both the Senate and the House of Representatives, it is sent to the president. Once the president signs a bill, it becomes a law.

Sometimes a proposed law is presented directly to citizens as a public question. Public questions appear on voting ballots as *propositions*. When citizens go to the polls to vote for public officials, they may also vote on one or more propositions. If the majority of voters accept a proposition, it becomes law. If people vote down a proposition, it does not become law.

Another method of making laws is sometimes used on the local level. A town council member may introduce a bill by reading it at a public meeting. The bill is then printed in the local newspaper. The bill is read again at a second public meeting. Citizens are given time to make comments and express their opinions about the bill. After the discussion period, the council members vote on the bill. If passed, it becomes a law.

Types of Laws

The laws in the United States are divided into two categories: civil laws and public laws. *Civil laws* define a person's rights in relation to other people. Civil laws relate to cases involving such issues as contracts, inheritances, and the business of corporations.

31-2
The U.S. Congress is responsible for making laws at the national level.

Public laws define a person's rights in relation to government. Public laws are divided into four groups.

- *Criminal law* relates to punishments for failure to obey the law.
- *Constitutional law* refers to the basic laws of the nation. See 31-3.
- *Administrative law* pertains to the duties and powers of the executive branch of government. The executive branch includes the highest office at each level of government. Presidents, governors, and mayors are members of the executive branches of federal, state, and local governments, respectively.
- *International law* relates to the relationships among nations.

bill
A proposed law.
proposition
Public questions appearing on voting ballots for the consideration of voters.
civil laws
Laws that define a person's rights in relation to other people.
public laws
Laws that defines a person's rights in relation to government.

31-3
In the United States, constitutional law relates to the Constitution and its amendments, including those listed in the Bill of Rights.

When You May Need a Lawyer

At some point, you may need a lawyer to help you interpret the laws that affect you as a citizen. If you need help finding a lawyer, you might ask friends and family members. They may be able to recommend lawyers they have used. You could also look in the Yellow Pages of the phone book for a listing of attorneys in your area. When looking in the phone book, you may find a number for a state legal association. Such an association is another source of help for finding a lawyer to meet your specific legal needs.

Lawyers specialize in the types of legal services they offer. Some lawyers specialize in defending criminal cases. Some deal primarily with tax laws or corporate lawsuits. Others primarily handle divorce cases. When choosing a lawyer, it is important to look for one who is qualified to deal with your particular type of problem. See 31-4.

Legal advice can be quite costly. Ask about fees before you hire an attorney. If you are unable to afford a lawyer, you may be able to get free legal help from a public service agency.

You might want to seek the advice of a lawyer if you are involved in any of the following situations:

- If you buy or sell a house, a lawyer will review all the legal documents involved. He or she can make sure that your best interests are being served.
- If you get a divorce, a lawyer can help you arrive at a fair settlement.

31-4
Lawyers generally specialize in a specific legal area, such as real estate transactions, divorces, or personal injury.

- If you rent an apartment and wish to break the lease, a lawyer can help you understand your options.
- If you buy a service or product and fail to receive it, a lawyer can help you resolve the problem.
- If you receive a summons or subpoena to appear in court, you may need the services of a lawyer to protect your rights.
- If you are arrested, you may need a lawyer to defend you and represent you in court.
- If you wish to make out a will, a lawyer can help make sure it is a valid document.
- If a loved one dies, you may need a lawyer to help settle the estate.

Consumer Rights and Responsibilities

As a citizen of the United States, you are entitled to participate in the economy. You do this by working to produce goods and services. You also participate by consuming goods and services produced by others.

The economy of the United States is based on free enterprise. To make this economic system work, both businesses and consumers must be treated fairly. Many laws have been passed to protect the free enterprise system. As a result, you have both rights and responsibilities as a consumer.

The Right to Information

As a consumer, you have the right to accurate information. Product labels, claims, and advertisements must be truthful. Instructions for the use and care of products must be clear and understandable, 31-5.

Along with this right to information comes the responsibility to use it. You should read product labels and service contracts. You should compare items carefully. Know what to expect from a product or service before you pay for it. Once you buy a product, follow the instructions for its use and care.

The Right to Choose

You and other consumers have the right to choose from a variety of products and services. The government protects that right with laws against monopolies. A *monopoly* is total control over a product or service.

Suppose Company AZ held a monopoly on cars in the United States. In that case, the company would be the sole U.S. manufacturer and seller. Company AZ might decide to make only two-door, compact cars to save money. Meanwhile, the company would charge whatever price it desired. If you wanted a car, you would have to buy an AZ car at a fixed price.

The government has laws against monopolies to encourage a variety of products and services to exist. When monopolies are outlawed, competition reigns. *Competition* is the effort of two or more parties acting independently to offer the most favorable product or terms.

31-5

Consumers have the right to expect clear and accurate directions on product packages.

Variety is a sign of a free enterprise economy. You and other consumers have the responsibility to select wisely. You should compare different features, qualities, and prices. Then make choices that best meet your needs. See 31-6.

The Right to Safety

Consumers have the right to be protected from unsafe products. You can expect foods, drugs, toys, appliances, and tools to be safe.

You also have the responsibility to use products safely. Use them as they are meant to be used. Do not share prescription drugs. Do not use items past their expiration dates. Follow directions for the safe use of products that are potentially dangerous. You also have the responsibility to report products that you find to be unsafe. Notify the store where you bought the product. Notify the product's manufacturer. You may also want to notify an appropriate government office.

monopoly
The exclusive possession and control of a product or service.
competition
Two or more parties acting independently to offer the most favorable product or terms.

31-6   *Walgreen Co.*

Consumers have the right to choose from a variety of products.

The Right to Be Heard

If you buy a product or service, and it does not meet your expectations, you have the right to recourse. ***Recourse*** is the right to complain and receive an appropriate response.

If you purchase an item that is defective, you should return it to the store where you purchased it. Bring the merchandise and the sales receipt. It is a good practice to save the receipts from all your purchases.

Most stores have a customer service representative. You should explain to that person the problem you have with the merchandise. He or she will follow the store's policy for defective merchandise. Most stores will exchange the item for another. Some stores will issue a store credit for the returned item. You can use that credit to buy something else from the store. Many stores will refund your money. It is a good practice to inquire about a store's return policy before you make a purchase.

If you are not satisfied with the response of the customer service representative, ask to speak to the supervisor. If after talking to the supervisor, you are still not satisfied, ask to see the store manager. You should be prepared to go as far as necessary to reach satisfaction.

If your problem is not resolved by the store manager, write a detailed letter to the main office of the company. In your letter, explain in detail the facts pertaining to the problem. List the names of all the people to whom you spoke, and describe their responses to your problem. Also state in your letter what you expect from them to bring the matter to a satisfactory close. See 31-7.

If you still do not get satisfaction, consider contacting the area's Better Business Bureau (BBB). Usually there is a small fee to file a complaint with the BBB.

For matters that may involve unlawful behavior, contact the consumer protection bureau in your city or state. This department is usually located within the office of the attorney general. The name of the protection group can be found in the telephone book.

Generally, the BBB and a government agency will not handle the same complaint at the same time. If you do not get satisfaction through one channel, you may contact the other. Send copies of all your correspondence and ask for their review of the matter. If you still do not get satisfaction, you may need to retain the services of a lawyer to help resolve your problem.

23 W. Taft Drive
South Holland, IL 60473
May 18, 2004

Nancy Milan
Consumer Services
Contemporary Communications, Inc.
2121 West Main Street
Mesa, AZ 85201

Dear Ms. Milan:

One month ago I purchased a Chit-Chat Telephone from your Small Talk Collection, Model #012988 in Whispering White. This purchase was made at the Contemporary Communciations store in my hometown.

To my disappointment, the quality of the newly purchased telephone did not live up to its reputation. After only one month's use, the deluxe spiral cord of my Chit-Chat Telephone has loosened and become completely uncoiled. In addition, as the cord loosened, the telephone line weakened.

To solve my problem, I ask that you please replace my Chit-Chat deluxe spiral cord. It would be greatly appreciated, as I love my Chit-Chat phone and do not want to return it. Please find a copy of my pruchase receipt and warranty enclosed.

I hope to hear from you soon with a resolution to my problem. I will wait another month for your response before I return the phone and cord for full reimbursement. You may contact me at the above address or by phone at 708-555-7200. Thank you.

Sincerely,

Jennifer Sims
Jennifer Sims

enc.

31-7

A complaint letter written to the manufacturer will often resolve a consumer's problem with a faulty product.

recourse
The right to complain and receive an appropriate response.

Summary

Citizenship involves both rights and responsibilities. One of the most important rights of U.S. citizens is the right to vote. To exercise this right, you must register first.

Laws are rules by which people live. They are made by the people elected to public office. The two categories of laws in the United States are civil laws and public laws. At various times in your life, you may need the services of a lawyer to help you interpret laws.

Another part of being a responsible citizen involves being a responsible consumer. Consumers have rights and responsibilities related to product information, selection, safety, and recourse. If you buy an item that is defective, there are certain steps to follow to solve the problem.

Reviewing the Chapter

1. True or false. The law requires every eligible U.S. citizen to vote in all elections.
2. True or false. To register to vote, a person must be a citizen of the United States and at least 18 years old.
3. True or false. Federal laws are made by the United States Congress.
4. Name and define the two categories of laws in the United States.
5. List three sources of help for finding a lawyer.
6. List four situations that may require the services of a lawyer.
7. Describe consumers' rights and responsibilities related to product information.
8. Explain how the government protects the rights of consumers to choose from a variety of goods and services.
9. List three responsibilities consumers have concerning product safety.
10. If you have a problem with an item you purchased, you should first contact _____.
    A. the Better Business Bureau
    B. the store's manager
    C. the store's consumer service representative
    D. a lawyer

Building Your Foundation Skills

1. Research the right to vote in a country other than the United States. Find out what percentage of eligible voters voted in the last U.S. presidential election. Include this information in a written report along with your own ideas about the right to vote.

2. Prepare a pamphlet describing why, how, and where a person should register to vote. Distribute copies of the pamphlet throughout your school and community.

3. Design a bulletin board showing the steps involved in making a federal law.

4. Describe a situation that might require the services of a lawyer. Make a list of the kinds of information a person in this situation would need to bring to the lawyer.

5. Ask class members to play the parts of customer service representatives, store managers, presidents of companies, and customers. Create different situations for making and resolving complaints.

Building Your Workplace Competencies

Working with three or four classmates, write a skit that demonstrates a store's reluctance to grant a consumer's right to be heard. Include actions a consumer can take at all levels of a store's management until a consumer is satisfied. Incorporate characters into the skit so that each member of your team also performs in the skit. Have the class evaluate whether the consumer problem demonstrated in the skit was appropriately handled in the end. *(This activity develops competence with resources, interpersonal skills, information, and systems.)*

GLOSSARY

A

abilities. The skills a person has developed. (7)

accessories. Items that complement a wardrobe, such as shoes, handbags, belts, neckties, and jewelry. (20)

acne. A skin disorder caused by the inflammation of the skin glands and hair follicles. (20)

addiction. The never-ending obsession to use a drug more often. (21)

advanced training. Special skills and training required for a specific job. (4)

Age Discrimination Act. Law that prohibits employers from not hiring people simply because they are older. (3)

agenda. An order of business that lists activities that will occur during a meeting. (22)

alternatives. Options a person has when making a decision. (8)

Americans with Disabilities Act. Law that prohibits employers from discriminating against people with physical disabilities. (3)

annuity. A form of investment that lasts 10 or 15 years and provides insurance as well as savings. (26)

apprenticeship. Occupational training involving learning a trade by working under the direction of a skilled worker. (9)

aptitudes. The natural talents a person has or the potential to learn certain skills easily and quickly. (7)

argumentative. Easily creating arguments. (14)

assets. The valuable possessions a person owns, such as a house or a car. (27)

associate degree. The award granted after completing a two-year college program. (9)

attitude. How you react to a situation. (7)

B

bachelor's degree. The award granted after completing a four-year college or university program. (9)

balanced diet. An intake of food that supplies the body all the necessary nutrients in the needed amounts to maintain good health. (21)

bank statement. A balance sheet listing deposits, withdrawals, service charges, and interest payments on an account with a financial institution. (25)

bill. A proposed law. (31)

body language. A form of nonverbal communication in which a person "speaks" with the use of body movements, facial expressions, and hand gestures. (19)

budget. A plan for the use or management of money. (24)

C

CAD/CAM. Systems that use computer technology to run manufacturing systems. (2)

car pool. A group of people who take turns driving, usually to work. (30)

career. A series of jobs, usually in the same or related fields. (1)

career cluster. A group of careers that are related to each other in some way. (5)

career ladder. An illustration that shows a sequence of work in a career field, from entry to advanced levels. (1)

career plan. A list of steps a person takes to reach his or her career goals. (10)

career/technical program. A program that teaches students skills necessary for entry-level employment. (9)

career/technical student organization (CTSO). School groups that help students learn more about certain occupational areas. (22)

carrier. An organization that operates a transportation system. (30)

cashier's check. A check drawn on a bank's own funds and signed by an officer of the bank. (25)

certificate of deposit (CD). A savings certificate earning a fixed rate of interest that is purchased for a specific amount of money and held for a set period of time. (26)

certified check. A check for which a bank guarantees payment. (25)

check. A written order instructing a bank to take a specified amount of money out of the account on which the check is drawn and give it to the person whose name appears on the check. (25)

citizen. A person who owes allegiance to a government. (31)

civil laws. Laws that define a person's rights in relation to other people. (31)

civil service job. Government jobs obtained by taking a competitive exam. (5)

closed ad. A classified ad giving general information about a job. (11)

collateral. Something of value held by a lending institution in case a loan is not repaid. (27)

commission. A percentage of the money received from a sale. (16)

communicate. To share ideas, feelings, or information, both verbally and nonverbally. (19)

competent. Having the ability to respond appropriately. (1)

competition. Two or more parties acting independently to offer the most favorable product or terms. (31)

compound interest. Interest figured on the principal plus the earned interest of a financial account. (26)

computer revolution. The total change in the way people live and work caused by computers. (2)

concentrate. To focus attention and effort on something. (11)

conflict. Hostile situation resulting from opposing views. (14)

cooperative education. A program between schools and places of employment that allows students to receive on-the-job training through part-time work. (9)

corporation. A business that can legally act as a single person, but may be owned by many people. (6)

cosigner. A person who signs a loan with a borrower and is held responsible if the borrower does not pay back the loan. (27)

cost of living. Amount of money needed for rent, food, travel, and other everyday expenses. (4)

credit agreement. A written contract that legally binds a lender and a borrower to specific credit terms. (27)

credit bureau. An organization that gathers financial information on individuals for businesses to use as a credit reference. (27)

credit line. The maximum amount that can be charged on a credit card. (27)

credit rating. An estimate of how likely a person is to pay bills on time based on past records. (27)

criticism. Judgmental comments about your work. (14)

D

decision. A choice or a judgment. (8)

decision-making process. A seven-step guide for making decisions based on careful thought and planning. (8)

deductible. The amount a policyholder must pay before an insurance company will pay a claim. (28)

degrees Celsius (°C). The basic unit of measuring temperature in the metric system. (17)

dependable. Being reliable. (13)

dependent. A person, such as a child or nonworking adult, who relies on a taxpayer for financial support. (23)

deposit slip. A form filled out before depositing money into a bank account. (25)

direct deposit. Program that allows an employer to deposit a paycheck directly into an employee's account. (26)

disability. A temporary or permanent physical or mental condition that prevents an employee from working. (15)

discrimination. Unfairly treating a person or group of people differently. (3)

dismissal. Another term for being fired. (15)

diversity. The positive result of people of different racial, ethnic, and cultural backgrounds working together. (2)

dividend. A payout, usually annual, on money earned on whole life insurance. (28)

doctoral degree. The most advanced degree, often requiring three years of study beyond a bachelor's degree; also called a doctorate. (9)

dress code. A set of clothing rules that workers must follow while at their places of employment. (20)

drug. A chemical substance that brings about physical, emotional, or mental changes in a person. (21)

drug abuse. The use of a drug in a way that can damage a person's health or ability to function. (21)

drug screening. Tests that can reveal the presence of drugs in a person's body. (21)

E

economy. The way goods and services are produced, distributed, and consumed in a society. (1)

education. Gaining knowledge to live and work in today's society. (4)

e-mail. A feature of the Internet which allows people to send and receive messages via computer. (2)

endorse. To sign the back of a check in order to deposit or cash the amount specified. (25)

entrepreneurship. The starting and owning of a person's own business. (6)

entry level. A job that requires no previous training. (4)

EOE. Equal Opportunity Employer. (3)

Equal Employment Opportunity Act. A law that makes it illegal for an employer to discriminate because of race, color, religion, sex, or national origin. More recent laws make it illegal to discriminate against

people for other reasons, such as disabilities, age, and marital status. (3)

Equal Pay Act. Law that prohibits unequal pay for men and women who are doing essentially the same work for the same employer. (3)

evacuate. To empty or vacate a place in an organized manner for protection. (15)

F

fads. Clothing items or styles that are popular for a very short period of time. (20)

family-friendly programs. Work programs that help employees to balance the demand of work and family. (2)

Family and Medical Leave Act. A law that allows 12 weeks off without pay per year in certain cases to handle special family matters.(3)

Federal Insurance Contributions Act (FICA). An act that allows the federal government to reserve a percentage of a paycheck for social security tax. (23)

feedback. The return of information to a sender by a receiver trying to understand the message. (19)

fire triangle. A symbol representing the three elements that provide the necessary condition for a fire: oxygen, fuel, and heat. (15)

fired. To lose a job because of unacceptable work or behavior. (16)

first aid. Immediate, temporary treatment given in the event of an accident or illness before proper medical help arrives. (15)

fixed expense. Something for which a set amount of money must be paid regularly, such as rent, insurance, or tuition. (24)

flammable liquid. A liquid that can easily ignite and burn rapidly. (15)

flexible expense. An expense that varies in amount and does not occur on a regular basis, such as food, transportation, or entertainment. (24)

flextime. A work schedule that permits flexibility in work hours. (2)

follow-up letter. A brief letter written in business form to thank an interviewer for an interview. (12)

Form 1040EZ. The simplest income tax return form to complete. (23)

franchise. The right to sell a company's products in specified areas. (6)

free enterprise system. An economy in which individuals and businesses play a major role in making decisions. (2)

fringe benefits. Extra rewards given to workers in addition to salary or wages, such as insurance coverage and paid vacation time. (4)

G

global economy. Goods and services created by companies in one country are sold to customers in other countries. (2)

global positioning system (GPS). A highly accurate satellite-based tracking system. (5)

goals. The aims a person tries to achieve. (10)

gossip. To tell personal information about someone. (14)

graduate degree. An advanced degree requiring education beyond a bachelor's degree. (9)

gram. The basic unit of measuring weight in the metric system. (17)

grapevine. An informal and unofficial flow of information. (14)

grooming. The way in which people take care of themselves. (20)

gross pay. The total amount of money earned during a pay period. (23)

grounded. Connected to the earth to avoid electrical shock. (15)

H

health maintenance organization (HMO). A health insurance for which members pay a set fee and receive medical care, as needed, from a participating doctor or hospital. (28)

human resources. The resources that people have within themselves. (10)

I

identity. The sum of traits that distinguishes a person as an individual. (1)

illiterate. Being unable to read or write. (17)

implement. To put a plan into action. (8)

impulse decision. A decision made quickly, without much thought. (8)

income. The amount of money a person receives for doing a job. (1)

income tax. A tax on all forms of earnings. (23)

interest. The money paid to customers for allowing a financial institution to have and use their money. (26)

interests. The ideas, subjects, or activities a person enjoys. (7)

Internet. The global computer linkup of individuals, groups, and organizations in government, business, and education. (2)

internship. An occupational training program, usually unpaid, a college student or graduate gains practical experience under supervision. (9)

interview. A talk between an employer and a job applicant. (12)

interviewee. A job applicant who receives an interview. (12)

interviewer. An employer who talks with a job applicant. (12)

Internal Revenue Service (IRS). The agency that enforces federal tax laws and collects taxes. (23)

IRS time (individual responsibility for saving time). Taking whatever steps are needed to make the best use of time. (11)

J

job. Work a person does to earn money. (1)

job application form. A form completed by a job applicant to provide an employer with information about the applicant's background. (11)

job description. An explanation of tasks to be performed by an employee in a specified position. (12)

job shadowing. Accompanying a person to his or her job to learn about that person's job. (4)

L

laid off. To lose a job because the employer must release the employee for financial reasons. (16)

leader. A person who influences the actions of others. (22)

leadership. The ability to lead or direct others on a course or in a direction. (22)

lease. A written rental agreement, which defines the rights and responsibilities of the tenant and the owner of a rental property. (29)

letter of resignation. A formal letter stating plans to quit or resign from a job. (16)

lifelong learning. Continually updating your knowledge and skills. (2)

lifestyle. A person's typical way of life. (1)

liter. The basic unit of measuring volume in the metric system. (17)

M

mass transportation. Transportation, such as buses or trains, used routinely by the general public. (30)

master's degree. An advanced degree involving one to two years of study beyond a bachelor's degree. (9)

meter. The basic unit of measuring distance in the metric system. (17)

metric system. A decimal system of weights and measures. (17)

money market account. A type of savings account that is similar to a CD, but has no time restrictions. (26)

money order. Used like a check, this is an order purchased for a specific amount to be paid to a certain party. (25)

monopoly. The exclusive possession and control of a product or service. (31)

multitasking. Doing more than one job at a time. (19)

mutual fund. A long-term investment that provides a way to invest in stocks and bonds. (26)

N

needs. The basics a person must have in order to live. (1)

net pay. The amount of money left after all deductions have been taken from the gross pay. (23)

nonhuman resources. All the material resources around you. (10)

nonverbal communication. The sending and receiving of messages without the use of words. (19)

nutrient. A chemical substance in food that nourishes the body. (21)

O

online. Connected to the Internet. (4)

open ad. A classified ad providing specific information about a job. (11)

OSHA. A government agency and a federal law that calls for safe and healthy working conditions. The Occupational Safety and Health Administration is the agency, while the Occupational Safety and Health Act is the law. (15)

outsourcing. The practice of one company contracting with another to handle some work. (2)

overdraw. To write a check for more money than what is in the account. (25)

overtime pay. The wages earned, usually one-and-a-half times the regular wage, for working additional hours beyond the normal 40-hour week. (16)

P

parliamentary procedure. An orderly way of conducting a meeting and discussing group business. (22)

partnership. A business owned by two or more people. (6)

pay period. A length of time for which an employee's wages are calculated. Most businesses have weekly, biweekly, semi-monthly, or monthly pay periods. (23)

PC. Personal computer. (2)

penalty. A loss or hardship due to some action, such as breaking company rules or policies. (13)

personal interview. A face-to-face meeting between an employer and a job applicant. (12)

personality. The group of traits that makes each person unique. (7)

personal priorities. All the beliefs, ideas, and objects that are important to an individual. (7)

physical fitness. The ability to easily perform daily tasks with enough reserve energy to respond to unexpected demands. (21)

piecework. A job in which something is produced by an individual that can easily be counted. (3)

policy. A legal contract describing the rights and responsibilities of a person purchasing insurance and those of the company offering it. (28)

preferred provider organization (PPO). An organization of doctors or hospitals that contract with an insurance company to provide health services. (28)

premium. The amount of money paid for insurance. (28)

principal. A savings account deposit. (26)

priorities. Everything that you consider highly important. (19)

private employment agency. A business that helps people find jobs for a fee. (11)

privilege. A right that is given as a benefit or favor. (13)

procrastination. The delaying or putting off of decisions or activities. (18)

profit. The money left in a business after all expenses are paid. (2)

promotion. A move up to a higher position within a company. (4)

proofread. To read something, check for mistakes, and mark any errors found. (17)

proposition. Public questions appearing on voting ballots for the consideration of the voters. (31)

public employment service. A government-supported group that helps people find jobs for free. (11)

public laws. Laws that define a person's rights in relation to government. (31)

punctual. On time. (13)

R

real estate agency. A business that assists customers in the buying and selling, and less often renting, of apartments or houses. (29)

recourse. The right to complain and receive appropriate response. (31)

references. People who can speak about a person's character and skills. (11)

register. To submit one's name to the official list of citizens eligible to vote in elections. (31)

rental agency. A business that assists customers in the renting of apartments for a fee. (29)

reprimand. A severe expression of disapproval. (13)

residency requirement. A specification demanding a job applicant to live in a certain area. (5)

resource. Anything a person can use to help reach his or her goals. (7)

resumé. A formal written summary of a person's education, work experience, and other qualifications for a job. (11)

retail business. A business that sells products, such as clothing or cars, to consumers. (6)

ridicule. To tease or belittle. (14)

Robert's Rules of Order. The most common reference book used to describe the parliamentary procedure used at business meetings. (22)

routine decision. Decision made often. (8)

rumor. Information passed from one person to another without proof of accuracy. (14)

S

salary. A set amount of money paid to an employee for a full year of work. (16)

sarcasm. The use of cutting remarks. (14)

savings club. A savings plan into which a set amount of money is deposited regularly until a savings goal is reached. (26)

schedule. A list of the expected arrival and departure times and locations for buses, trains, and airplanes. (30)

security deposit. An amount of money usually equal to a month's rent initially paid to the owner of rental property by new tenants. It is used to cover the costs of any damages that may occur during the renter's stay. (29)

self-concept. Recognition of both your strengths and weaknesses. Acceptance and feeling good about yourself. (7)

self-esteem. The confidence a person has in himself or herself. (1)

self-sufficient. Individuals who can take care of themselves; who can earn a salary that will support their needs and wants as well as those of their future families. (2)

semiskilled labor. In manufacturing, a position requiring experience and/or vocational training. (5)

service business. A business that performs tasks for its customers. (6)

services. Nonmaterial assistance for which people are willing to pay. (2)

sexual harassment. Unwelcome sexual advances, requests for sexual favors, and other verbal or physical conduct of a sexual nature when it is made a condition of employment or of a person's work performance or environment. (3)

skills. Abilities that result from education and training. (4)

skilled labor. In manufacturing, a position requiring formal training beyond high school. (5)

sole proprietorship. A business owned by one person. (6)

stockholder. A person who owns a share of a corporation's stock. (6)

stress. A feeling of tension, strain, or pressure. (21)

T

teamwork. Two or more people working toward a common goal. (14)

technology. The application of scientific principles. (2)

telecommuting. Working at home through an electronic linkup with the central office. (2)

telephone interview. A telephone conversation between a company representative and a job applicant. (12)

term life insurance. An insurance plan that offers coverage for a limited period of time. (28)

termination. The end of employment or the loss of a job. (13)

time log. A written record of a person's use of time. (18)

time management. The planning and using of time. (18)

trade-off. The giving up of one thing for another. (8)

training. Applying knowledge through practice. (4)

traits. Noteworthy characteristics. (4)

transfer. To change from one bus or train route to another. (30)

transferable skills. Skills used in one career that can be used in another. (1)

traveler's checks. Checks purchased in common denominations that are replaceable if lost or stolen. (25)

U

unskilled labor. An entry-level job in manufacturing. (5)

U.S. savings bond. A certificate of debt issued by the federal government that serves as a safe way to save money. (26)

V

verbal agreement. The simplest form of an agreement in which certain terms are specified but not written down. (29)

verbal communication. Communication involving the use of words. (19)

vocabulary. The group of words known and used by an individual. (17)

W

W-2 Form. Wage and tax statement, a form showing how much a worker was paid and how much income was withheld for taxes in a given year. (23)

W-4 Form. Employee's withholding allowance certificate, a form filled out by an employee when beginning a new job. It determines how much of the employee's pay should be withheld for taxes. (23)

wages. The money earned for doing hourly work. (16)

want ad. A source of information about available jobs, found in the classified section of the newspaper. (11)

wants. The items a person would like to have, but are not required. (1)

wardrobe inventory. A list of all the clothes and accessories found in a person's closet and drawers. (20)

whole life insurance. An insurance plan that offers the insured permanent coverage. (28)

wholesale. A large quantity of items packaged in bulk with a per-item cost below the retail price. (6)

wholesalers. Businesses that sell to retailers. (5)

working capital. Money needed to start and maintain a business. (6)

work. An activity done to produce or accomplish something. (1)

work ethic. A standard of conduct and values for job performance. (13)

workers' compensation. An insurance against loss of income from work-related accidents. (15)

workplace competencies. Skills needed for workplace effectiveness and success. (1)

INDEX